GANGSTER

Mark A. Stuart spent fifteen years searching for the man behind the charm, personality and grace which Zwillman presented to the world. He searched public records, ploughed through FBI files and court documents, and interviewed countless former associates and employees of Zwillman. Many agreed to talk only on the promise of anonymity — even today they fear gangland retribution!

Mark A. Stuart is a Pulitzer Prize nominee and lives in New Jersey, USA.

GANGSTER

The Story of Longy Zwillman, the Man who invented Organized Crime

Mark A. Stuart

A STAR BOOK
published by
the Paperback Division of
W. H. Allen & Co. Plc

A Star Book
Published in 1987
by the Paperback Division of
W. H. Allen & Co. Plc

44 Hill Street, London W1X 8LB

First published in the United States of America
by Lyle Stuart, 1985

First published in Great Britain by
W. H. Allen & Co. Plc, 1986

Printed and bound in Great Britain by
Anchor Brendon Ltd, Tiptree, Essex

ISBN 0 352 31808 2

TO MY FRIEND MELBA
for 40 years of pure joy

Acknowledgments

Any book this complex has to be a team effort. I was helped by a group of all-stars, and this acknowledgment doesn't begin to pay the debt I owe them all. To mention just a few:

To the cohort of librarians, especially the gentlemen in the New Jersey Room of the Newark Public Library, who dug up long-discarded material with missionary zeal. To the former bootleggers, now respectable business executives, and the erstwhile gangsters, now retired and still alive, who shared their experiences with me and asked only one thing in exchange – that I protect my sources.

To Malcolm A. Borg, my boss, for 20 years of support and belief in my talents. To Donald G. Borg, late Editor of *The Record*, for teaching me how to tell gold from dross. To William A. Caldwell, Pulitzer Prize-winning editor and friend, who insisted the gold was there. To Allan Wilson, who sweated over getting this book ready for the public.

To my mother, who's always proud of my work, but worriedly kept asking me: 'Do you *have* to use the real names of all those gangsters?' To my children, Jane, Tom, and Chris for bugging me – but oh, how lovingly – to keep going. To Rachel and Jonathan for just being. To my brother and sister-in-law, Bill and Elizabeth, for understanding why I couldn't come on retreat. To my brother-in-law, Stan, whose 'What chapter are you on now?' was a much-needed goad. To John O'Hara, good guy, for his help interpreting IRS minutiae.

To all of them, thank you from a brimful heart.

Contents

	Preview	8
1.	The Young Defender	15
2.	The Banker	21
3.	The Reinfeld Connection	27
4.	A. Zwillman, Businessman	33
5.	Young Man in a Hurry	45
6.	War and Peace in Newark	56
7.	A Hoods' Convention	66
8.	The Jean Harlow Story	78
9.	The Making of a President, 1932	92
10.	Benevolent Racketeer	102
11.	Love and Marriage	115
12.	Gangs, Gambling, and Labor Goons	127
13.	Business Is Business	143
14.	Strange Bedfellows: Longy and the Politicians	157
15.	The Kefauver Shadow	165
16.	The IRS Hits	196
17.	The Trial	215
18.	The Bribe	228
19.	Over the Edge	236
	Epilogue	243

Preview

I first heard of Longy Zwillman in 1949 from a neighbor of mine in New York's Stuyvesant Town. This neighbor had just been hired as office manager for a Staten Island brickyard. He barged into my apartment one Friday night.

'I just met my boss,' he blurted excitedly.

'I thought you met him when he hired you,' I said.

'No, no! The guy hired me is just a front. I mean my *real* boss. The one who *really* owns the place is Longy Zwillman.'

'Who?' I looked perplexed. My neighbor looked astonished.

'You mean,' he asked incredulously, 'you never heard of Longy Zwillman? Abe Zwillman? Longy the gangster?'

He had a right to be surprised. He thought I was a hip New York newspaperman. I thought I was too.

My beat as a reporter covered Manhattan's West Side from Columbus Circle to Columbia University, from the Hudson to Central Park. In the Nineteen Forties and Fifties, this was a residential neighborhood favored by successful garment manufacturers, wealthy thugs and con men, sports figures, people in the performing arts.

Babe Ruth lived on Riverside Drive. The Beresford on Central Park West and 81st Street was home to stars of stage and radio – and to gang chieftain Meyer Lansky. The Ansonia Hotel on 73rd Street and Broadway was favored by concert artists and opera singers; its thick walls made apartments virtually soundproof, and ideal for practicing at all hours. Successful lawyers and high-ranking judges lived at the Apthorp on 79th Street, between Broadway and West End Avenue. City political figures preferred the block-square building at 200 West 86th Street.

For two weeks one summer, I spent every night hanging around the side door of the Majestic Apartments on 72nd Street and Central Park West. I was hoping for an interview with Frank Costello, one of the biggest figures in the rackets. I got close to him once, and was rudely dissuaded from trying again by Costello's beefy chauffeur-bodyguard. Only the fact that one of the doormen recognized me saved my kneecaps from a painful pounding.

I knew all about dapper Joe Adonis, who ran the big-stakes gambling games on the East Coast. I learned about Lucky Luciano early in my career. I practically grew up with Lepke Buchalter and Gurrah Shapiro of Murder, Inc. I thought I had inside information on the Mob because my aunt was dating racket-buster Tom Dewey's No. 1 assistant, Jacob Rosenblum.

And I never heard of Longy Zwillman.

Stupidly, I didn't bother to follow up on my neighbor's story about the Staten Island brickyard. The following year, this same neighbor got a new and better job as office manager of a meat-processing plant in Brooklyn. He wasn't on the job three weeks when he came bouncing up to me outside our apartment building on 14th Street near Avenue B.

'Guess who owns the new place I work in,' he asked. He didn't wait for an answer. 'Longy Zwillman!' he blurted.

This time he had me. A guy I never heard of who is supposed to be a gangster turns out to be the secret owner of a brickyard in Staten Island *and* a salami factory in Brooklyn. Was he a clever investor, or really a power in the rackets, as my knowing neighbor insisted?

I checked the clips in the library at my paper (only in the movies is a newspaper's files called a morgue). Longy's envelope held a modest inventory – one story. He had been questioned in 1935 about the gunning down of Dutch Schultz in a Newark restaurant. The request to have Longy come in came from New York's police commissioner, Lewis Valentine. Longy, living in Newark, told the commissioner he had no objection to being grilled. He didn't even mind when two FBI agents chased all the cops from the room. They wanted an hour with Longy all to themselves.

And that was it. Nothing in the one story in our files hinted that Longy Zwillman was in a class with Lansky, Luciano, Costello, Adonis, or the bully boys of Murder Inc.

So, I forgot about Longy Zwillman – until 1951, when Senator Estes Kefauver of Tennessee began his committee hearings on organized crime.

Abner 'Longy' Zwillman spent a total of two hours testifying before the Special Committee to Investigate Organized Crime in Interstate Commerce. Longy's performance, critics said later, was far superior to that put on by a nervous Frank Costello, whose raspy voice, poor diction, and wringing hands – with their well-manicured fingernails – were a caricature of the public's idea of a mobster's appearance.

Zwillman, on the other hand, was described as a self-assured witness who controlled his temper, even under severe provocation. He used impeccable English, and liberally sprinkled 'sirs' through all his answers. He wore a dark, well-cut suit by Benham, a starched shirt by Sulka, and a hurt-puzzled expression all his own. Longy seemed anxious to answer any questions, even those that might incriminate him – although, it was noted, he *did* invoke his constitutional rights against self-incrimination five times.

Those two hours on the stand didn't reveal the true Longy Zwillman. Three months of testimony before the committee by others – licit businessmen and bootleggers alike – did a much better job.

They unveiled Longy Zwillman, the bootlegger who made millions during Prohibition. Longy, who switched to equally lucrative involvement in gambling and other shady occupations after Repeal. The witnesses told of a man who stayed in the shadows, allowing trusted associates to accumulate large chunks of real estate for his benefit. Longy's portfolio of legitimate businesses included a steel mill, a General Motors truck franchise, a Wall Street investment firm, and a railroad.

These revelations were followed by two articles in *Collier's magazine, August 25 and September 1, 1951, exposing Zwillman's extraordinary political power in New Jersey. Then came a lengthy Wall Street Journal* story detailing Longy's acumen in the legitimate business world. Abner Zwillman was beginning to interest me.

In 1956, I went to work for a New Jersey newspaper. Longy Zwillman had just been indicted for income-tax evasion. I spent some time as an observer during his trial. I was in the courtroom on March 4, 1956, when the jury came in to tell Judge Reynier Wortendyke that it was hopelessly deadlocked after 30 hours of deliberation.

I didn't pay too much attention to Longy Zwillman after that, even when two of his henchman were indicted for trying to bribe jurors during his income-tax evasion trial.

All that changed on February 26, 1959. That was the day I went up to Longy's English Tudor mansion at 50 Beverly Road, West Orange, to report on his suicide.

Abner Zwillman was 55 years old when he tossed an electric cord across a rafter in his cellar, wound it around his neck, and strangled himself. Rumors began as soon as news of his death became known. The most persistent was that Longy didn't kill himself – the boys in the Mob called in his chips. They were worried he would make a deal with federal prosecutors and tell all he knew, instead of facing a new trial on the income-tax evasion charge.

I examined Longy's career, off and on, for the next 20 years. I studied his appearance before Senator Kefauver's committee, his income-tax evasion trial, his death. I wrote several short pieces about him.

After talking with childhood friends, buddies from his old bootlegger days, former employees of his businesses (legitimate and illicit), prosecutors, and law-enforcement agents familiar with his career, I'm convinced that Longy Zwillman *did* commit suicide.

It was the last act of a human drama that could play as a Greek tragedy. Abner Zwillman was blessed with brains. Forget the stories you've heard about organized crime in this country. It isn't an import. It wasn't brought from the hill towns of Sicily to the streets of America.

Gambling and bootlegging run on a wholesale scale was Abner Zwillman's refinement of what had been very messy businesses. The idea of how they *should* be run came from the fertile brain and managerial imagination of a Newark street kid smart enough to realize that cooperation in crime pays far bigger dividends than flamboyant, macho individualism.

Abner Zwillman had charisma. It drew people to him, men and women alike. Leaders in the world of finance, the law, medicine, and education worked for him eagerly, often against their better judgment. Beautiful women fell in love with him. One of them was the most beautiful movie star of her era. Another was a socialite with impeccable breeding and background.

He was proud, brave, handsome, dignified, cool, polished – and ruthless, tough, unforgiving, mesmerized by money. Although he quit school in the eighth grade, he was well-read, interested in the arts, an opera buff. He could not be called self-educated because he had help. Msgr. John Delaney of the Newark Diocese was his mentor, hiring Father Hugh Mulcahy and other teachers at Seton Hall University to tutor Zwillman in English, literature, and music.

Zwillman had the business acumen of a chief executive for a successful multi-national conglomerate. He could delegate authority, attract competent subordinates (and reward and punish them with fairness and good judgment). He spotted business opportunities – legitimate and illegitimate – long before competitors even thought of them. He knew the banking business, and handled security investments with the deftness of a professional trader.

He understood how American government and politics worked as astutely as the shrewdest professional politician. He used that knowledge to help one historic figure secure the Democratic Party's nomination for president.

But, like the ill-fated heroes of Greek tragedy, Abner Zwillman had that fatal flaw, the Achilles heel: he didn't trust his own ability to succeed.

Abner Zwillman could have become a truly wealthy legitimate businessman with the coming of Repeal, like so many other bootleggers did. Joseph Kennedy grasped the chance, and became America's ambassador to England. Joseph Reinfeld (Longy's partner in rum-running) did, and became Sir Joseph Renfield, knighted by the Crown of England.

Longy Zwillman chose to remain a racketeer. It was a conscious decision. When Prohibition ended, Zwillman was making more than $2 million a year, more or less tax free, bringing whiskey to Americans craving drink. He couldn't trust his ability to make that much money legitimately. He chose the rackets instead. And, like the Greek heroes of old, he fell. This is the story of his rise – and fall.

Chapter 1

The Young Defender

The year is 1918. The scene is Newark's Prince Street. It's a mirror image of the crowded, fetid, immigrant-inhabited streets of New York's Lower East Side. As they do on Orchard, Ludlow, and Rivington streets in Manhattan, pushcarts line the curb in Newark's Jewish ghetto from Springfield Avenue on the north to Waverly Avenue in the south. On these few short blocks, peddlers sell everything from bottom-of-the-barrel fruits and vegetables to wire-rimmed eyeglasses.

A mother pushes a pram along the crowded sidewalk. In the carriage, her young child is half-concealed under the day's purchases – soup greens rolled in newspaper, a loaf of seed-covered corn bread, a chunk of kosher soap, wrapped in a piece of broadcloth that eventually will become a shirt. The young woman strains to spot other bargains – Sabbath candles in wax paper, a few overripe cucumbers, a cheap pencil.

The tenements on the sidewalk behind her rise three and four stories. Behind the pediments that loom above the top floor are the poor people's air-conditioners – mattresses strewn on the roof for hard-working men and women who, on hot summer nights, use them to snatch a breath of fresh air.

In the shops on the ground floor of the tenements are Zaretsky the grocer, Neibart in his poultry market, Eisler rearranging his fish on ice, Greenberg and Keller in the yard-goods store. They've come up in the world. They no longer rent a pushcart by the day from Columbus Brothers on Court Street. Now they preside proudly over a counter in a regular store.

The young mother, shopping, ignores the stores behind

her until it's time to go home to start the evening meal. That's when she will stop at Greenfield's for a quart of milk, ladled into an aluminum can hanging from her child's carriage. Maybe a small chunk of pot cheese, as a treat for her husband.

She stops in front of a pushcart selling carrots and peas, the dregs of that morning's batch. As she begins to inspect a bunch of faded carrots, she hears a commotion up the street – a woman's piercing scream, male voices shouting hoarsely.

'*Gevalt!*' A desperate call: Help!

The little man selling the carrots and peas begins to push the young mother away from his pushcart. At the same time, he pulls a large section of canvas from beneath the cart and begins to cover his withered goods. Other peddlers at the curb scurry to do the same.

'*Gayt shoin avek*,' the peddler growls at his young customer. Go away, quickly.

Trouble is on the way. The peddler recognizes it. He wants to avoid the trouble, to protect himself. He's learned from bitter experience. He knows what those hoarse cries mean. The hoodlums are coming.

A block away, the trouble is swirling in from Montgomery and from Broome. Thin, acne-scarred Irish youngsters from 18th Street and 5th Avenue are engaged in a favorite caper: rading the peddlers of pushcart row. They're not interested in stealing the pitiful wares on sale. There's more fun in plain, safe Jew-baiting – pulling beards and snatching skullcaps.

It's been a bad day all around for the peddlers between Kinney and Court Streets. Business had been slow. Arguments with customers had been fierce. Now come these young toughs to make things worse. A few of the angrier peddlers call for help.

'*Reef der Langer!*' The shout goes up from half a dozen throats. Go get the Tall One, the defender.

Somebody always knows where the defender is. This time, his horse and wagon is parked in front of Joe Mann's Cafe. Alderman Mann had taken a shine to the defender right after the tall one's father died. The boy was fearless. He could keep his mouth shut. He knew how to carry messages, especially those that might require the use of his big, thick knuckles before they'd be answered.

The cry for help has reached Mann's Cafe. The tall defender, alerted to battle, comes out running, followed by two pals, one tall and thick-faced, the other small and hawkish. The smaller one yells to a huddle of comrades lounging in front of Berlin's barbershop. They fall in behind their leader, all running toward the commotion on the pushcart-filled street.

The leader, a handsome youngster, is 6 feet 2 inches tall. His thick, curly black hair is parted in the middle. He's wearing clean, faded work pants, a blue denim shirt, and sturdy shoes – his uniform on the route when he's peddling fruit and vegetables. He looks well-groomed, even in humble clothes.

The dozen Irish attackers pull away from their peddler-victims and huddle in a circle as soon as the defender and his gang are spotted. The Irish kids know their reputation.

The tall leader wades into the Irish circle without a word. He punches, gouges, kicks. He stomps one invader who has been pushed beneath a cart. His buddies, who called themselves the 'Happy Ramblers,' have been getting in their own licks.

The fight is over in less than 10 minutes. The Irish kids run toward sanctuary beyond Springfield Avenue. The tall leader and his boys head back to Mann's Cafe. His rescue mission was an obligation he had accepted without question. His dead father had been one of these street merchants. The defender wants no protection fee, expects no thanks from these poor pushcart peddlers trying to eke out a living.

Abner Zwillman had always been the tallest kid in his age group, as early as the fourth grade. He was chosen for teams organized by older guys in the playground at the corner of Prince and Waverly, and at the gym of the Young Men's Hebrew Association, when he was as young as 12.

He was not just tall, but wiry and strong. Whatever he was asked to do – play ball, run errands for Alderman Mann, or fight – he did with reckless zeal.

Der Langer, Yiddish for 'The Tall One,' became his nickname. This quickly was transliterated by English-speaking kids to 'Longy,' and it was as Longy that he was known to the gang on streets called Prince, Charlton, Broome, and Stratford in Newark's decaying Third Ward.

Longy's parents, immigrant poor, had come to Newark from Russia before the turn of the century. They settled into a small apartment on the middle floor of a gabled building at 84 Charlton Street, in the heart of Newark's poorest Jewish neighborhood. Abner Zwillman, born in 1904, was their third child. First had come his sister, Bessie, and his brother, Barney. Then came Abner, Larry, Irving, Ethel, and Phoebe.

The father, Avraham Zwillman, peddled live chickens from a stall in the public market on Prince Street. He made a pitifully small living. Longy in later years was asked why he was fiercely addicted to making money.

'All I remember is that as kids my brothers, sisters, and I were always hungry,' he said.

From the time he was 12, Abner pitched in to help supplement his father's meager income. He did it mainly by running errands for Alderman Mann.

The alderman's cafe was political headquarters for the Third Ward. It was also a hangout for pimps, prostitutes, and gamblers. Young Abner never asked questions when ordered to run an errand. Nor did he worry about how the person who paid him made a living.

The boy's reputation for speed, strength, accuracy, and the ability to keep his own council was appreciated. Longy's reputation for toughness and reliability spread beyond Newark's Third Ward.

In 1918, Longy was in the eighth grade at the Charlton Street School. He was an average student, at 6 foot 2 inches the tallest boy in the school. His report card showed he was never absent, seldom late. This was unusual in a neighborhood where truancy was high. Proper deportment –

outwardly – was a fetish with Longy from his earliest years.

Longy's father died before school ended in the summer of 1918. Immigrant workers carried no insurance, had no death benefits. Even a burial plot depended on benevolent societies made up of immigrants who came from the same region in the old country.

The Zwillman household was no better off than that of any of the other immigrant families in Newark, and worse than most. Avraham Zwillman's chicken stall seldom brought in more than enough to cover the barest necessities. By temperament, Longy's older sister and brother were unable to assume the responsibility of caring for an entire family. With the father gone, it was up to the biggest, strongest, most capable of the children to accept the role – and burden – of breadwinner. For Longy, it meant quitting school before graduation. That didn't bother him until many years later. At the time his father died, it was imperative that Longy bring money into the house. He was 14 years old.

Longy recognized that he couldn't earn enough running errands for Alderman Mann to feed eight people. He discarded the idea of taking over his father's market, smothered by the smell of chickens and their droppings. Instead, he rented a horse and wagon, stocked it with fruits and vegetables, and traveled the better streets of Newark as an itinerant peddler.

'He was quick, that Longy,' said a childhood friend. 'He didn't peddle in our neighborhood. For two good reasons – one, we were all too poor to be good customers; and two, he would have been competition for the pushcart peddlers. So, he went to sell his goods up on Clinton Hill and other better neighborhoods.

'He was a handsome kid. He looked a lot older than 14. The housewives would come out to his wagon, or greet him at the door, and he would kid with them, you know, make joking remarks about their good looks, pay them compliments about the way they dressed. He was as smart as a whip. He could sell those women anything.'

Newark had goons preying on even the poorest peddlers

trying to make a living. Some peddlers paid protection to stand at the sidewalk unmolested; others paid for the right to sell in certain neighborhoods. Not Longy. He went wherever he thought he could find business. Most of the goons already knew his reputation as a battler. They stayed away from the tall, wiry youngster. Those who didn't know him soon found out that it didn't pay to pick on the kid called Longy.

Longy didn't have a career in mind. He didn't think about leaving the immigrant neighborhood where he was born and where all his friends lived. Selling vegetables on Newark streets, however, wasn't his ambition. He wanted more than just enough to take care of his family. He recognized that having plenty of money meant freedom, respect, and power.

Longy had studied the men in the neighborhood. They were either immigrants like his father, or the sons of immigrants like himself. Those who worked in factories, hauled goods, or sold from pushcarts made just enough to pay rent, feed their families, buy some clothing twice a year for the holidays. Those who owned little stores earned enough for a few extras – a weekend at Bradley Beach, a day-trip to Manhattan, a pair of tickets to one of the theaters on Branford Place.

The men in the Third Ward who made *real* money, the kind of money Longy was after, were either in politics or in gambling. The ones who used brawn were feared, and made money. Those who used their brains were respected, and made even more money. By the time he was 16, Longy Zwillman knew his own strength. He had brawn *and* brains. He only needed to find the right place to use the combination.

Chapter 2

The Banker

Longy Zwillman discovered his first path toward wealth in 1919. It began modestly, with 'policy', or the numbers game. This was a variation on the lottery. It could be played by small bettors for pennies, nickels, and dimes. The big spenders played for quarters.

A player selected a three-digit number. He placed his bet with a neighborhood collector. The collector passed his bets to a runner, who brought them to the 'bank'. The banker paid off when the winning number was announced each day. Today, the winning number is derived from racetrack parimutuel betting figures or stock market averages. In Longy's day, it came down to the street from the banks to the collectors, arrived at by a mysterious process that every bettor accepted.

Today, states run their own lottery, but bettors still throng to the illegal numbers collector in poor neighborhoods. The illegal banks have met government competition by raising the winner's take. And winners in the street lottery pay no taxes.

The housewives who lived in modest homes on Belmont, Chadwick, Hedden, or Seymour, the neighborhoods where Longy began peddling his fruits and vegetables, always had an extra nickel or two to play the numbers. If they won, they would make enough money for an embroidered dress, a pair of fancy pumps, or an ostrich-feathered hat. If they lost, no one noticed. An astute, well-organized homemaker could always make up a few nickels a week.

Before Longy came on the scene in Newark's Third Ward, bettors would have to find the local collector, then risk neighborhood gossip by being seen betting. For a housewife, gossip was the enemy.

Longy refined the process. He brought the numbers game right into the home, door-to-door. His service did more than save a woman the few steps she had to take to take her bet to the candy store, the barber, the shoemaker. He built a new clientele.

Housewives who had envied bettors, who were dying to bet but were too embarrassed to be seen handing their money over to a neighborhood bookie, could now play the numbers discreetly. Longy came right into the house in the guise of a peddler. This pick-up service soon was earning the 15-year-old boy as much money in a day as he had made peddling fruits and vegetables in a week.

Longy began as a collector for the hoods who ran Newark's numbers banks. It didn't take the young man long to figure out that the men who owned the banks he collected for were no braver or smarter than he was. But they were making real money; all he got was a small commission on his customer's play. Why not, he reasoned, run a bank himself?

Zwillman already had the nucleus of his own organization. They were childhood friends, the old neighborhood bunch who played ball together at the local schoolyard and at the YMHA. Longy, the street-fighter, had organized them into a mutual protection society with a reputation all over the Third Ward. It took the form of a social club, known as 'The Happy Ramblers'. Longy said later he picked the name out of a newspaper story describing the ramblings of a group of nature-lovers who hiked the hills of Essex, Bergen, and Passaic counties.

Longy's ability to organize, to attract competent help and inspire their loyalty, to recognize opportunities for making money, went into use. He was 16, with the physical build of a full-grown, athletic male. His intelligence and native shrewdness were far beyond his years.

The gang Zwillman headed spread out to neighborhoods beyond the ghetto, beyond Clinton Hill, to every part of Newark except the First Ward in the north. Longy wasn't ready – yet – to tackle the Italian gangs who were in control there. Within a year, Longy had built the biggest policy bank in the city, if not in all New York.

Numbers collectors were, in the main, small merchants who were paid a tiny commission for receiving bets daily and handing them over to a runner who carried the money and slips with betting record to the numbers bank.

Collectors worked long hours for little money. The few dollars a week they earned from collecting for the numbers people made a big difference in their lives. A collector who had a good spot, in a lower middle-class neighborhood where bets were nickels and dimes rather than pennies, could earn perhaps $25 to $30 a week.

There were risks. Numbers banks were notoriously sloppy about keeping records or paying commissions. Some banks would welsh when a number held by too many bettors would hit big. Bettors complained to collectors, the only one in the chain they knew. If a collector complained to a bank, he had a choice – either lose his collection job and its commissions, or have his ribs kicked in. Even when a collector dealt with an honest bank, he was never sure of his income. And he could always be nabbed by a rookie cop, hot for a reputation.

A shopkeeper hit with this catastrophe had double trouble. Once arrested, his policy bettors would find themselves another collector. And many of his regular store customers would melt away. Longy had different ideas about running a bank. He organized it along legitimate business lines. Instead of commissions, he paid his collectors a flat wage each week. At first, it was little more than the collectors could have earned in commissions under the old system. But to a storekeeper accustomed to earning, at most, $50 for an 80-hour-week on his feet running a store, a guaranteed additional $30 was a golden egg.

Longy's collectors enjoyed an additional advantage – safety and security. From his days as a protege of Alderman Mann. Longy learned the indispensable element in running a successful racket – the payoff. With the cop on the beat on the bank's payroll, policy collectors didn't have to worry about being arrested. Even if they were picked up by some mistake, the bank would have a lawyer ready to defend them. At most, a collector could look forward to being fined.

Longy would pay the cop's bribe, the lawyer's fee, the fine and court costs – and never deduct it from the collector's weekly reward. These fees, Longy told his companions, were merely the cost of doing business. They built loyalty among his people. Better yet, they built political clout. Once bribed, officials – cops, aldermen, legislators, even judges – were compromised. You could call on them at other times, for other reasons.

Sometime in 1919, Longy Zwillman gave his numbers bank an extra added boost. He decided to manipulate the winning number for his own advantage. His buddy, Doc Stacher, had a marvelous mathematical facility. In later years, Stacher used this gift to help run Longy's chain of New Jersey gambling emporiums; he also acted as caretaker of Longy's Las Vegas investments.

In the days of the Newark policy bank, Stacher would wait until Longy's bank collected all the slips for the day. Then, in a lightning calculation, he would figure out which number had drawn the fewest bettors or the least number of bets. That became the daily winning number.

In the same year – 1919 – Longy built his policy bank into a modest money-making machine, Congress gave him his big chance at the brass ring. It passed the act imposing Prohibition on America.

The itch to prohibit the sale of alcoholic beverages – beer, wine, whiskey – is almost as old as the republic. It came from different sources, with different motives. 'Temperance' campaigns urging people not to drink alcoholic beverages began almost the day the Pilgrims landed at Plymouth. The push to prohibit the manufacture and sale of liquor started a little later.

The nation's growth, its reputation for freedom and opportunity, was a magnet for impoverished immigrants. They flooded into the country in successive waves of migration. Poor housing was all the immigrants could afford. As immigration increased and began choking the cities, poor housing became slums. Slums brought disease that threatened entire regions, not just the poor.

Those who preached against 'demon rum' didn't blame the plight of the poor on exploitation. Drink itself was the evil; it must be eradicated. The fact that the poor often drank to escape their misery was ignored. The upstanding citizen drank in private; the poor fell down in the streets. Since many of the immigrants happened to be Roman Catholics, bigots joined the ranks of those demanding an end to lawful drinking.

The demand for Prohibition increased in the 1830's and 1840's. Drinking was popularly believed to be the cause of mental illness and physical disability, as well as a spur to increasing crime and the proliferation of slums. Maine became the first state to pass a prohibition law in 1846. By 1855, twelve more states had become dry.

Support for Prohibition waned during and after the Civil War. The major political parties ignored the issue. Irked, the 'drys' formed the Prohibition Party in 1869. It went nowhere. The opening of the West eased the plight of the cities somewhat, and the drys lost more ground. By 1900, only five of the original 12 Prohibition states still banned public drinking.

The battlers against 'demon rum' made a big comeback when the United States entered World War I. The drys adopted a new, more popular argument. Using grain to make liquor, they shrilled, would deprive the armed forces of food. Congress bought the argument. It passed laws limiting the manufacture and sale of liquor for the duration of the war. That was all the opening the drys needed. They began an all-out drive for a constitutional amendment to prohibit the making and selling of whiskey. And they were successful.

Congress approved the 18th Amendment late in 1917. It prohibited the import, export, manufacture, sale, and transport of alcoholic beverages in the U.S. and its territories. By January 1919, three-fourths of the states had ratified the amendment, and it was added to the Constitution. In October 1919, Congress passed the Volstead Act, which spelled out the penalties for defying the 18th Amendment. It took effect on New Year's Day 1920.

Prohibition gave Abner 'Longy' Zwillman the chance to use all his native shrewdness, his courage and skill, to organize an illicit operation that earned him, by government estimates, at least $20 million in a ten-year period.

Chapter 3

The Reinfeld Connection

Joseph Reinfeld arrived in Newark with his family 1910. His father was a tailor. Young Joe and one of his brothers, Abe, were taught the trade, but never really practiced it. As soon as they accumulated a little money, Joe and Abe opened a tavern on the corner of Eighth Avenue and High Street, at the edge of Newark's predominantly Italian First Ward.

Joe Reinfeld, the older of the two tavern-keeping brothers, was tall, brown-haired, and swarthy-complexioned. He could easily pass for a Sicilian or Calabrian. Actually, Joe Reinfeld was Jewish.

Daily life for the hard-working Italians who came to Newark's First Ward in great numbers from the 1880's onward revolved around home and family. Mealtime was family time. Children and the church were the women's interests; bocci and a glass of wine after work were the male's recreation.

These were people with the gumption to escape the poverty of their native Italy, uprooting themselves to struggle for a better life in the New World. They cultivated tiny garden plots in their backyards in the First Ward. They pressed and fermented wine in their basements the old-fashioned way. Few of the men of these toil-worn families ever set foot in a saloon.

Reinfeld's tavern catered to a different set. Along with the bricklayers, hod-carriers, mill workers, and ditch-diggers, the old First Ward had its share of hard, stony-eyed young men who lived by terror and intimidation. They disdained physical labor of any sort, except when wielding an ax-handle or baseball bat to teach someone a bitter lesson.

The more enterprising of these tough guys made money by using their wits as well as their fists. They branched out into lending money at usurious rates, into gambling, prostitution, and the numbers racket. The toughest of them would rise to the top of a loosely organized gang that adopted the name 'Black Hand.'

Back in the old country, this was a feared Neapolitan underworld organization. Some of the members emigrated to New York before the turn of the century, bringing their old-country trade along. Their racket was selling 'protection' to the poor merchants in the Little Italy sections of the larger cities. If you paid them a weekly retainer, your goods wouldn't be contaminated, your windows wouldn't be smashed. If you were stubborn, you might find your store burned during the night.

Few of Newark's First Ward tough guys were actually members of the Black Hand in the old country. Those who adopted the guise used it to frighten timid shopkeepers, or to impress rival loan-sharks and pimps.

The 'Mafia,' as it's known now, existed in Sicily. It began as a secret revolutionary brotherhood determined to protect poor peasants from outrageous exploitation by absentee landlords. When Italy became unified and independent, the Mafia didn't disappear. It remained underground. Its members became brigands, preying on the helpless.

The First Ward's gamblers, politicians, city employees, and strong-arm boys considered Reinfeld's Tavern their home away from home. Joe Reinfeld, a congenial host, had a reputation for being fair, impartial in the many factional feuds that wracked the neighborhood. He was also known for being discreet.

When Prohibition went into effect in January 1920, Reinfeld's saloon continued to do business as if nothing had changed. Customers wanted beer and whiskey. Reinfeld had both to sell. He also had protection from harassment and prosecution because of his friendship with – and payoffs to – city officials and the police.

Joe Reinfeld's prosperous business wasn't all problem-free, however. An indispensable part of his trade required good, reasonably priced liquor and beer. At first, Reinfeld's supply came from a variety of local sources. Illegal breweries flourished in Newark. The police on a brewmaster's payroll were adept at protecting their benefactors, warning of raids by federal Prohibition agents. Big breweries shut down when federal agents came snooping. Smaller ones kept brewing; they knew how to disguise their activity.

Whiskey was a different problem. Some saloons got their supplies from legal distilleries. Many prescription medicines in those years had as much as a 70 percent alcohol base. Federal law permitted the manufacture of alcohol for medicinal purposes. It was to be sold only to pharmacies and physicians.

The Treasury Department issued permits to legitimate distillers, to doctors, and to pharmacists. It tried to keep a close check on how much alcohol was made and where it was shipped. It was relatively simple, however, to divert legal alcohol to bootleggers who would doctor the product with additives, caramel coloring, and plenty of plain water. That would transform a gallon of pure good whiskey into a case of illegal 'hootch.'

Joe Reinfeld began by buying this 'cut' whiskey, as it was called. He disliked it thoroughly. It was horrible stuff. It wasn't uniform in taste. It wasn't reliable. Unscrupulous bootleggers were known to cut their whiskey with chemicals that sometimes resulted in blinding unwary drinkers. Reinfeld looked for another source of whiskey – and found it in Canada.

It isn't clear whether Reinfeld was the first American to approach the Bronfman brothers in Montreal, owners of a medium-sized distillery called Seagram's. But he was there right at the beginning; Reinfeld's saloon was selling real Canadian whiskey (only slightly cut) as early as the summer of 1920.

Reinfeld was the genius who developed the system of shipping whiskey directly from the Bronfman distillery in Montreal to the New Jersey shore.

St Pierre and Miquelon are two tiny islands in the mouth of the St Lawrence River, just off the southwestern tip of Newfoundland. They are the last remaining fragments of what had once been France's North American empire. They are inhabited mainly by fishermen who prowl the Grand Banks. Prohibition brought the islands a new notoriety.

The Volstead Act of 1919 had no force in Canada, although the Canadian government – to satisfy Washington – did ban the direct export of alcoholic beverages to the United States. Reinfeld showed the Bronfmans a simple way around their government's edict. Liquor intended for the US was shipped to fictional consignees on St Pierre and Miquelon. Freighters carrying the goods from Montreal made a token run to the islands. They never stopped. Once through Cabot Strait, they swung southeastward toward their real destination, the New Jersey shoreline.

The freighters laden with whiskey would heave to outside the three-mile limit off Port Newark. Speedboats would race out to the freighters anchored beyond US jurisdiction. Loaded, the small boats would head back to port where wagons (in the beginning) waited to be loaded with the precious cargo.

Longy Zwillman soon realized that the arrival of Prohibition presented a faster way to make money than collecting pennies, nickels, and dimes in the policy racket.

He became involved in beating Prohibition's strictures almost as soon as the Volstead Act went into effect in January 1920, by delivering bootleg whiskey picked up at the docks for importers like Reinfeld and others. He sold his horse and wagon and bought a truck. With motorized transportation, Longy realized, distances were no longer a problem. A bootlegger need not be confined to one neighborhood, one city.

Soon, Longy applied the lesson he learned when he was collecting bets for policy banks. Selling liquor yourself was much more profitable than hauling it for others.

'We started in the Third Ward, where we knew everybody,' said one of Longy's old bootlegging sidekicks. 'We'd go around to the different joints to take orders. Longy would take his trucks – we soon had three – down to the docks where he knew the people bringing the stuff in. He'd buy a few hundred cases and bring 'em back to a warehouse we had near Prince Street.

'It was a cash-and-carry system. We'd go down to the port with half a $5 bill. The guy on the dock had the other half. They had better be a match. If our bill matched his, he'd turn the stuff over to us. If it didn't, you could get killed right on the spot.

'The guys we used to load the truck,' recalled the old Newark bootlegger, 'would be picked up on the streets. Unemployed guys, winos, some young punks glad to make an extra buck. We'd cram them into the trucks that were tightly covered by tarpaulins. We always made the trips at night. The guys in the trucks couldn't see which docks we used.

'After the stuff was unloaded from the speedboat and put on the trucks, we'd bring the loaders back to the same street-corner in Newark where we'd pick them up, pay them off with a couple of bucks and a bottle of real hootch. We used people from our own neighborhood to unload the truck in our warehouse. We didn't want pick-up loaders to know where we kept the stuff. We only trusted a few guys, mostly neighborhood people, for that.

'We didn't trust the loaders for another reason. We were afraid of hijackers. We were afraid they'd grab one of our pick-up workers and make him tell where the warehouse was, where we had the stuff stashed. A lot of hijacking went on in those days.

'That's when people got killed. The hijackers were vicious bastards. They didn't have the connections or the organization to get the whiskey on their own. So they tried snatching other people's. If they pulled a successful hijacking during a big shipment, they'd have a couple thousand cases to sell without spending a nickel to get 'em.'

Longy's truck was hit only once by a hijacking gang. He was ready. Zwillman had foreseen such an attempt, had drilled his boys in how to defend their merchandise.

'It wasn't enough to fight off the hijackers,' said another old Zwillman pal who had been on his first raid. 'You had to protect the goods. You had to keep the hijackers from shooting up our stuff on the truck.

'Longy had some of us ride shotgun, just in front and behind the truck carrying the goods. Just like in the Wild West pictures. We were going up the hill toward Reinfeld's place on High Street that one night when the hijackers jumped us. They tried to block off the cross-street, but one of our guys up front rammed right through their barricade. We all had guns, and when we started shooting, they took off, fast. They thought Longy was some punk kid – he was only 17 years old – who'd run as soon as they had him hemmed in. They never expected us to be ready with our own guns.'

The warning to stay away from Zwillman's trucks spread quickly through Newark. Here was a kid who was not only smart enough to use trucks to move his goods. He was ready to fight to protect his property.

Longy had been hauling whiskey for Joe Reinfeld for only a few weeks when the hijack attempt was beaten off. Reinfeld recognized a good thing. His connection with the Bronfmans in Montreal gave him a golden chance to spread his business beyond his own saloon. He was to become the biggest importer of good – and illegal – whiskey on the East Coast.

Reinfeld offered a deal. He asked Longy to become his chief of transportation.

Chapter 4

A. Zwillman, Businessman

The end of World War I brought a quick release of pent-up emotions in the United States. Europe was weary, bled white by war. Its best young men lay under shell-scarred fields in Flanders, at Verdun, near the Somme and the Marne.

America was on the verge of world leadership. Those who foisted Prohibition on the country had used the war as their major weapon. The war was over and won, and all America reached for a big drink to celebrate the victory. People stormed the saloons and speakeasies that sprouted throughout the country, trying to satisfy this enormous national thirst. Prohibition agents discovered that telling people not to drink whiskey was about as easy as trying to tell them not to enjoy sex.

Federal officials tried and failed to stem the flow of beer and whiskey that was drowning the country. They begged for help from state and local agencies. They got very little. Local officials soon knew that the public was dead against Prohibition.

In Longy Zwillman's New Jersey, special state prosecutors had to be named in most of the larger counties because local law-enforcement officials simply refused to enforce Prohibition.

A typical case involved Moe Katzman, a well-known basketball player and promoter who knew just about every official in Bergen County. In 1925, Katzman decided to open a restaurant directly across from the county courthouse in Hackensack.

'I had to get permission to sell whiskey and beer, of course,' said Katzman. 'You know, from guys in the prosecutor's office, the sheriff's men, the local cops. But I knew everybody in town, so I got the word.'

Katzman called his place the Mansion House. It did a brisk business, especially when court was in session.

'I never paid anyone a nickel for the permission,' said Katzman. 'They just did me a favor. And I was protected. One day, a guy comes in the place and wants a beer. He takes one swallow, then asks the bartender for the boss. I was sitting at a table in the corner. I never saw this guy before. He comes over to me and asks if I'm Moe Katzman. I said I was. He tells me I'm under arrest for serving him an illegal drink.

'I was surprised. I told him I had the permission, but he paid no attention. He dragged me across the street and told me to sit inside the courtroom and wait while he talks to a clerk. Judge Charley McCarthy wasn't on the bench, but the minute he walked in, he took one look at me and asked, "What are you doing here, Moe?" I told him that this guy pulled me in for selling beer. The judge looked around to see if anyone was listening. "Get out of here, Moe," he said. I never was bothered again.'

The public had no use for federal agents who tried to enforce the Prohibition laws. Some 40 people were having a high old time in the dining room of a hotel in the suburban town of Oradell. The hotel restaurant had a reputation for serving good, uncut liquor with its food. While everyone was busy eating and drinking, the locked dining-room doors suddenly came crashing down.

'Federal officers,' barked a big man in the doorway. 'Everybody, clear out. This place is padlocked from now on.'

Padlocking – officially closing a business – was the favorite form of punishment for a place caught selling illegal liquor. The diners, grumbling, finished whatever whiskey or beer was left on their tables and began to leave. The agents made no move to stop them. They were after whiskey, not drinkers.

It took the agents a long time to collect the bottles of fine imported stuff stacked in the hotel's cellar. It took them even longer to haul the contraband away. The diners, on their way out, had slashed every tire on the cars belonging to the federal agents.

In Paterson, one of New Jersey's largest cities, local police had to summon the riot squad to protect Prohibition agents who were dismantling the Lido Venice Club, a popular local drinking joint. About 2,000 people had gathered, and the local cops actually feared a lynching.

By 1922, Newark, New Jersey, was the bootleg capital of the country. Newark was chosen over other east coast ports for good reason. It had the most corrupt police, prosecutors, and courts in the country.

Kingpins in this illegal booze traffic were Longy Zwillman and Joe Reinfeld, mainly because they had developed the payoff into an art. The payoffs began at the basic level, with the cop on the beat. These cops didn't just look the other way when whiskey was involved. Uniformed motorcycle cops convoyed trucks from the docks to warehouses to prevent hijacking. Other cops guarded warehouses where liquor was stored.

Prosecutors were equally helpful. When they were forced to consider cases, they 'misplaced' evidence, or made amateurish errors in drawing up indictments, so that a case would be dismissed. Judges, too, did their part. In cases where dismissal would have created a ruckus in the local press, they levied tiny fines. The cruder judges bargained for bribes right in the courtroom.

One of Longy Zwillman's men was sent to lease an empty warehouse in downtown Newark. The young punk was so impressed with being given this important job that he forgot to notify the local precinct commander about Longy's interest in a warehouse in his district.

The night the booze arrived at this warehouse, two plainclothes detectives showed up right behind the first trucks. Jimmy Rutkin a friend of Longy's, was overseeing the unloading.

'You the boss here?' one of the cops asked Rutkin.

'Yeah. What's up?' asked Rutkin.

'You're under arrest,' said the detective.

'What for?' Rutkin wanted to know. He had no idea the fix wasn't in.

'Storing illegal liquor,' said the cop.

'You must be out of your fuckin' mind,' Rutkin said, pulling away from the cop. 'You know who rents this warehouse?'

'I don't give a shit if Calvin Coolidge rents it, wise guy. Come on along,' said the cop.

'Lemme call my lawyer first,' said the surprised Rutkin.

The call made, Rutkin appeared in court that afternoon. Zwillman's lawyers were ready. They had the case put before a certain judge. It was well prepared.

Rutkin stood up when his name was called in court. The charge against him was read. The defense attorney could hardly wait for the last sentence to be finished. He jumped up.

'Your honor,' he said loudly, 'I can give 500 reasons why my client deserves to be on the street right now instead of in this courtroom.'

The judge looked at the lawyer's hands, stuffed deeply in his pockets.

'I'll hear your arguments in chambers,' said the judge. The prosecuting attorney, head bent, was busy shuffling papers in his briefcase.

Rutkin's attorney strutted into the judge's chambers. He reappeared in less than five minutes. His hands were out of his pockets. The judge ascended the bench, rapped for order. He asked Rutkin to stand.

'The case against Mr Rutkin is dismissed,' intoned the judge, 'due to exculpatory evidence.'

Rutkin picked up his coat, patted his lawyer on the back, and walked out of the courtroom. The judge, behind the bench, rubbed his trouser leg, feeling for the 500 crisp, new reasons why James 'Niggy' Rutkin belonged on the street.

Longy's arm extended into every precinct in Newark. The owner of a large warehouse, an immigrant who hadn't lived in this country long enough to qualify for the citizenship he coveted, declined an offer from Gerardo Catena, one of Longy's trusted henchmen, to rent his property. When Catena persisted, threatening violence, the warehouse owner raced down to the local precinct to report the threat.

'Look,' said the sergeant at the desk when he heard the story, 'don't make a fuss. Were you offered a fair rental price? Why make a stink? Let 'em have the place. You'll make a good profit, and you won't get in any trouble.'

Longy learned the payoff art from a master practitioner. Joe Reinfeld had developed this skill in the years his First Ward tavern was the hangout for many of Newark's politicians.

Reinfeld used to give Longy lessons in the art of payoff on Sunday mornings, before the hour when saloons were permitted to open. Reinfeld, polished and worldly, enjoyed playing surrogate father to young Zwillman.

'Any cluck can wave money in front of somebody he wants to buy,' Reinfeld used to say. 'The trick is to learn who to bribe, and how much the guy is worth. A judge is more important than a prosecutor. A city attorney is more important than a cop. Some cops are important, though, because of the information they have, like when and where raids are planned. They're worth almost as much as a prosecutor. If you spread the money around right, you cut out the waste and get the most value.'

Longy was a quick study. It didn't take him long to become as smooth and as sharp as Reinfeld. In addition, while Reinfeld didn't like to beat the bushes for customers, Longy was an adept salesman. He liked mixing with saloonkeepers and politicians, drinking with them, quietly swapping stories. His sales efforts helped Reinfeld's bootleg business grow beyond Newark into the rest of the state.

Zwillman's sales technique was simple. He'd walk in on a potential account, a couple of his boys trailing behind. All were well-dressed, but oozed menace. Conversation was carried on in low tones. Longy would do all the talking.

'Our firm carries only the finest merchandise. No mixtures, no cutting. You can test it.'

This was no boast. Most bootleggers paid $25 for a case of Scotch off the boat. That included the cost of bribery. They sold it for $30 a *bottle*. That was a profit of $28 per bottle. The greedier rum-runners would open the sealed bottles, add water and other adulterants (a trick known in the trade as 'cutting') and rake in $1,000 for each case they sold.

Too often, adulterants included industrial alcohol or other poisons that sickened or killed patrons. That was bad for business all around. Zwillman and Reinfeld claimed their merchandise was uncut, as pure as when it left the distillery. They charged a little more for their goods, but their customers knew they were getting trustworthy liquor.

Longy had another persuasive sales argument. His strength and controlled rage were a Newark legend. Muscle was his investment capital. His customers learned that a deal with Longy was honest and safe. But, once a customer signed up with Zwillman, he'd better not go looking for a deal elsewhere.

Leo Kaplus was a neighborhood Newark gunsel ready for any job that promised even the smallest payoff. He was a braggart, big and bulky, who liked to think he was the toughest man in the city. He free-lanced around Newark, picking up change by squeezing pimps and numbers runners, or beating up storekeepers who refused to pay for 'protection.'

Some of Longy's numbers runners complained that Kaplus was harassing them. Niggy Rutkin, who ran Longy's numbers racket, called in another small-time hood, George Haber, who was known to be a friend of Kaplus's.

'Your buddy, Kaplus,' Rutkin told Haber, 'has been bothering my people. Tell him to cut it out.'

Haber, a wise owl, rushed to give Kaplus the word, Kaplus was not only loud; he was also stupid. He believed his own propaganda.

'You tell Niggy he can kiss my ass,' Kaplus told Haber.

'Don't be a schmuck, Leo' said Haber. 'You don't know what you're in for.'

'There ain't anybody,' bragged Kaplus, 'who has enough guts to tell me what I can and can't do in this city. You tell that Niggy son of a bitch that if he or his boss fucks with me, I'll kick 'em both in the balls to teach 'em a lesson.'

'Leo,' warned Haber, 'you're out of your fuckin' mind.'

'If Niggy and Longy want trouble,' said Kaplus, 'they know where they can find me.'

Haber delivered the message to Longy.

'Where does that big ball of shit hang out?' Longy asked. Haber mentioned a tavern behind the Shubert Theater on Branford Place. 'Let me know when he's in there,' Longy told Haber. Longy preferred handling discipline problems himself.

'I enjoy the exercise,' Longy told Gerry Catena, 'and I know the discipline is done right the first time.'

Kaplus was sitting in the Branford Place saloon one night, still boasting about how tough he was. Another Zwillman henchman, Big Sam Katz, walked by, looked in, made a phone call, then waited in a nearby alley. It took Longy five minutes to ride from his office in the Riviera Hotel. Katz slipped something into his pocket as Longy walked in the saloon door.

Silently, Longy glided over to the table where Kaplus was sitting. Kaplus looked up, started to say something. Longy never gave him the chance. He took a gun from his pocket, pointed it at Kaplus, and fired.

The single shot went right where it was intended – into Kaplus's testicles.

Kaplus was rushed to the emergency ward at Beth Israel Hospital, where the bullet was removed. Big Sam Katz had followed the ambulance. Tall, heavy-set, with a square jaw and an ever-present grin, Katz walked brazenly into the emergency room. He confronted the young doctor who had removed the bullet from Kaplus's scrotum.

'I'll take that,' said Katz, holding out his hand for the bullet.

The doctor, assuming Katz was a detective, meekly handed over the only bit of evidence that could have connected Longy to the shooting.

Kaplus took the lesson to heart. He never pressed charges against Longy. George Haber, who had helped finger Kaplus, was repaid by being put on Longy's payroll as a chauffeur and bodyguard.

Longy knew top bootleggers and gamblers in New Jersey – Willie and Sal Moretti in Cliffside Park, and Al and Tony Anastasia in Fort Lee. The Morettis introduced him to Joseph Doto, known as Joe Adonis, in Brooklyn.

Willie Moretti and Longy became close, even though they had totally different personalities. Moretti was tiny, just over 5 feet. Clever, witty and loud, Moretti was deadly when crossed. He could laugh as he shotgunned a rival to death. He liked living in style. His suits were tailored in Rome. He wore a diamond stickpin in silk ties. He frequented the $100 betting windows at racetracks, but baseball was his favorite sport. Moretti was a heavy contributor to his church. He controlled a trunkful of politicians in North Jersey, and admired Longy's attitudes.

Moretti got a kick out of the Kaplus shooting. He bragged about being friendly with a guy who had such high style. He was fond of telling his pals in Duke's Restaurant how well Longy trained his people.

'Longy's pal, Big Sue Katz,' Moretti told Adonis one night, 'found a rookie cop nosing around one of their warehouses. The kid was just learning his beat and nobody gave him the word yet. This cop was trying to get a look into the warehouse through one of the windows when Big Sue spotted him.

'Sue came running out of the warehouse, grabbed the cop by the arms, and screamed at him, I mean he really yelled: "What the fuck are you doin' around here? Didn't I pay you last week." The rookie was so bewildered, he could shit. He just shook his head.

' "All right," said Sue, "here's $200, $100 for this week, $100 for last week. Next time, pick up your money on time." Of course, Sue realized the kid was new, otherwise he wouldn't be sticking his nose around. This way, he not only scared the shit out of him, he never came near the place again until it was payday. Now that's what I call quick thinking,' went on Moretti, 'and it all comes from the way Longy trains his people.'

Through Moretti, Longy also met Meyer Lansky and Salvatore Lucania, better known as Lucky Luciano. They introduced him to Frank Costello, who controlled the biggest gambling joints in the city, and Benjamin 'Bugsy' Siegel, the smoothest killer in Lansky's crowd.

Later, Longy met the Capone brothers and Jake Guzik in Chicago, King Solomon in Boston, Moe Dalitz, Lou Rothkopf, and Charley Polizzi in Cleveland, Boo Boo Hoff and Niggy Rosen in Philadelphia, Abe Bernstein in Detroit, and John Lazia, who was Boss Pendergast's man in Kansas City.

In South Jersey, Longy ran into Irving Wexler, known as Waxey Gordon, a Philadelphia bootlegger with delusions of grandeur. Gordon wanted to set up a brewery in Paterson, and he knew enough to ask Longy's permission.

Gordon and Longy never really liked each other. Waxey, alternately loud and sniveling, was born on New York's Lower East Side, and was shipped to a reformatory for picking pockets when he was only eleven. His police record filled a folder at New York police headquarters that was five inches thick. When Gordon and Longy met, Zwillman still didn't have an entry in any police file.

When Gordon got the go-ahead, he paid a pittance for Sprattler and Mennel's, an old-line Paterson brewery that had been brewing German-style beer for 44 years. The partners were worried about brewing illegal beer, so they practically gave their business away to Waxey Gordon.

Waxey knew how to market booze. He began paying off people in Passaic and Bergen counties. His bagman was William 'Big Bill' Brady, who ran a taxi service used by the Bergen County prosecutor's office. Brady was later gunned down by a quartet of hoods. His offense: keeping too much of the payoff money for himself. As the assassins' bullets sprayed him, Brady was heard screaming: 'I'll give it back! I'll give it back!'

Waxey Gordon got more than the permit from Longy to brew beer in North Jersey. Longy let him in on a favorite

Zwillman method of bringing beer out of a brewery or a warehouse without federal agents spotting it. He taped clay pipes to the city's sewer system, leading from a brewery or warehouse to a delivery point at the other end of town, where tank trucks waited to haul it away.

Joe Reinfeld knew from the time they first met that Longy Zwillman wouldn't be content to remain a mere employee.

'The kid is not just smart,' Reinfeld told his brother. 'He's also got a lot of drive. He's loyal, up to a point. One day, he'll decide he doesn't need us, and he'll walk out. I wouldn't want to be his competitor. I wouldn't want to cross Longy if our whole business depended on it. He's a killer who doesn't look the part.'

'What are you going to do?' asked Abe Reinfeld. 'He already gets a bonus on the number of deliveries, besides his big salary. What more can you give him?'

'My biggest mistake,' said Joe Reinfeld, 'Was sending him to Montreal to meet Sam Bronfman. Now he's got the connection, too.'

'And Sam really admires the kid,' chimed in Abe. 'Last time I was there, he kept telling me how well-behaved Longy is, how studious-looking. You'd never guess he was a *shtarker* (Yiddish word for strong-arm man), Sam tells me. Also has a head on his shoulders, Sam said. Sounded to me like he was ready to marry off one of his daughters to Longy.'

'That's the big problem,' said Joe. 'If Longy quits us, he has the suppliers he needs. He can even get the Scotch. I told Joe Kennedy that his shipment, the one that was hijacked outside Brockton, that couldn't have been done by one of our people. I don't think he believed me. Oh, he didn't blame us. Said it must have been that punk kid Zwillman, making a deal to hijack his whiskey and give it to the King, Solomon. Said he'd get Longy if it was the last thing he did.'

Joseph P. Kennedy, later American ambassador to Great Britain, father of a president and two senators, controlled the import of all whiskey from the Haig & Haig distillery in Scotland during Prohibition. To his dying day, Longy denied that his men had done this hijacking, one of the largest ripoffs of a shipment of whiskey ever. He often blamed his troubles with the Kefauver Committee on the proddings of Bobby Kennedy, then a Senate aide. Bobby, said Longy, was carrying out his father's orders to settle an old grudge.

The Reinfeld brothers mulled over what to do about Zwillman all summer and fall of 1923, not wanting to make the first move. Longy finally asked for the meeting the brothers dreaded. It was set for Thanksgiving Day. Longy showed up at Joe Reinfeld's home giving no sign of what he was going to ask.

Barely nineteen, Longy had the poise of a much older man. He got right to the point.

'I've been thinking,' said Longy, 'of going into my own business.'

'What business?' asked Joe Reinfeld, parrying.

Longy was aware that he carried the upper hand into the room. Reinfeld may not have been a street fighter, but he was tough and shrewd just the same. He had backbone, Longy knew. Zwillman also knew that Reinfeld didn't hold all the cards in this game.

'I been thinking about buying, selling, and delivering the goods myself.' The challenge was down, all the way, just as Reinfeld had feared.

'You want the problems also?' he asked. 'The payoffs, the payrolls, the lawyers. It's a big nut. You're making as much now, without all the headaches.'

'I got a hard head,' shot back Zwillman. 'I don't mind taking aspirin when it hurts too much.'

Longy could see Reinfeld sag into his chair. The boss tried one more gambit.

'I'll give you 20 percent of the gross,' Reinfeld said. 'That way, you'll be a partner without the expenses and without the headaches.'

Longy shook his head, even as Reinfeld spoke. His

stone-cold eyes looked down on the man who three years before had offered him $200 a week to protect his trucks from hijacking.

'Half,' he said, slowly and distinctly, 'Fifty-fifty. A full partnership.'

Reinfeld's face reddened. He caught himself before spitting out a curse and words he knew he would later regret. He looked at this nineteen-year-old *pisher*, a kid he thought he could buy and sell like hundreds of others in the city. His eyes glazed over. His bootlegger's instincts came to the rescue. He took control of himself, looked down at his well-manicured fingernails. He was getting an offer he couldn't very well refuse, and Joe Reinfeld knew it. Refusal meant war, and Longy had the troops, the guns, the ammunition, and held the high ground. The battle was over before it began. Reinfeld held out his hand.

Longy shook it.

'And,' said Longy Zwillman, the new partner, magnanimously, 'I'll share the expenses too, fifty-fifty.'

In less than two years, Abner 'Longy' Zwillman, poor immigrant's son from Charleton Street, neighborhood rackets man, had become a full partner in one of the biggest, most profitable bootlegging operations in the country. In five years from the Thanksgiving Day agreement, the Zwillman-Reinfeld combine went on to earn more than $20 million, tax-free.

Chapter 5

Young Man in a Hurry

By 1927, Longy Zwillman was a wealthy man. He was still running the numbers racket, which had spread beyond Newark to the surrounding suburbs. His bootlegging deal with Joe Reinfeld was an even better source of income, all tax-free.

Longy was nearing his boyhood goal – to be rich *and* respected. It was what he had thought about when he was hustling vegetables in the streets of Newark with horse and wagon. The morality of reaching his goal didn't concern Zwillman.

Zwillman had grown up in a rugged neighborhood where you lived by your wits. The strong survived and prospered. Longy was strong. He had killer instincts. Those around him knew it even when Longy was a youngster. Sam Katz watched him take on a tough Italian in the schoolyard on Charlton Street who was teasing younger kids by snatching the basketball they were using.

'We were shooting crap up against a wall in the schoolyard,' said Katz. 'Longy must have been 13 or 14. This other guy, the Italian, he had to be 17 or 18 because he had a thick five-o'clock shadow on his face. He had a shirt with the sleeves cut short, just so he could show off his muscles.

'One of the kids who was playing had a little more guts than the others. When this big guy grabbed at the ball, this kid walked over and asked for it back. The Italian just laughed, held the ball out, teasing like, then snatched it back when the kid reached for it. The kid, frustrated, yanked at the big guy's shirt and tore off a button. The guy threw the ball, with all his force, at the kid's head. Then he grabbed him by the hair and started slapping his face, cursing him in Italian.

'Longy wasn't paying too much attention until he heard the slaps and heard the kid howling. He got up slowly and started over. You know the way he walked. It looked slow, but he sure could cover a lot of ground with those long legs of his. He said something to the Italian, so low I didn't hear. Then the Italian guy told Longy to get the fuck out of there or he'd get some of the same medicine.

'Longy didn't say another word. His leg shot out and caught the other guy's shin, right in the bone. Longy was wearing them pointy shoes with lead taps on the tip. The guy doubled over, howling, as if he was shot in the stomach. Longy rabbit-punched him in the back of the neck, and the guy went down like he was clubbed. He was surprised by the attack, but he had enough left to reach out and try to grab Longy's arm. Longy kicked him again, in the stomach this time. He grabbed the guy's hair and started pounding his head on the pavement. We had to pull him off. He would've killed him if we didn't.'

This show of almost uncontrollable rage was rare for Longy. Normally, he was cold and calculating when he wanted to punish someone. But he flashed into violence from time to time, most often when someone challenged him.

'Why didn't you let me kill the fuck?' Longy asked Sam Katz when he was pulled off the Italian. His face was white. 'He called me a kike son of a bitch.'

Longy always felt that his selling bootleg whiskey was morally more defensible than someone else's squeezing the guts out of poor workers in a sweatshop.

'The law against selling whiskey is stupid,' he would say. 'Everybody ignores it, the people who want to drink – and that's almost every grownup in this country – and the cops too. You got to be crazy not to try and make money selling something everybody wants.'

Gambling, to Longy, was another universal urge, as compulsive as sex.

'You find these suckers all over the place. They bet on a card, a number, a horse, a game. They're all trying to beat the odds. They all think they're smarter than the book, they have the system, they're going to make the big hit. But the house always comes out on top. So why not take the money from the suckers?'

Zwillman didn't have any illusions that he was a man of destiny. He recognized, even as a teen-ager, that he was smarter than the petty hoodlums around Newark.

'They were all big shots in their own mind,' he once told Mike Lascari, Charlie Luciano's best friend and Longy's partner in the cigarette machine business. 'All they were doing was running penny-ante games, or pimping, or pushing small storeowners around for 'protection' money. They were dirt, and they always wound up in dirt.'

Longy's horizons spread across the river. He became acquainted with the younger gangsters in New York, guys near his own age. It didn't take long for Longy to realize he was as cool and smart as any of them.

'They got connections,' Longy told Gerry Catena, one of his aides, after he'd been to New York to visit Costello and Luciano. 'They're not using them right. They're not businessmen.' Zwillman believed, without being arrogant, that he could teach the New Yorkers a few things about business tactics.

Longy got his chance through the Moretti brothers, who controlled big gambling in North Jersey. They also had a loose alliance with their powerful friends on the other side of the Hudson. Willie Moretti, an admirer of Longy's style, respected Zwillman's ability to corrupt politicians.

Longy's political clout in New Jersey derived from the Third Ward Political Club at 88 Waverly Place in Newark. It was a hangout for Essex County Democrats and Republicans alike. Party affiliation didn't matter to Longy. If you needed a favor, you got it, regardless of party label. You only had to remember where the favor came from, and that some day you'd have to pay it back.

Longy's reputation as the political 'czar' of Newark fed off his bootlegging business. He was an easy touch for campaign funds. The state Democratic leadership grew into the habit of turning to Longy whenever it came up short. His money helped to finance statewide political campaigns from the late Twenties through the Forties.

In the late Twenties, a succession of reform district attorneys in New York created problems for big-time gambling games in Manhattan and Brooklyn. Meyer Lansky talked to Willie Moretti about the idea of moving the Lansky-Luciano-Costello-Adonis gambling operations across the Hudson into New Jersey, where the climate was more favorable. Moretti suggested bringing in Zwillman.

'The big guy,' Moretti told Lansky about Longy, 'knows his way around New Jersey politics better than anybody in the state'.

Lansky brought Moretti's suggestion to Luciano and Costello. Lucky Luciano liked the big, quiet boy from Newark. Most of the Italian gangsters in New York were anti-Semites; not Luciano. He and Meyer Lansky had been friends since both were still in their early teens. Their friendship blossomed when Lansky helped Luciano get a parole from reform school.

Luciano agreed that the partners should talk to Zwillman. The meeting was held in Moretti's headquarters, Duke's Restaurant in Cliffside Park, across from the entrance to Palisades Amusement Park. As far as an unsuspecting patron could tell, Duke's was an ordinary neighborhood restaurant, a nondescript place where patrons could find a beer and some talk. Some diners boasted about Duke's lasagna. They must have had cast-iron stomachs.

The back room of Duke's, where the Moretti brothers Willie and Salvatore, or Solly, as he was called, had their 'office,' was something else again. It was lavishly furnished in what is popularly called 'Italian provincial.' There isn't a province of Italy that features such furniture.

The door to the back room was a double thickness of steel. The windows, all high above head level, were thickly barred. The walls, nine inches of stone reinforced with concrete, could have served as a bomb shelter – which they were.

Whenever the Morettis were in residence, a couple of their pals like John 'Kid Steech' Bongiorno or Joe 'Chicago Fats' Szabio could usually be found lounging at the end of the bar nearest the door to the 'office.' Since the office was uncomfortably close to the men's room, the hoods at the bar had to stay alert to prevent drunks from wandering through the wrong door. Solly Moretti, the quieter of the two brothers, tried to talk Willie into renovating the restaurant to make a better arrangement. Willie wouldn't hear of it.

'That's why we got three fuckin' locks on the steel door and two guys sitting outside,' was Willie's argument. 'If that can't keep a drunk out of the office, let the bastard walk in and we'll take care of the stupid fuck.'

Longy arrived alone for the big meeting with the New York boys. He had been driven up from Newark by Georgie Haber, his regular chauffeur.

'Take a ride into the country for a couple of hours,' Longy told Haber when he got out of the car in front of Duke's. 'This won't take long. If I'm not in the restaurant when you come back, just sit in the car. Don't come inside. If you want a drink or a bite to eat, go over to the park and wait for me. I'll come out to the car.'

Longy wanted to go to the meeting alone. It would show confidence in his own ability to stand with the others as an equal. It would also show trust, a good way to start any business association. The New Yorkers were impressed. They all knew Longy by reputation. They had never done business with him before. Luciano expressed their pleasure aloud.

'Good to see you, Abe,' he said. The choice of name was significant. Only his family and his closest confidantes called Zwillman 'Abe.' Even his partner Joe Reinfeld called Longy 'Abner.'

Moretti beamed. This kid from Newark was Willie's kind of man. He liked Longy's behavior. It showed the others that Willie was a good judge of a man he had been touting as a possible partner for the New Yorkers.

There were handshakes all around while Willie called for drinks. Solly broke out a well-aged bottle of Chianti Classico that he had been saving for a special occasion.

'Take a look,' he told Adonis. 'It has the medallion

under the name. This is no homemade junk. You can't get a better bottle in Rome.'

Adonis, dapper, self-contained, smacked his lips in appreciation after sipping the wine. Luciano looked at him, tasted the wine, licked his lips, said nothing. He was a man in a hurry, didn't brook small talk, was always ready to get to the heart of the matter when a meeting was called. He looked across the table at Longy.

'You hear the proposition?' he asked Longy.

'Coming to New Jersey makes sense,' Longy said slowly. He stopped, looked around the table. He wasn't committing himself until he knew what was in it for him. Nobody else spoke.

Zwillman had come up from Newark expecting to be cut in to whatever operation they had in mind. He had made up his own mind that he wouldn't take a subordinate position. He knew the others could go into business on his side of the Hudson without him. He also knew they wouldn't have asked him to show up unless they felt he had concrete, profitable contributions to make to the common cause. He spoke right up.

'What's the deal?'

'This is a straight partnership,' Luciano shot back. 'We all contribute equally, and the payoff is equal shares.'

Longy relaxed. They were talking his language. His gamble in coming alone had paid off. His first suggestion showed the New Yorkers they had bought a partner of worth.

'The best way to go,' said Zwillman after a handshake on the agreement, 'is to buy a string of roadhouses across the area, in spots closest to New York. We open good-looking joints. We sell liquor to the gamblers, and we make money on both ends. We take 'em at the tables, and by the bottle. The places I have in mind would attract the best people. No riffraff. We let the word out that any gentleman can bring his best girl or his wife to our places, and not be ashamed they did it. We get the most prominent citizens from the big city and from the suburbs, and we make 'em feel comfortable. They'll come back, bring their friends, advertise the places for us, and bring plenty of money. A class place builds its own reputation.'

The details, the partners agreed, would be left to Moretti and Zwillman while the others took care of closing out their New York properties that were under the most heat. Using dummy real-estate firms, Zwillman selected the sites – from the rim of the Palisades through Bergen and Hudson counties to the far reaches of Morris County. Some of these casinos were large, shapeless structures, like Costa's Barn in Lodi. The partners put sawdust on the floor for atmosphere as much as cleanliness. Gamblers frequenting these casinos said they had been 'hitting the Sawdust Trail.'

Others were more elegant, like the Carriage Club in Florham Park. It was so posh that, after being sold, it was transformed into the Florham Park Country Club without much alteration. Clients in these fashionable clubs included high-ranking state officials and business executives, many of whom were socially prominent scions of 'old money' families.

Gaming at the tables and drinking uncut liquor weren't the only vices available at these clubs. The young gangsters who worked there had a special attraction. The sleek women who came to the clubs soon learned to thrill at their touch, to boast to their female friends of the men's prowess as studs. Romancing a young gangster became the fashion of the day among a certain class of woman.

One wealthy young widow became deeply attached to Zwillman. Her late husband, a nationally prominent industrialist, had left her a small fortune that she had invested wisely, building her own wealth. She didn't flaunt her money, wore simple, tailored clothing, lived modestly, gave liberally to charity, endowed college professorships. Her one vice was Zwillman. His quiet good looks and the aura of danger he carried, the widow told a friend, fascinated her. She showered him with gifts, invited him to parties at her home, had him escort her to charity dinners and theater parties.

Longy, at first reluctant, began to enjoy these outings. He was seeing a new and different life-style, and he liked what he saw. He began to read widely in the widow's excellent library. His natural love for music was steered by the widow into a taste for grand opera.

One patrician figure who with his wife made weekly visits to the gaming tables was wealthy Charles Edison, son of the famed inventor-industrialist, Thomas Alva Edison. They came, said Edison, who was later to be a governor of New Jersey, purely for fun. When the Edisons won at the tables, they distributed some of the winnings to employees of the club. The rest went to charity. When they lost, Mrs Edison would write out a check to the house for the correct amount.

The boom years of the Twenties saw Longy's firm import about 40 percent of the booze that crossed the border from Canada. He and Reinfeld ran 30 chartered ships to help supply most of the East Coast. The Internal Revenue Service later estimated that the Reinfeld-Zwillman combine earned $40 million from rum-running during the five-year period between 1928 and 1933.

Longy was never showy with his money. He preferred to live quietly in a suite at a downtown Newark residential hotel, the Riviera. He dressed conservatively, spoke quietly, preferred owning two- and three-year-old automobiles, smaller Buicks and Chryslers instead of the larger, showy limousines some of his henchmen sported.

Zwillman moved his mother and his unmarried sisters and brothers from their humble Stratford Place apartment into a new house at 120 Hansbury Avenue in the wealthy Weequahic section of Newark. He paid all the bills for his family, which included a couple of brothers-in-law.

'He was a sucker for that family,' the notoriously cheap Meyer Lansky once said. 'None of the brothers is worth a shit. They don't want to work, couldn't handle a job if he gave them one. Only his mother and his sisters appreciate what Longy does for the family. But you can't say a word against them. Longy says it's his obligation to support them all.'

Longy's reputation for violence had never resulted in any appreciable police record. He was picked up in Newark in

December 1925, charged with disorderly conduct, specifically with 'using loud and indecent language,' but received a suspended sentence.

Between June 1927 and March 1928, Longy was arrested three more times, in each case on a charge of atrocious assault and battery. The complaints were all withdrawn a day after being filed.

On June 18, 1928, Preston Buzzard of 194 Charlton Street walked into Newark police headquarters.

'I want Abner Zwillman arrested,' said Buzzard, a pimp who was also a runner for Longy's numbers racket. The cops were amazed. They knew who Buzzard was, and listened uncomfortably to Buzzard's story.

'Longy attacked me, hit me a dozen times with a blackjack,' said Buzzard to detectives, who tried to look the other way. 'Look at my face. Hospital says I got three broken bones here in my cheeks. My whole body is one big bruise. I thought I was going to die after Longy finished hitting me.'

With reluctance – and only because several reporters were on hand after they had been tipped off about Buzzard's beating and his determination to squeal to the police – two detectives named Conlon and Thomas were assigned to bring in Longy. They worked slowly and methodically, so slowly that it took them a week to find one of Newark's most prominent, most visible residents. Longy finally appeared voluntarily on June 25, and was held in $1,000 bail on the assault charges. He put up his bail – in cash – and was bound over for trial.

While Longy awaited trial, several men showed up at police headquarters. Each one insisted that he, not Zwillman, was Preston Buzzard's assailant. The most reasonable story, according to the police, came from Lewis Reich, known in the Third Ward as Leibush. He had beaten Buzzard, Leibush told the cops, because the man owed him a lot of money, and refused to pay up.

The police were inclined to believe Leibush. They were ready to hold him and let Longy off the hook. However, they couldn't push this ploy by a newly appointed judge named Daniel Brennan. Longy's trial, ruled Judge Brennan, would go on as scheduled.

Leibush's story was true – up to a point. Buzzard did owe a lot of money, but to Longy, not to Leibush. Zwillman later revealed that Buzzard held out a week's worth of collections from his numbers route.

Nobody held out on Zwillman; it was suicidal. In Buzzard's case, Longy made an exception. He said later he felt sorry for the pimp because Buzzard was black. Zwillman taught the pimp a lesson with a severe beating, but let Buzzard live. This bit of charity cost Zwillman his freedom for the first and only time in a 30-year career of crime.

Longy's attorney in the Buzzard assault case was Harry Weinberger of the firm of Weinberger and Minturn, one of the most prestigious in the state. But this time, not even prominent lawyers could help. Zwillman was found guilty of atrocious assault and battery against Preston Buzzard on February 11, 1929. He appealed the conviction, and lost. He was ordered to appear on December 2, 1930 for sentencing before Judge Brennan – and didn't show up. He was, it turned out, in Montreal on rum-running business.

The judge ordered that Longy be picked up at once, and issued an arrest warrant. Up stepped a young lawyer of the Weinberger and Minturn firm named William J. Wachenfeld, later to become a Superior Court assignment judge. He asked for a conference with Judge Brennan. It was held in the judge's chambers. The prosecutor strangely, didn't ask to attend. A few minutes after the conference, Judge Brennan ordered the arrest warrant cancelled. He ruled that Longy had a week to turn himself in.

Longy showed up at the appointed date. He was sentenced to six months in the Essex County Penitentiary in North Caldwell. He could have gotten a year and a day.

Longy was driven to North Caldwell in one of his cars, a huge 16-cylinder Cadillac, by Sam Katz, who lived near the prison. Zwillman knew how to drive but seldom, if ever, drove himself. He said it could only bring him problems because of his 'prominence' in the community. He would be, Longy maintained, an open target for every ambulance-chasing lawyer in the state if he became involved in even a minor accident.

Longy was assigned to work in the prison laundry until his political cronies could exert influence. Within a week, he was transferred to the prison hospital, where he worked as an orderly. He was paid $5 for the three months he served. He also had a private deal with the warden. Zwillman was allowed illegal weekend furloughs – on one condition. He had to spend his free time in Katz's house in Caldwell, where the warden could find him if unexpected trouble developed. Longy scrupulously lived up to this agreement.

Zwillman was released from the penitentiary at 7:59 A.M. on March 31, 1930. He was dressed in a white shirt, gray tie, dark gray suit, a pearl gray hat and was carrying a dark overcoat over his arm. Two friends were on hand to escort him.

As he waited to be released, Longy bantered with his guards, who seemed extremely friendly. Reporters hanging around heard Longy say to one guard that he was going back to Newark, 'the greatest city in the world.' He also told reporters he was 'through with politics,' and denied he was 'in the rackets.' As reporters pestered him, he shouted, 'A box of cigers if you leave me alone.' The reporters refused the offer, and some of Longy's friends threw an overcoat over the racketeer's head as he ducked into a Cadillac. The shades in the car were drawn as it raced out of the prison courtyard.

A big public welcome-home dinner had been planned by friends. Longy demurred, 'because of the publicity,' he told his friends. Instead, he was feted at a private hideout. Only his closest friends were on hand, including his New York partners and some of the handsome women who were regular patrons at the Carriage Club.

One chapter in Zwillman's life was ending. Another, bigger one, was about to begin. First, he had to settle an old score, and that meant a battle to the death.

Chapter 6

War and Peace in Newark

The war was short and brutal, raging only a few weeks. Bullets plunked into soft flesh, ricocheted off buildings, exploded in breweries and speakeasies all over Newark. The beastliness, the spying, the lying that was part of this conflict was like the combat between two mighty countries. In reality, it was only a war between two rival gangs.

When the battle was over, the rival gang leaders agreed on a treaty of peace. It lasted more than a quarter of a century. That's longer than a lot of treaties between nations have lasted.

Abner 'Longy' Zwillman declared the war. It began, like most wars, over a question of territory. His opponent was Ruggiero 'Richie the Boot' Boiardo, the flashy, snarling, brutal crime boss of Newark's Little Italy, the First Ward.

In the early post-World War I days, the First Ward in Newark was home to a large Italian immigrant population. They were mainly hard-working construction laborers, tailors, and shoe-makers. A few of the earlier arrivals had graduated to the status of small shopkeepers.

Few, if any, families in this neighborhood of hard-working immigrants had a telephone in the house. Outgoing calls were usually made from the pay phone at the local corner candy store. Each block had at least one such store with a messenger-phone setup. Good customers were given a special privilege – they could also receive incoming calls at the store.

When an incoming call would arrive, a neighborhood boy would always be hanging around, glad for a chance to run an errand or call a customer to the phone in return for a penny tip, a piece of candy, or even (when the customer was a pretty female) a simple smile.

Ruggiero Boiardo, among his other traits, was a committed Don Juan. He would receive more than his share of calls at the corner candy store, not only from friends and henchmen but also from female admirers.

Boiardo was called to the phone so often that it became a standing neighborhood joke. Invariably, the answer to the query 'Where's Richie?' would be followed by the phrase: 'He's in the phone booth.'

The last word was pronounced, in inimitable North Newark dialect, without the last letter – as 'boot.' The word relating to Boiardo caught on.

Ruggiero Boiardo was anglicized to Richie Boiardo. And the nickname became 'Richie the Boot.'

Boiardo had been a milkman, delivering bottles for babies from door to door. It was just as easy for Richie the Boot to collect bets on his milk route as it had been for Longy Zwillman to pick up numbers from housewives to whom he delivered fresh fruits and vegetables. In time, Richie the Boot developed a flourishing local business in the numbers and protection rackets. When Prohibition came in, Boiardo expanded into the whiskey business.

Boiardo, however, never made the big jump out of his own neighborhood. While Longy's wealth and influence grew through his ties with Joe Reinfeld and the New York mob, Boiardo remained stuck in North Newark, where he had grown up.

Boiardo, naturally, was jealous. It took him a few years, but eventually he thought it was time to challenge Longy on Zwillman's home ground. Toward the end of the Roaring Twenties, Boiardo's boys went swaggering through Longy's Third Ward fiefdom, harassing bartenders, threatening saloon owners, holding up numbers runners.

The first warning came from Hymie 'The Horse' Klein, who ran speakeasies in a couple of Newark hotels. He came into Longy's Riviera Hotel office looking worried.

'I got a visit,' said the Horse, 'and I don't like it.'

'What kind of a visit?' asked Gerry Catena, one of Longy's close associates and friends.

'From one of Richie's boys,' said Klein. 'He started

asking me all sorts of questions about how much beer I buy, what I pay for a barrel. What is this shit? I asked him. You know where my stuff comes from. Well, he tells me, from now on you've got a new supplier.

'Then he tells me,' continued Klein, 'what the price for beer is going to be from now on. I look at him like he's crazy. I asked him who sent him, anyway. He snaps his fingers and two guys come off the wall. I never even saw 'em come into the place. Two big bastards. One grabs a stein and smashes it on the bar. Then he throws the broken pieces on the floor and squashes 'em like you would squash a pumpkin. The other guy, the one I recognized, comes from Richie's gang, tells me there'll be no more trouble if I just pay attention. Then they leave. What happens now?'

Longy had been sitting behind his ebony desk as if he hadn't been listening to Klein's story. Catena turned around to his boss. Longy looked out the window for a long minute.

'I don't get it,' he said finally. 'That crazy bastard knows it's our stop. You sure they were Richie's boys?' The last question was addressed to Klein.

'Abe, I know the guy who came in first. I don't remember his name, but he lives up on North 7th Street. I've seen him. He belongs to Richie. He told me he's sending in a salesman Thursday to sign the deal.'

'Get me Jake Rosenthal,' Longy said to Sam Katz. Rosenthal was a muscle man. He once worked for anyone who would pay him, but gradually, Rosenthal stuck to Longy's side. It was his guarantee of steady work. 'Tell Jake I want him in Klein's place Thursday, when that salesman shows up.'

Zwillman had never had any trouble in the First Ward. He had kept out of Boiardo's home territory as a matter of courtesy. Longy couldn't understand what was happening – at first.

Jake Rosenthal came back with the answer.

'This fat little fuck walks into Klein's place today,' he told Longy the following Thursday. 'He has a card he slaps on the bar and tells the Horse that's his price list. The Horse gives me the sign, so I walks over and asks this guy what's happening. He tells me to mind my own fuckin' business. I tell him this *is* my business, and if he don't get his fat ass out of the place, I'll throw him through the window. He's alone, so he just looks at me and walks out. I pick up the card. It has Richie the Boot's name on it.'

It didn't take long for Rosenthal's action in Klein's place to have a repercussion. The Horse walked into his place Friday morning to find that someone had smashed in the back door and raked the back bar with a submachine gun. Hotel employees had heard the noise, but didn't bother to investigate. It wasn't their business.

Richie the Boot's answer was typical of his logic. Longy's partner, Joe Reinfeld, built his multi-million dollar business from a saloon in Boiardo's home territory, the First Ward. Now the Reinfeld-Zwillman combination was doing business all over New Jersey. Why couldn't he, Ruggiero Boiardo, therefore do business anywhere in Newark?

Longy didn't declare war on Richie the Boot until a second provocation took place. Barney Goldfarb, who made a good living lugging whiskey for Longy, was bringing a load of booze from a warehouse to a saloon owned by a Third Ward character named Meyer Rosenberg. It was a warm day, and before unloading, Goldfarb stepped inside to cool off with a draught beer.

'I heard a shot,' he told Longy later, still shaking from the experience, 'then breaking glass. It sounded like it was coming from my truck. Then I heard a scream – I knew it was the kid I hired to ride along with me – and some more shooting. I ran out, and there was the kid, hanging half out the door with a hole where his eye used to be. The bastards killed him, then they turned a Tommie on the truck. They just shot up half the cases I had. I ducked inside Meyer's place. I didn't know if them fucks was coming after me, too. I knew I couldn't do anything for the kid anyway.'

The last straw for Longy came when some of Boiardo's boys walked into the Third Ward Political Club, Longy's home away from home on Waverly, between Avon and Mercer streets, and held up the few members sitting around schmoozing. Longy's response was quick and typical. He struck directly at the head and heart of his enemy.

Richie 'The Boot' Boiardo was walking leisurely along a street in downtown Newark. It was spring, and Boiardo had been to visit his tailor. Surrounding him were four of his best men, all well-armed. Just as the Boiardo party reached the southwest corner of Broad and Market Streets, they spotted three men ambling toward them across the aptly named Broad Street.

The four Boiardo bodyguards took a few steps into the street toward the oncoming trio, then saw who they were. All four Boiardo gangsters melted swiftly away.

'They disappeared,' said a Zwillman henchman, 'like thin smoke rings from a lousy cigar. They just melted away, leaving The Boot all by himself in the middle of the sidewalk. He didn't have a chance. Our guys started banging away before Richie could get his gun out of his holster.'

Some witnesses said later they heard 16 shots. Others claimed they counted 12. Verified by a surgeon was the fact that eight bullets were lodged in Ruggiero Boiardo's bulky body.

Doctors at St Michael's Hospital, where The Boot was taken, said it was a miracle that Richie hadn't died. He lived, although Boiardo carried two of those eight slugs in his body until the day he died, aged 95, in November 1984.

Boiardo ordered retaliation from his hospital bed. His gunmen had a standing order – get Longy Zwillman. They roamed the streets, searching out Longy in candy stores, policy stops, saloons, anywhere they thought they could find him.

Longy didn't wait around to be hit. His own men searched through the First Ward for Boiardo's boys. Three were trapped in a restaurant on Bloomfield Avenue, dragged into a waiting car, and driven into Newark's industrial section, known as Ironbound. Behind the barrelhouse of the Ballantine Brewery, the three Boiardo boys were hauled out of the car, sure they were going to die. Instead, they were bashed across the knees with baseball bats until their patellas had been reduced to gritty mush. They were crippled for life.

The war went on unabated for three weeks. Boiardo, in his hospital bed, was beside himself with rage because his men couldn't get to Longy and wipe him out. Richie knew he was alive only through a miracle. Any one of those eight bullets that hit him could have been fatal.

Boiardo ordered his men to rent an apartment opposite the Riviera Hotel, where Longy lived. He had them set it up with enough artillery to sack a city, while they waited for a crack at Longy. Their chance never came. Zwillman's protection was too tight. Nothing seemed to work.

The dayside desk clerk at the Riviera Hotel was going over some bills one morning during this war when two young women came in. They were tall, fairly good-looking, probably call girls, the clerk decided.

'Mr Zwillman,' said one of the women. She had a husky, pleasant voice.

'Have an appointment?' asked the clerk.

'Of course,' was the reply. The second woman didn't show her face. She seemed to be interested in checking the exits leading from the lobby.

'One minute, please,' said the clerk. The Riviera was a family hotel. The management, however, made discreet concessions to tenant Zwillman and his men when female visitors were involved.

The clerk called the Zwillman suite on the third floor, turning his back to the women. His conversation with the voice at the other end was low.

'A couple of people here asking for Longy,' the clerk said. 'No, women. But there's something fishy. They don't *look* like women. I don't know. Yeah, you want me to send 'em up?' The clerk was surprised, but did as he was told.

'You can go up,' he said, turning to the women. 'Use the left elevator, please. The other one is out of service just now.' It wasn't, of course.

As soon as the elevator door closed, the clerk was back on the phone.

'The two are coming up,' he told whoever answered in Longy's office. 'Yeah, something fishy about the way they walk.'

The door to Longy's suite on the third floor of the Riviera was protected by two layers of tempered steel. In addition, a 'watchman' stood guard in the corridor. This day, it was Joe Caprio, the barrel-chested brother of Newark city commissioner Ralph Caprio.

Caprio was waiting beside the elevator when its door opened. As the two 'women' stepped out, they found themselves staring into the barrel of Caprio's .38 caliber Police Positive. Behind the bodyguard and in front of the door to Zwillman's suite was chauffeur George Haber, also with a gun held ready.

'Mr Zwillman,' said Caprio sweetly to the visitors, 'is waiting for you. Inside, you pricks!'

By this time, the two well-dressed visitors were trembling so violently that Caprio later swore he could hear their bones rattling. They were, of course, not women at all, but two young, handsome Boiardo buckos. Each had a snub-nosed Smith & Wesson tucked into the waistband of a flapper-style panty.

The boys, no more than 18 years old, were relieved of their weapons and marched into Longy's office. Their eyes rolled, and they sweated, teeth chattering. Zwillman walked from behind his desk, stood and stared at the terror-stricken youngsters. Zwillman's reputation for instant punishment was known to every hood in Newark. One of Boiardo's young soldiers was already moving his lips in silent prayer.

'Sit down!' Zwillman said softly, after a long interval. His voice was a sibilant purr, cold and controlled. The two youngsters almost fell into two chairs against the wall. The one who had been praying before began to retch. Caprio walked over and slapped his face. Longy waved his hand in annoyance. Caprio backed off. A dark stain spread over the front of the young hood's costume as he wet himself in fear.

Longy walked closer to the two cringing would-be assassins. He put his hands in the pockets of his immaculately tailored jacket, bent slowly from the waist to get closer to the two boys.

'I'm not going to hurt you,' Longy said. 'I want you to listen closely, and remember exactly what I tell you. I have a message for your boss, and I want you to promise you'll give it to him.' Each gunman nodded, his head jerking with anxiety. 'Tell Boiardo I want a meeting. Tell him all this is bullshit, and it's time to talk. Got that?'

Both boys nodded again, more vigorously.

'Repeat what I said,' said Longy.

In unison, the gunmen parroted Longy's message. When they finished, he nodded again.

'I'll give you a number. You tell Boiardo, if he doesn't call it in 24 hours, you're all dead. My people will clean every one of you rats off the streets of Newark. Now, get out of here.'

The two jumped to their feet. They took one sidelong glance at Caprio, who still held his gun in his hand, then almost knocked each other down in their haste to get to the door.

'Wait!' The youngsters froze.

Longy glided over to them. 'Let me,' he said, 'hear that message again.' One boy began crying, so hard that he could only mumble. The other stuttered out Longy's message to Boiardo. 'Okay, Joe,' said Zwillman to Caprio, 'take 'em downstairs.'

The messengers must have been persuasive. Or maybe it was because Longy spared their lives that Boiardo realized Zwillman was serious about a meeting. He was also a little flattered that Longy wanted the meeting, despite his threat to wipe out the Boiardo gang.

A meeting was arranged. Neither boss would attend. Mutual distrust was still too strong. Each chose a representative to do his talking.

Boiardo, determined to show Zwillman that he wasn't just another Newark punk, convinced Ralph Capone, brother of Chicago boss Al Capone, to be his representative. Zwillman didn't feel any need to impress Richie the

Boot. He selected one of his younger lieutenants, Gerardo Catena, as his negotiator. Catena had risen rapidly in the Zwillman organization. He was imposing looking for all his youth, sharp and cool, as well as fiercely loyal to Zwillman. By choosing Catena as his representative, Longy made two statements. One: he thought it good form to have someone of Italian extraction do his negotiating with Richie the Boot. Two: Catena's choice was a signal of his promotion to the Zwillman inner circle.

Negotiations, surprisingly, took only two days. Zwillman's proposal made eminent sense. He wasn't seeking hegemony over all of Newark, he let it be known. Why couldn't both sides profit from the action in the city? As rivals, they could only destroy each other, at great cost. Sharing the city, they could each make more money than was possible individually, and without bloodshed.

It made a kind of hard sense. Longy, a more important figure than Boiardo, was also more resourceful. A war in Newark, he saw, would only mean diverting resources that could be better used elsewhere in his newly expanding rackets. He tucked the idea of cooperation away in the back of his mind, to be used elsewhere later, even if Boiardo spurned the offer.

Boiardo, surprisingly, saw the value of cooperation even though he was lusting for blood and power. Longy's argument was convincing. And, as Ralph Capone explained to Boiardo, it was Longy, after all, who was asking for peace.

'That's a point for you,' said Capone, who reasoned that, if peace didn't work out, there would always be time for Boiardo to return to war.

The peace treaty was celebrated at a private catering establishment on Newark's Seventh Avenue, a regular hangout for mob figures. It was one of the wildest parties seen in Newark in generations. It lasted two whole days. It was attended by both gangs and their leaders, by city officials, and by Paul Moore, the Democratic candidate for Congress, among other politicians from all over New Jersey.

Boiardo discovered, after the peace treaty, that he really liked Zwillman. Longy, in turn, gave Richie a huge diamond mounted on a belt buckle as a gift. That buckle was later to save Boiardo's life when a gunman took a shot at him. The bullet glanced off the diamond instead of striking Boiardo in the gut. Who fired that shot was never discovered.

Boiardo and Niggy Rutkin, one of Longy's top aides, then went into business together operating stills where illegal whiskey was distilled until Repeal and after. These stills continued to operate into the Forties; the whiskey they produced wasn't subject to federal or state taxes.

Chapter 7

A Hoods' Convention

The most profitable American industry in the high-flying late Twenties was a blue chip unlisted on the nation's stock exchanges. Bootlegging produced bigger profits on a smaller capital investment than anything Wall Street or Main Street could offer.

The biggest boom years for bootlegging were 1928 and 1929. Profits were enormous, close to $350 million a year, according to federal estimates. And the government didn't get a dime in taxes out of all that income. Bootleggers lived high, spending money like profligate pashas. And for some of them, living for today was the right philosophy. Tomorrow truly never came.

It took a long time for some of the old-time racketeers to recognize that rum-running was far more profitable than the money they had been squeezing from small-time gambling, prostitution, and terrorizing small shopkeepers.

These gangland hotheads had a nasty habit of killing anyone who disagreed with them, or insulted their 'honor.' Known as 'Moustache Petes' if they were Sicilian or 'Potato Heads' if they were Irish, they took off after each other for minor reasons, spilling blood in the streets and causing a public uproar when they killed innocent people.

Gangsters like Zwillman, Lansky, Luciano, and Costello, on the other hand, were not averse to rubbing out their eliminating rivals. But they did it with discretion.

'I've got a good thing going in whiskey,' Longy Zwillman once told a dinner companion who was a Wall Street broker. 'It's a protected business. I take care of the right people, and they don't bother me. I want the cops to spend their time catching crooks and murderers. The prosecutors try 'em. The judges do their thing. It doesn't upset them when I sell whiskey. They drink, just like everybody else. They know I'm providing a service. So, they don't bother me. So I pay 'em a few bucks. That's nothing, just expense money to the cops, who have families. It's campaign money to the guys running for office. I'm paying because they provide a service – to me.

'But, when my people start causing them grief, look out. The public don't give a damn if hoodlums knock each other off. But, if too many bullets start flying around near a school, if they start finding bodies on the front lawns in Maplewood or South Orange [fashionable suburban neighborhoods], if you have to step over bodies on the sidewalk, it's embarrassing to the guys I'm paying off. That's not what they bargained for.

'They hear screams from the public, and they put the squeeze on us. A couple of times, we had to give them people to prosecute because it was just too hot. Look, we had to give them Al Capone when he went crazy in Chicago. We didn't want to do it. But he became a menace to our business. We had to convince him it would be a shorter rap if he got pulled in for income-tax evasion. If he didn't go, we'd turn him over for something more serious, and he knew it. That's why he went quietly.

'Another time, we had to play ball was when the Lindbergh baby was kidnapped. A lot of bull was being thrown around that the mob did the job. That was crazy. Just the opposite; the Lindbergh family asked some of our people to help 'em find the baby when the State Police couldn't do it.

'The last thing any of us wanted was to have the whole country get excited about us because of a lousy thing like snatching a baby. There's no ransom big enough to pay for such a stupid trick. We passed the word through Frank Costello – we want the guys who did this thing, and we better get them fast. The answer soon came back – it was an amateur job. Not even the cheapest goon in the rackets would have done this thing. He'd be dead the minute he tried passing any of the ransom money.'

FBI files verify this account. They report that Longy

Zwillman had offered first $50,000, then $100,000 for information that would assist in finding the Lindbergh baby. One of his men, Al Silvers, reported that he heard some people in the Hotel Victoria in New York claim they knew where the baby was. Abe did some checking. It turned out to be a false claim, a con game by some small-time crooks who thought they could grift some money.

'We sent word into the Lindbergh family that we were trying to get at the guys who did the job,' continued Longy. 'Then they found the baby dead, and they knew the child died before the ransom money was paid. That's when Colonel Lindbergh said he believed us that it was an amateur job, just like we told him.

'Later, Frank Costello told me he got a "thank you" note from the family, after that guy [Bruno Richard] Hauptmann was caught. Lindbergh always believed someone in our organization fingered Hauptmann. Maybe we did, maybe we didn't. I always thought that Nazi Hauptmann was caught buying gas in the Bronx with a ransom bill.

'The point I'm making is that when the public gets too pumped up about killing, our business is in trouble. I always liked it calm and quiet on the streets. Those politicians are like jackals. The first time there's trouble, they turn on you, while they're still taking your money.'

Longy's explanation glossed over his own method of eliminating bootlegging rivals or acquiring rum-running businesses he coveted. Longy's early reputation in the industry was earned purely as a '*shtarker*,' a strong right arm for others in the business. He developed finesse as he grew older and more sophisticated. But the old habits would return when he was thwarted.

Take the case of Max Hassel and Max Greenberg, partners in a successful brewing operation in Elizabeth. They had purchased the large Peter Hock Brewery, operating in Harrison as well as in Elizabeth.

When you own an operation that big – in bootlegging as in any business – you're bound to run into rivals. Hassel and Greenberg soon found themselves irritated at an operation run by young Abner Zwillman, who was building his own illegal business out of Newark. This upstart, as Hassel called Longy, was getting too big for his own good. The partners arrived at a business decision simultaneously – Longy had to be eliminated.

Hassel and Greenberg equated Longy's youth with inexperience. They made a fatal mistake. Longy had planted several of his own men in the Hassel and Greenberg organization. The information was passed back that the partners were going to have Longy machine-gunned to death in Port Newark the next time he went out to supervise the unloading of a shipment of whiskey.

Longy didn't retaliate immediately. That would have revealed his hand to other potential rivals, those he wanted to keep guessing about the way he operated. As a matter of fact, Zwillman waited a full four months – taking care to be on guard – before he moved.

On April 12, 1933, the two Maxes, Hassel and Greenberg, were sleeping in their suite at the Elizabeth Carteret Hotel in Elizabeth. Bodyguards were ensconced in rooms on either side of the two bosses. Hotel employees were on duty at their desks. Everyone swore later that they heard nothing, saw less.

Nevertheless, there were the two Maxes, stretched out on their bloody beds, dead as beached mackerel, their necks cut from ear to ear. The two murders were never solved.

Within weeks after the Hassel and Greenberg funerals, their brewery operations were taken over (without a murmur from anyone in the dead partners' organization) by Longy Zwillman. Longy eventually expanded his operations in Elizabeth to take in the Rising Sun Brewery. In charge was a friend, Nick Delmore.

At the time, a Treasury agent named John G. Finelli was assigned to the Elizabeth region. He began snooping around the Rising Sun Brewery to see what he could see. It's hard to know what Finelli was looking for; everyone in the city – in the East – knew illegal beer was being brewed at the Rising Sun.

In any case, Finelli was killed. Nick Delmore was tried

for the murder, and acquitted. Another Zwillman employee, William Weisman, had been indicted in the same murder. His indictment was quashed. The murder of Finelli was never solved.

Years later, an old friend of Zwillman's related how Finelli was eliminated.

'The guy was a real pain in the ass. He was always whining, then getting in the way, making it tough for Nick. One day, a couple of the guys came in and found Finelli snooping around. They grabbed him, and strung him up by his heels over one of the brewing vats. They let him dangle there for 15 minutes while he begged and pleaded for his life. He swore he'd never tell anybody what he found, that he would be good. He swore on the life of his family.

'It didn't do him any good. They let him down slowly into the vat by the chain around his legs. Then they rolled his body out into the street. I guess they didn't dump it far away because they wanted the guy to be a lesson to his pals in the area.'

A word here about the popular conception of organized crime in America. It has been tabbed by impressionable journalists and a sensation-oriented press by a variety of names: Black Hand, Mafia, Cosa Nostra. You read constantly of 'families' dominated by '*capos*,' advised by '*consiglieri*,' assisted by '*caporegimos*' and 'soldiers,' or hit-men known as 'buttons.'

These 'families are said to be organized into a national 'Syndicate,' with a '*capo di tutti capi*' as the top boss to whom inter-regional disputes are brought for adjudication. You have five families in New York (the biggest crime market) and various others all over the country. The names of leaders and soldiers are always Italian (a non-Sicilian, it is said, can work for Cosa Nostra, but not be a 'made' member).

That may or may not be true today, depending on which law-enforcement agency you're talking to. In 1929, it was pure nonsense to speak of organized crime in terms of the Mafia. Sure, there were Italian gangsters – the Capone brothers, Johnny Torrio, Big Jim Colosimo, Joe Masseria,

Sal Maranzano, Adonis (born Joseph Doto), Costello, and Luciano.

But, they weren't organized into anything like a national 'trust' until Longy Zwillman arranged the 1929 convention in Atlantic City. And they weren't exclusively Italian, not by a long shot.

Gangsterdom in America – big-time rum-running, numbers racketeering, loan-sharking, labor union subversion, and gambling, mainly big-bet gambling – was in the hands of more Irishmen and Jews than Italians.

Just look at the names of the well-known early hoods: Moses Annenberg, Meyer Lansky, Ben Siegel, Moe Dalitz, Legs Diamond (whose real name was John T. Noland), Big Bill Dwyer, Dutch Schultz (really Arthur Flegenheimer and Jewish), Jake Guzik, Dandy Phil Kastel, Mickey McBride, Owney 'The Killer' Madden, Dion O'Bannion, Arnold Rothstein, Charlie 'King' Solomon – these were hardly sons of Italy.

These men all had criminal organizations they either headed or worked with. Their interests, however, were local or regional, at best. If they conferred, it was haphazardly – chance meetings at racetracks or spas, for example. In some cases, they were bitter rivals to the death, ready to murder not only each other but every member of a rival's gang.

Then came Longy Zwillman, the organizational genius, translating his personal experience with Ruggiero 'Richie the Boot' Boiardo into national terms.

The 1928 presidential election was a turning point in bootlegging history. Herbert Hoover, the Republican candidate, was a staunch defender of the 18th Amendment. Democrat Al Smith was a 'Wet' who favored legalizing the sale and manufacture of liquor. Hoover's handy Election Day victory convinced the younger rum-runners that Prohibition would be around for four years at least, perhaps eight.

'We're in for some big money,' Longy Zwillman told Lansky and Luciano, 'as long as we keep our heads. We need better organization. Something like the National Association of Manufacturers. We stake out territories, reduce competition so we can keep prices steady and avoid battling, and keep the public off our backs.'

'How do you set something like that up?' Lansky wanted to know.

'We call a conference,' was Longy's answer.

Luciano, who was having his own troubles with a couple of 'Moustache Petes,' quickly approved Zwillman's proposal. It was a way, he realized, of shucking the shackles of the old guard that still had strength in New York and Chicago. Luciano told Zwillman that he'd use his connections to sound out bootleggers around the country.

It didn't take long for Luciano to get replies. They flowed into New York from one bootlegging boss after another. They were all having territorial troubles. The convention was long overdue, was the word. Where and when was left to Zwillman.

Atlantic City was Longy's natural choice as the site of the first national convention of bootleggers. The resort city was playland for the rich, for honeymooners, and for rum-runners. It held much the same attraction for bootleggers in the Twenties as Miami Beach did in the Thirties and Forties, when Prohibition ended and gambling became king. Zwillman had other reasons for his choice.

Longy took advantage of all the angles whenever he planned something. Holding the convention in Atlantic City, which Longy considered his home grounds even if the others thought of it as neutral territory, gave him the tiniest edge. Atlantic City was controlled by an old friend, someone Longy could count on if things didn't go just right.

Enoch 'Nucky' Johnson was Republican boss of the city and the county, a New Jersey original. His mother was a Higbee, a hard-working tribe who lived in the northeastern corner of the county in a town that bore their name. Mom Higbee had tuberculosis as a young girl, fought it off, and lived to be 83. For the last 20 years of her life, she delighted in bouncing around from nightclub to nightclub, wearing high-heeled slippers, and offering crackling personal opinions on the politics of her day. When she died, 6,000 attended her funeral.

Nucky's father was Smith Johnson, descendant of Revolutionary-era pioneers who founded Smithville, an Atlantic County village that is now a national historic shrine. Smith Johnson was first elected sheriff of the county in the 1890's, then re-elected four times even though county law forbade sheriffs from succeeding themselves.

When Nucky Johnson was 21, his father appointed him under-sheriff. For 12 years thereafter, father and son alternated jobs. Nucky gradually supplanted his father in influence. He became head of the county GOP machine, and a Republican state committeeman. He always had one county job or another; which one didn't seem to matter. Nucky rarely cashed his county paychecks until he had accumulated a year's worth.

The six-foot two-inch, gravel-voiced Nucky lived in an oceanfront mansion adjoining the fabulous Ritz Hotel. He wore a $1,200 raccoon overcoat in winter, and gave his $300 suits, after wearing them only two or three months, to his favorite boardwalk bootblack. Waiters made Nucky an honorary member of their union because he always left a $20 tip after a meal. He rode in a $14,000 chauffeur-driven, 12-cylinder Cadillac, and donated large sums to charity every year.

In 1929, some 40,000 adults lived in Atlantic City, headquarters for Nucky's county fiefdom; 4,500 of them were on the county payroll. That didn't include the thousands with municipal jobs, or the hundreds on the state and federal payrolls. In 1928, a congressional committee asked Nucky to explain the presence of so many people in government service in his county.

Nucky shrugged. 'Ask the guys who appoint them,' he told the committee counsel. It was an inside joke. Nucky selected everybody who had appointing powers.

Nucky's money came mainly from the numbers racket and prostitution in a city he kept wide-open, as long as he could enjoy his share. He received tribute from every ounce of whiskey sold in the resort city, and was on a first-name basis with every mobster in the country. His special favorite, though, was Longy Zwillman.

When Zwillman broached the idea of a bootleggers' convention, Nucky Johnson was delighted.

'Leave it to me,' he told Longy. 'You just come down and enjoy yourself.'

Only the best would do for the top gangsters in the country. Nucky reserved several dozen rooms at the Breakers, the most exclusive hotel on the boardwalk. He was careful to use pseudonyms for all his guests. Nucky knew the Breakers didn't accept any reservations from anyone who wasn't white, Anglo-Saxon, and Protestant.

The date of the convention was left to Meyer Lansky. The Little Man, as he was known, planned to get married. He didn't want to waste his time or his money. Since Nucky Johnson was picking up the tab, Lansky thought it would be nice to hold the convention during his honeymoon.

Lansky, who was born in Poland, became an American citizen in October 1928. His wedding to Anna Citron, daughter of Moses Citron, a respected produce wholesaler from Hoboken, New Jersey, took place on May 9, 1929.

The crime convention began five days later, May 14. From Chicago came Al Capone, Jake 'Greasy Thumb' Guzik, Frank Cline, and Frank Nitti. King Solomon came from Boston. Moe Dalitz, Lou Rothkopf, and Charley Polizzi arrived from Cleveland. Max 'Boo Boo' Hoff showed up from Philadelphia with Waxey Gordon and Niggy Rosen. Abe Bernstein brought a crowd from Detroit. John Lazia represented Kansas City. The New Jersey partners, Zwillman and Willie Moretti, were already at the scene. The New York delegation was impressive – Luciano, Lansky, Costello, Adonis, Ben Siegel, Johnny Torrio, Lepke Buchalter, Frank Erickson, Dutch Schultz, Al Anastasia, Vincent Mangano, and Frank Scalise.

When the first of the delegates arrived at the Breakers, the desk clerk took one look at guys like Al Capone and Niggy Rosen and called the manager, who said he was sorry, but there had been a mistake. All the hotel's rooms were occupied.

Rosen sputtered, Capone roared, and Nucky Johnson came running. Nucky didn't want any commotion, no adverse publicity. In a brilliant extemporaneous maneuver, Nucky told his guests that it was *he* who had made the terrible mistake. He never intended for them to stay at a fussy old place like the Breakers. He organized a cortege of limousines that carried all the guests to the flashier, less prejudiced Ritz. None of the guests thought this was odd, especially when they discovered that the Ritz was where the Lanskys were honeymooning.

Nucky provided each delegate's wife or girlfriend with a fur cape, his personal gift. Champagne was placed in every suite. Lansky complained; he didn't recognize the label. Zwillman's eyes smiled when he heard the complaint. Nucky bought his champagne from Longy. For the convention, he had removed all the labels so that none of the guests would feel offended at not being consulted.

The eating and drinking parties lasted far into the night for three days. On the fourth, the delegates came out of their rooms, climbed into those famous Atlantic City roller-chairs, and were wheeled down to the southern end of the boardwalk. There they got out, took off their shoes and socks, and walked onto the sand. Boardwalk strollers could see little knots of well-dressed men walking at the edge of the ocean where no eavesdropper had a chance to listen.

The decisions reached that week were momentous. Co-operation was the key word. A monopoly was created that would have warmed the heart of that old trust-designer, John D. Rockefeller – no competitive bidding for supplies, no invasion of designated territories. Prices were to be kept stable all over the country.

Control was exercised through a federation. The Mid-westerners were gathered into one regional grouping, including Kansas City and the South. The Easterners had their own setup, from Washington north, and west to Pittsburgh. Equally important, gambling was to be handled along the same lines. Arrangements were made for the regional heads to confer on a regular basis on national affairs. What they did inside their own federation was their own business.

The federation system was Longy's idea. He devised the organizational charts. He suggested that gambling, as well as bootlegging, be handled by the same method. His subtle maneuvering created the Big Six in the East.

Zwillman, Luciano, Lansky, Costello, Adonis, and Siegel – the Big Six – held their miniconvention in Zwillman's suite. In addition to splitting up the metropolitan area among themselves, they bound themselves into a tighter confederation.

'What we had,' Longy later told his aide, Doc Stacher, 'was a board meeting to plot future strategy.'

Longy didn't use fancy words with his partners. They had to respect the territory of the other delegates at the convention. But, he reminded them, their area was the biggest market in America. It had potential for far greater growth than any of the others. He saved his master stroke for last. The way the Big Six could protect themselves against possible catastrophe was to diversify.

'Go legitimate,' was his advice.

This concept was still foreign to the bootleggers gathered in Atlantic City in 1929. They were making too much money to wonder what they would do if illegal whiskey stopped flowing, and the gold ceased falling into their laps.

Longy's cold calculation took in every possible contingency. His background of poverty and privation had made a lasting impression. In later years, when he was at his peak financially, with investments in steel mills, railroads, real estate, film-making, and truck dealerships, he told an old friend that his memory of childhood hunger could never be wiped out.

'I still remember,' he said, 'what it felt like to skip meals, to go to sleep early because there wasn't enough in the house to feed all of us any supper. I swore I'd never let that happen to me, or any of mine, ever again.'

Patiently, Longy explained his theory. The Big Six would

invest in legitimate businesses. They would take equal risks, get equal shares, divide profits equally. Instead of taking a little individual chunk of business on their own, they would use their considerable capital resources to divide up the whole pot.

Longy had one advantage. Outside of the shrewd Lansky, none of the other members of the combine had much experience in the intricacies of legitimate enterprise. They had trusted Lansky, at that point in their careers, to take only a tiny portion of their profits and to invest them in the Sawdust Trail gambling casinos in New Jersey. By and large, they were still thinking only of their fabulous profits from whiskey.

Longy had been studying the stock market, watching stock issues being floated, checking out utilities, railroads, new industrial products, the burgeoning chemical industry.

Longy wanted to use that knowledge to safeguard his money. If one part of his business would go down, he wanted to have another at hand to pick up the slack. Longy, unlike the others in the Big Six, had hired bookkeepers. They were ordered never to write anything down. They checked everything, but always in their heads. He ran a tight ship, knew his inventory up to the minute, knew sales figures, costs, profit margins. It was experience he was to use later.

Longy added one more idea for the others in the Big Six to think about. If they were the biggest in the business, they wouldn't have to fear anyone trying to muscle in. Financial strength has as much, if not more, muscle than bullets.

The Big Six went home with a healthy regard for the brainy kid from Newark who was now their partner. Willie Moretti had the last word. Longy had already left the room. Moretti looked right at Lansky.

'All the smart Jews,' he said to Meyer, 'don't come from New York.'

Chapter 8

The Jean Harlow Story

Longy Zwillman first saw Rose Hanigan when he delivered a load of fruits and vegetables to the back door of Christian Feigenspan's mansion on High Street in Newark, New Jersey.

Rose was plump without being fat, and 16 years old at the time. She had arrived from County Roscommon after her father died; she had been an extra mouth for the Hanigan family, and as the oldest child, felt her future to be in America. She found a job as a cook's helper in the Feigenspan home through an aunt, the wife of a lace worker in Paterson.

Longy admired Rose from the moment he saw her. He liked the uninhibited way she walked and talked, the way she did her job effortlessly, and the candid look in her eye. She was a young woman with deep blue eyes, creamy white skin, and long black hair.

Longy was 15 at the time, had never been involved seriously with a female. Rose interested him more each time he stopped at the house to deliver an order. And Rose, on her part, admired the tall, well-built, handsome youth with the direct gaze.

Three months after he first saw Rose, Longy was bold enough to ask her to go out with him. She had one afternoon a week off, each Thursday, and Longy proposed that they spend the time at Olympic Park. It was, at the time, the largest amusement park in the nation.

The outing was more fun than either Rose or Longy had imagined. Olympic Park was a fairyland – dance-hall, motorcycle races, picnic groves, wild animal shows, and dozens of amusement-park rides like the Chair-O-Plane, the Tilt-a-Whirl, the Bug, and the Leaping Lena.

The couple had a delicious meal, walked along the brook under the trees near the park's entrance, and kissed behind a mulberry bush. On subsequent dates, Longy became bolder, took Rose to Eagle Mountain in West Orange on the trolley, to a show in downtown Newark, to dinner at restaurants in Orange. Within a month, the couple made love. It was the first experience for both of them.

Longy stopped going out with Rose after he overheard her talking to some of the other household help in the Feigenspan mansion, mentioning marriage. He wasn't ready for such a commitment, and quietly dropped out of Rose's life.

Marilyn Cohen was a honey-haired, green-eyed youth worker at the Newark YMHA. She was 22, a widow, and new in her job when Longy met her, and quickly asked her for a date. Marilyn was originally from Chicago. Her husband of six months had been killed in a railroad accident, and she had come east.

It was Marilyn Cohen who, on their first date, introduced Longy to music and the theater. She suggested that they go to see an opera performed by the Aborn Opera Company, whose home base was Olympic Park. It was one place Longy had never taken Rose Hanigan.

Her love for opera touched a responsive chord in Longy. Soon, he was accompanying Marilyn to New York, to the Metropolitan Opera, to the theater, to concerts at the Educational Alliance.

Marilyn enjoyed instructing Longy in the fine arts; he enjoyed being taught. He had never gone beyond the eighth grade, and the young social worker was the first person to introduce a taste of culture into Longy's life. And Longy's enthusiasm for the arts touched a responsive chord in the young widow.

Longy mistook her interest in his artistic development for emotional attachment. He told her he loved her, and the young woman recoiled. She was six years older than her 'date,' never thought of him in a romantic sense – or so she told him.

Longy was disappointed. He wasn't the kind to press his

suit against the girl's will. He thought of dropping Marilyn as he had done Rose. But the girl's vitality and kindness kept drawing him back.

It wasn't long before Longy's ardor and natural charm broke through the older woman's defenses. He sent her little gifts, notes filled with expressions of longing, flowers. Longy was in love, and he didn't hesitate to let Marilyn know how deeply.

One night, sitting in Zuckerman's Restaurant on Mercer Street in Newark, Longy proposed marriage. Marilyn was shocked, then flattered, finally flabbergasted. She was fond of him, she told Longy, but she didn't love him. She thought it would be better if they just continued as they had before, without deeper entanglements.

Disillusioned, the boy kept away from Marilyn for a week. Then he approached her once more, entreating her to change her mind. Harshness, the young woman felt, was her only defense. She began to excoriate him, make fun of his taste, call him cry-baby.

Stung, Longy felt like beating the woman. Instead, he turned his back on her, vowed he'd never let a woman make a fool of him again. He walked into Pop Meisner's saloon, got drunk, and had to be dragged into the Mercer Baths to be sobered up.

Longy Zwillman avoided permanent attachments to any woman for years after his experience with Marilyn Cohen. The attachment had wounded him, made him extra wary of making any more commitments. He had no dearth of affairs at the height of the Prohibition era. Spice was in the air, and as he was introduced to the bright lights of Broadway, Longy took his chances on short, sweet, meaningless arrangements with a series of show business personalities.

His next long-term, serious entanglement with a woman began in 1930.

Doc Stacher saw her first. He had gone to the Adams Theater that summer night in 1930 to see *Hell's Angels*, a Howard Hughes blockbuster production. He fidgeted through the few acts of vaudeville – the whiskey tenor, the jugglers, the sloppy magician. Then it was the girl's turn.

Her act was terrible, and the crowd shifted in its seats, anxious for the picture to start.

'She was lousy,' Stacher said later to Longy. 'She had these stupid lines about life in Hollywood, then she told a few lousy jokes about directors, and read a dumb poem. If she wasn't so fuckin' good-looking, the crowd would have booed her off the stage. Whoever did her makeup ought to be in jail. She looked good anyway. And that dress she wore – it looked like she picked it up at a rummage sale.

'The thing that got me was that hair of hers; you should see it. It's not blonde. More like the color of eggnog, know what I mean? I never seen hair like that. Boy, would I like to see her snatch to find out if it's really her own color!'

Longy was intrigued. Doc Stacher seldom spoke so glowingly about a particular woman. Ben Siegel and Joe Adonis, yes. They were cunt-crazy. Doc liked women, all right, but he didn't talk about any one of them all the time the way some of Longy's other pals did. This girl must really be something special.

Longy went backstage to watch the girl's act. It was no problem; the manager of the Adams Theater knew who Longy was. He was honored, he said, to do Longy a favor.

The girl's act was even worse than Doc Stacher had described. Longy, since his days with Marilyn Cohen, had become a theater *maven*. He attended opening nights, had invested in a few shows. He had come to know all the important theater people – writers, directors, producers, actors – as much because of his bootlegging business as his devotion to the stage.

The girl's act was amateurish. It gave Longy what a friend of his used to call *fontrum*, an invented word to describe that queasy feeling you get when someone you know is making an ass of himself in front of a large audience. Her lines were horrible. The only saving grace was the fact that she delivered them in a tinny nasal twang that somehow sounded sexy. Her dress was even cheaper looking than Stacher had said it was. That hair, though, was glorious. It had a beige sheen that was really like the color of rich eggnog, thought Longy.

Her act finished, the girl walked past him toward her tiny dressing room, actually a big closet with a sink and a lighted mirror. Longy had a close look at her hair as she went by. Her eyes were red; Longy couldn't tell why.

'What the fuck are you doing back here, mister?' Her tinny voice was bold and full of bluster, but Longy could see that she was frightened. He didn't like the profanity, but he let it pass.

'It's okay, Harlean,' he said soothingly, using her real first name. 'The manager is a pal, and he let me watch your act from the wings. It's worse than I was told.'

'Thanks a lot, buddy!' Tears formed in the blonde's eyes. No one knew better than she did that the act was lousy. It was that cheap bastard Howard Hughes. He not only was cheating her out of personal appearance money; he had stuck her with a 10-cent act. He was ruining her career even before it had a real chance to take off.

Howard Hughes, who had Jean Harlow under contract, was always looking for the edge. He shrewdly arranged a personal appearance tour for the youngster – she was only 19 – who he knew was destined for stardom after her performance in his picture, *Hell's Angels*. The screen had had its blond bombshells before, but Jean Harlow was something new and different. That glorious hair came over on film with even more sexy glitter than it had in person. Her piquant young face and her undulating body with its sexily broad behind had created more comment in Hollywood than any screen personality since Clara Bow.

Hughes had Harlow under a rigid contract. It paid her $250 a week for seven years. He was booking her for personal appearances at $3,500 a week, but Jean only got her contractual $250. Hughes's production firm kept the rest.

'I'm pissed,' Harlow had yelled when she found out what was happening. 'This fucking tour is costing me money.'

'Look at all the free publicity you're getting,' Hughes told her. 'It's worth millions.'

'Not to me,' shot back Harlow. 'You're getting my money. I'm getting the shaft.'

A contract is a contract, Jean was told, so off on the personal appearance tour she went. And it was turning out even worse than she had anticipated. Now here comes this big goon into her crummy dressing room in lousy Newark, NJ, to tell her that her act stank. For dessert, he'd probably try to put the blocks to her. Well, thought Jean, let him try. If he gets funny, I'll kick him in the balls and yell for the cops.

The big guy didn't try anything. He even turned his back while she struggled out of the dinky silver dress that did nothing for her hair. Jean never wore underwear, and when she slipped on a filmy dressing gown it fell into the crack of her ample behind. Her large nipples seemed to be forcing their way through the cheap fabric as if gulping air.

The big guy, she noticed, was paying no attention to her goodies. I wonder what he's after? Jean thought.

'Get dressed,' said Longy.

'What for?' the girl asked, defiantly.

'That was your last show today,' Longy said matter-of-factly, 'and we're going out. I'll get you something to eat.'

Jean thought of calling the manager and having this big donkey tossed out. Probably a friend of his like he says, she thought, so I can't get any satisfaction from the manager. What the hell, at least I'll get a meal out of it. And, with my mother out front waiting for me, how bad could it get?

'Something to eat' turned out to be an elaborate dinner in the Oak Room of the Plaza Hotel in New York. Jean was astounded by the attention given her escort. She gawked at the way the maitre d' fawned over the big guy when they walked in, how the captains and waiters came waltzing around their table, the best one in the room. The silver on the table shone. The tablecloth was snow-white linen. The dishes were real china. Who was this big guy, anyway?

Jean's mother was beside herself with glee, glad she hadn't been fluffed off the way things usually happened when Harlean was going out with a man. The big guy, who said his name was something that sounded like Abe Willman, was as attentive to Mama as to her blond-haired daughter. The dinner turned out to taste as good as the restaurant looked. All eyes were on Jean and her handsome escort, Mama noticed. Jean felt good about herself for the first time since she arrived in Hollywood from Kansas City.

The big guy wasn't through. After dessert, while they were drinking coffee, he excused himself, said he had to make a call. He returned 15 minutes later.

'Tomorrow,' he told Jean, 'you call Hughes and tell him you're sick and you have to postpone the trip for the next 10 days.'

'I can't do that,' said Jean. 'He'll kick my ass. The dates are all set. I have to be in fucking Philly in three days.'

Mama, ever the opportunist, tried to shush Jean. This was a gentleman they were with, and Jean shouldn't be using street language like that.

'You tell Hughes he can't make you go on with this tour when you're sick. Tell him you have to rest under doctor's orders. I'll have my doctor see you, and he can call Hughes.'

Then what? Jean stopped fighting the big fellow and started listening.

'You're going to start rehearsing a new act,' said the big guy.

Jean looked skeptical, but figured, what the hell, at least I'll get a rest, if nothing else. And this big guy looked like he knew how to treat a girl.

During the meal, Longy had pumped Jean ever so subtly. What kind of a guy was Hughes? Does he have much money? Who are his backers? Harlow told him as much as she knew. The big man was satisfied, she thought.

Jean Harlow didn't get the rest she had anticipated. She worked harder in that 10-day interlude than she had ever done on or off the screen. Longy Zwillman had arranged for two of Broadway's top cabaret writers to whip up a new act expressly for Jean Harlow's lithe body, nasal voice, big bosom, and bigger ass. Under the guidance of these pros, Jean's natural sexy talent was brought out. In suggestiveness, it was just this side of being in bad taste, titillating but nothing that a local censor could use to stop the show.

Longy hired a seasoned reporter to draw up a list of provocative questions. These would be planted with reporters called to a press conference. He called Niggy Rosen in Philadelphia, the next city in which Jean was to appear. Spread the news about this new bombshell, he told Niggy. Make sure that the theater is full for the first show. Get the press involved, even if you have to buy 'em to bring 'em into the house.

Longy didn't let Jean know the questions were plants. When the questions were asked, Jean's off-the-cuff answers, naturally risqué, began grabbing headlines on the entertainment pages. As she moved about the country, the Jean Harlow legend grew with each stop.

It was Longy who thought up the catchword for her hair. Someone asked Jean one night whether the color of her hair was real or 'touched up.'

'Never see a real blonde before?' she asked the reporter. The reporter was skeptical. Jean smiled crookedly and asked: 'What do I have to do to prove it's real, pull down my pants?'

The press conference nearly broke up in howls, with reporters and photographers whistling and yelling for her to do just that. Longy, who had been sitting quietly in the back row, got up and signalled Jean. She held up her hands for quiet.

'Look, I guarantee the color of my hair is real,' she said, '100 percent platinum.' Longy had told her to use the word if she was asked.

The description caught on. Longy made sure the story of Jean's answers, bawdiness and all, was spread by the wire services. The *New York Daily Graphic*, eager to break into the tabloid monopoly enjoyed by *The Daily News*, screamed the word that the platinum blonde bombshell had offered to give reporters the ultimate proof of naturalness. 'Platinum Blonde' became the hair-dye that beauty parlors all over the country began advertising.

Longy traveled with Jean to every stop on her six-week personal appearance tour. He booked her hotels – always the best one in the city – and arranged for her meals. Jean began receiving a bigger weekly paycheck, never suspecting that it was Longy's money that was being added to the $250 she was getting from Howard Hughes. Longy picked her wardrobe, hired a full-time hairdresser to accompany them on the tour, shielded her from her growing number of fans, arranged her press conferences.

The big guy – she now knew his name was Abner Zwillman – never seemed to spend time on his own business, and Jean began wondering what his angle really was. Not once in the three months they were together did he put the arm on her.

'He's too big to be a fag,' Jean told Mama. 'I can tell by the way he looks at me, like he wants to eat me up. But he hasn't touched me, not once. Not even a kiss. He's nice, and he's tough. I see how people in restaurants seem to be afraid of him, although he doesn't look threatening. I wonder where his money comes from?'

Jean, at 19, was naive. She had been pushed into show business by ambitious Mama when she was only 14. At 16, still not a success and bored, she married a young boy who messed up their first night together so badly that Jean never slept with him again. After her mother dragged her to Hollywood, Jean was pushed by Mama into sleeping with any phony who said he was a producer and maybe had a part for her. None of them satisfied her. When Jean Harlow, fast becoming America's favorite sex symbol, met Longy Zwillman she had never experienced an orgasm.

Longy was biding his time. He waited until the tour was over, then asked Jean to come back to New York with him.

'We're throwing a big party in honor of your success,' he told Jean. 'I have a room reserved for you at the finest hotel in town. But there's no room for Mama. She goes home without you.'

This is it, Jean figured. This is his payoff. What the hell, I owe him. And he's not bad looking at all.

The hotel 'room' was actually a suite at the Waldorf Astoria, filled with gardenias, with buckets of champagne in every corner, and a private maid and butler to tend to Jean's needs. She luxuriated in a warm bubble bath. Longy had told her, that first night at the Plaza, that she needed to bathe more often. She smelled sour, he said, like old herring. She had bathed twice a day since then. He bought her a special French perfume, taught her to apply it subtly, just a hint that wafted across a room.

Longy said he had to go out on business, would return in time for dinner. At 5:30, he was back. He ordered dinner in the room.

'We'll go out and see a show later,' he told Jean. 'You're famous now, and people will only spoil our evening if we go out to eat.'

The dinner finished, the dishes removed, Longy dismissed the butler and maid. He walked over to the window, looked down on the city's lights.

'Come here,' he said to Jean. 'I want you to see real beauty. Look at the way the lights shine from the windows, like diamonds. Play your cards right, and you can have as many diamonds as you see from this window.'

Jean came over, put her fingers on the pane of glass separating her from the street 14 stories below. She felt Longy's fingers brush across her bare back, rest on her neck. She leaned back against him. Here it comes, she thought.

Jean Harlow bloomed. Hollywood reporters remarked on how she exuded a sense of contentment in addition to creating sexual excitement wherever she went. She clung to Longy, couldn't get enough of him, demanded he make love to her when they went to bed, during the night, and when they awoke in the late morning. Now she knew why so many women talked and gossiped and ran after love.

Jean was in love, but Longy didn't lose sight of her career. He forced Howard Hughes to lend her to other studios to make pictures. They gave her juicier parts, enhanced her sex-symbol image. Her weekly paycheck quadrupled. Jean didn't know that Hughes was still paying her only the contractual $250 a week, and that Longy was advancing her the remainder. It was, he told Johnny Roselli, a Chicago pal, an investment in the future. Besides, $750 a week was pin money to Longy.

Roselli was imported by Longy to keep an eye on Harlow while he went back to Newark. Johnny could be trusted to protect Longy from being double-crossed by the Hollywood studio sharks.

The story of the double-cross goes back to the early days of movie-making. Jack Cohn, a New York lawyer, had one of the industry's pioneer distribution firms as a client. He prevailed on the company's officers to hire his brother, Harry, as a salesman.

Harry was the Cohn family's black sheep. He made unsuccessful starts as a streetcar conductor and a pool hustler before he latched on to a Tin Pan Alley music publishing company as a song-plugger. That didn't make him much money. In order to keep his brother out of further trouble, Jack Cohn arranged for Harry to go to work selling two-reelers to newly opened movie houses.

Harry, a quick study, soon saw enough of the new industry's wheeling and dealing to be able to convince brother Jack that they should form their own film sales company. They asked Joe Brandt, a theater owner, to join them. The company grew, changed its name to Columbia Pictures, and went into the production end of film-making as more and more movie theaters opened around the country.

As the company grew, so did the fights and rivalry between the Cohn Brothers. Joe Brandt, whose theater chain was slowly making him wealthy, couldn't stand the constant yowling of his two partners. He decided to sell out, offering his one-third interest in Columbia to the first brother who could come up with $500,000.

Jack, the lawyer, tried the conventional money sources – the banks. Most lending institutions had been severely hurt by the growing Depression. They wouldn't consider a proposition as risky as a movie company.

Harry Cohn, still a hustler, went to see Longy in Newark. Harry had been in debt to Longy before, as a gambler. His losses were large, but Longy never had to use his bone-breakers to get Harry to pay off. His credit, as far as Longy knew, was still good.

To get to Longy, Harry Cohn spoke to his bookie.

'I need to talk to the big man back East,' said Cohn.

'What for?' the bookmaker wanted to know. He wasn't going in over his head to talk to somebody he held in awe unless he knew what it was all about.

'Money.' Cohn was terse. He had owed as much as $400,000 to this bookie of his, so the man had a right to ask questions. But this was business, not gambling, so the less the bookie knew, the better. 'Big money, a business deal.'

The call went out to Longy. He waited until he had to be in Hollywood with Jean before calling Cohn. They met in Longy's bungalow at the hotel.

'I hear you want to see me about a business deal.' Longy opened thc conversation without preliminaries. He didn't particularly like Cohn.

'I have a chance to buy into the company, to buy out Joe Brandt,' said Cohn.

'How much?' Longy asked. He didn't want details, only the bottom line.

'Half a million,' said Cohn, watching Longy's face. The big man's eyes didn't even blink. This young *pisher*, thought Cohn, where's he come from? Cold as steel. Not even half my age. Has all the cunt he wants. How did he get so big?

Longy looked down at the movie-maker. 'What's the deal?' he asked.

'You advance the $500,000,' said Cohn. 'I buy the stock. I give you my personal note for the money, plus interest.'

'No, I give you the $500,000,' said Longy. 'You sign the stock over to me. I give you the note. When you pay me what you owe, I sign the stock back to you.'

Cohn thought fast. Sure, the guy could screw me out of the stock even if I pay him back. But he could take the whole ball of wax anyway, now that he knows Brandt wants to sell his share. What have I got to lose?

'Done,' said Cohn, holding out his hand. Longy walked to the door of the bungalow, ignoring the invitation to shake. He held the door open.

'I'll have the money delivered next Tuesday. In cash. Is that all right?'

Longy knew it would be. He knew how badly Cohn wanted to own part of Columbia Pictures. Longy cottoned to the idea of owning a studio himself, but he knew he was too busy with other things to pay a new investment the careful attention it needed.

Longy saw in Columbia Pictures the perfect vehicle for the repayment of his investment in Jean Harlow. Once he had his hands on a producing firm like Columbia, Longy figured to squeeze Howard Hughes into releasing Jean from her unfair contract.

But Jean Harlow had her own ideas. She trusted Longy, but another studio mogul named Joe Schenck convinced her that once Prohibition came to an end – and he insisted it would after the 1932 presidential election – Longy would lose his source of income and wouldn't be able to do right by her. Why not, he asked Jean, dump a small outfit like Columbia and join the studio of the stars, MGM?

Jean was dumbfounded. She had no idea MGM would even want her. When Joe Schenck told her that his brother, Nick, head of Loew's Inc., could buy her contract from Hughes and sell it to MGM, she fell for the doublecross. She insisted later that she thought Longy had engineered the whole deal, otherwise she never would have agreed. Longy, back in Newark, didn't know what was taking place. Johnny Roselli's job was to protect Jean from physical, not corporate, skullduggery.

When Longy finally learned what had happened, he didn't explode, or threaten the Schenck brothers (both heavy gamblers). His reaction was to stop sending Jean her $750 a week subsidy. Then he stopped calling her, stopped her protection by Johnny Roselli. It was as if Jean Harlow had died.

His revenge against Joe Schenck took three years. Through Meyer Lansky and his other Eastern pals, Longy trapped Schenck into a transaction with crooked leaders of the movie stagehands union. The information was leaked to the Internal Revenue Service. Schenck was tried and convicted of income-tax evasion, sentenced to a year in jail plus a large fine. Schenck could afford the fine. But even though he served only five months, Joe Schenck never really recovered from the prison sentence.

Chapter 9

The Making of a President, 1932

In its July 1932 convention, the Republican Party renominated President Herbert Hoover. The choice of Hoover was a reflex action. The country was being battered by the worst economic depression in its history. Almost 25 percent of the nation's work force was unemployed. Homeless people were living in shantytowns derisively nicknamed 'Hoovervilles.' Thousands of farmers in the Southwest were abandoning their land and heading westward, hoping to find relief and work in California. And the Republican Party felt it had no choice but to renominate the man who was being blamed, however unfairly, for bad times.

In the face of the Great Depression, President Hoover stubbornly refused to acknowledge that the system was breaking down. Prosperity, he told the American people, was just around the corner. Eventually, voters began asking 'Which corner?' and Hoover had to act.

The steps Hoover finally proposed were sound. The Reconstruction Finance Act, for example, already in operation when Franklin Delano Roosevelt took office, helped FDR's New Deal swing swiftly into action.

But Hoover's timing was off. The Republican Party had survived the scandals in the White House under Warren G. Harding. Calvin Coolidge helped the party regain some of its image by doing nothing while the boom of the Twenties lifted the country's economy into the stratosphere. Then came Black Thursday in 1929, and the country's economy plunged toward the cellar. Four years later, America had just about lost heart. Americans were looking for a rescuer, and they weren't about to trust anyone from the Republican Party as his messenger.

The Democrats, supremely confident that their day had come after 12 years out of power, were going into their convention in the summer of 1932 with three men vying for the nomination. Alfred E Smith, the Happy Warrior, former governor of New York, had run against Hoover in 1928. His loss to the Great Engineer was attributed as much to Smith's Roman Catholic faith as to the edge the GOP had acquired from the boom times. Still, Smith remained the party's sentimental favorite.

John Nance Garner of Uvalde, Texas, the tough, wiry Speaker of the House of Representatives, had built a large following in the South and West during his 30 years in Congress. He wasn't considered strong enough to challenge Smith; the best Garner could hope to do would be to bargain his Southwestern delegate strength for a position on the ticket as vice-president.

The most serious challenge to Smith came from the patrician Franklin Delano Roosevelt. A distant cousin of Teddy Roosevelt, and a former assistant secretary of the Navy, FDR was the popular governor of New York. James A Farley, who had played a big part in Al Smith's 1928 campaign, had been given the New York state Democratic chairmanship as a reward. Farley was a shrewd judge of popular opinion. Sensing Roosevelt's appeal, he switched his allegiance from Smith to FDR, and began canvassing the country for delegates who would back the Squire of Hyde Park.

Longy Zwillman, raking in the money from his liquor and gambling interests, recognized that whoever won the Democratic nomination would win the election. The Depression made that almost a certainty. The Democrats were already promising to repeal Prohibition if they won in 1932, and Longy knew it was time to hedge his bets.

That was the year – 1932 – in which Abner Zwillman made a decision that wrenched his life out of kilter, and indirectly led to his death. Some of the biggest bootleggers in the country had the same intuition as Longy did about the coming end of Prohibition. With the sale and manufacture of liquor legalized, the empires they had – and the millions they produced – would crumble. Their choice was logical. Why not go legitimate along with the liquor? They had a well-oiled distribution system in place. They had the connections with distillers overseas. Best of all, they had the financing, in cash. They wouldn't even have to go to the banks to set themselves up in a legitimate business.

Longy Zwillman and Joseph Reinfeld had spent hours discussing the future. Reinfeld had firsthand knowledge of his youthful partner's business acumen. He knew that together they could dominate the liquor importing business. He begged Longy to prepare for the day Prohibition ended.

Longy had prepared. Part of the reason he had thrown in his hand with the New York leadership of Luciano, Costello, and Lansky was their grip on gambling. It brought in almost as much money as bootleg whiskey, with a far smaller initial capital outlay. It was neat, nonviolent, as safe as any illicit business could be.

Longy was making millions, and he had grown to covet the money and the power it brought him. In his innermost heart, he didn't believe the liquor business would keep that kind of cash rolling in after it went legitimate. He told himself he could have it both ways by hedging. It was a tactic any Wall Street figure could recognize. Longy would retain a small partnership interest in Reinfeld's legitimate importing business, and keep his gangland ties at the same time. He would have his cake and eat it too.

It didn't work out that way. Joseph Reinfeld went legitimate, built a huge liquor importing empire, and was knighted by the king of England. Joseph P Kennedy went legitimate, built an impressive fortune fueled by legitimately imported Scotch whiskey, and became America's ambassador to Britain. Other, lesser fry in the bootleg whiskey trade went legitimate, and made themselves and their heirs comfortably rich. Longy Zwillman made his choice, stuck with crime, and wound up rich, powerful, and ultimately a failure.

Logic in 1932 dictated that Longy secure his gambling income any way he could. Since he didn't really trust legitimate liquor to continue bringing him the income to which he had become accustomed, he concluded that the end of Prohibition couldn't hurt him much. But if a real squeeze on his gambling interests were to take place, that could be dangerous. And the New York gambling empire was being threatened by a wave of reform.

Democratic politics in the city was in the hands of five county chieftains. Tammany Hall, Manhattan's Democratic headquarters, was the most powerful, the party ringleader when it came to state and national politics. Tammany Hall was run by Charley Murphy with shrewd discipline. Corruption was controlled. Boss Murphy made sure that it was thoroughly hidden from the public, that the life of the average man in the street wasn't threatened, that businessmen and financiers remained comfortable with the status quo.

Murphy died suddenly, and leadership of Tammany Hall fell into the hands of a succession of weaklings, none of whom were able to control Mayor James J Walker. Jimmy Walker was the kind of mayor New Yorkers seemed to want in the Roaring Twenties – handsome, fond of the bright lights of Broadway, always surrounded by beautiful women, winking at the abundance of speakeasies and the flourishing of gambling in the city.

But Walker was the exact opposite of a tough, shrewd city boss. He'd rather run off to Europe with a showgirl than discipline a party worker who stepped out of line. He paid little attention to ward politics. And he refused to curb the open theft of public funds by some of his closest friends.

Scandals exploded around City Hall, one after the other. When they touched the judiciary, usually passive newspaper editorialists thundered in indignation. A young congressman named Fiorello La Guardia, smelling a chance to move into City Hall, picked up the theme and inveighed against punks, pimps, and pilferers. The voters responded by appealing to the governor. They wanted the city cleaned up.

That was the last thing Longy and his New York pals wanted to see happen. A cleanup directed from Albany would put a severe crimp into their gambling and loan-sharking rackets. Longy called a meeting of his allies at the Claridge Hotel on Broadway.

Lucky Luciano had done his homework. 'This thing,' said Luciano, 'is gettin' all fucked up. That lousy Jimmy Walker, he's no fuckin' good. He lets them two-bit bastard friends of his sink their sticky fingers into every piece of shit in the city. Now they're selling judgeships. Like that bastard McCooey, the boss in Brooklyn. He wants four new judges for Brooklyn, and you know that's 'cause he's selling them to the highest bidders. So a bunch of lawyers who don't have enough dough to go for these job, they're yelling to Albany. The next thing, the Republicans smell they can make mileage. They yell for a fuckin' investigation. It's a good thing this Roosevelt killed it – this time.'

'Charlie, you're not going to keep this quiet,' said Longy Zwillman. 'The grand jury already has its hooks into Jimmy Walker. Some top money guys on Wall Street collected a 15-page list of shitty deals made in City Hall and filed them with the governor. It's got Walker and a couple of his judges dead to rights. Now, there's this Judge Samuel Seabury heading the investigation from Albany, and a lot of the punks around Walker are going to take a fall. If they go, he goes.'

'And that means,' said Meyer Lansky, 'we get hurt, bad. If some of the people we need get nabbed, we could be shut down for months, maybe years. We can't wait for this thing to blow over. We gotta move now.'

'Fine,' said Frank Costello, 'so we move. But where? We already tried to get a few guys. This Seabury gang, nobody's buyin'. They're all clean, like Bon Ami. You know we got somebody to go to Seabury. We asked, would he get off our backs for $2 million? Our man couldn't even get through the door. He says he's lucky they let him out alive.'

Longy went to a window, looked down on the traffic flowing through Times Square. He pulled on his lower lip. Everybody in the room knew what was going wrong. As

Longy Zwillman (UPI/Bettmann)

Joseph H. Reinfeld. (AP)

Ruggiero "Richie the Boot" Boiardo.

Vittorio Castle, the famous Newark restaurant-banquet hall owned by Richie "The Boot" Boiardo. It was here that Boiardo and Longy celebrated their famous gangland truce of 1930.

A pleasant luncheon. Dominick Di Maggio (Joe's brother, who played for the Boston Red Sox) flanked on his left by Sam Katz, Richie "The Boot" Boiardo, and a man known as "Peanuts." Behind Katz, standing, is Boiardo's son, Anthony "Tony Boy" Boiardo.

Charles "Lucky" Luciano. (AP)

Frank Costello. (AP)

Ben Siegel. (AP)

Meyer Lansky. (AP)

Joe Adonis. (AP)

A luncheon at Vittorio Castle. From left, clockwise, Longy; Sam Katz; unknown union official; Abe Lew, a union official and Zwillman cousin; two unknown men; Mike Lascari; and Gerry Catena.

Louis "Lepke" Buchalter.

Enjoying a social evening. Clockwise: Joseph "Doc" Stacher (back of head only); Mr. and Mrs. Sam Katz; Gerry Catena, Kay, his wife; Mary Zwillman; Longy; Carmine Battaglia, an associate of Longy's; Joe Rogers, who ran the numbers for Zwillman in Union County; and Miriam Stacher, Doc's wife. The occasion was a reception after the wedding of one of Longy's people.

Abe "Kid Twist" Reles, before his sudden death in November, 1941. (AP)

usual, Longy had been thinking about the solution, not the problem. He came away from the window to face his buddies.

'Okay, the only way we'll stop this thing and get rid of Seabury is through the convention next month.

'What convention?' Costello asked. He knew, of course, that the Democrats were to meet in Chicago to pick a presidential candidate. He hadn't connected the White House to his problems in New York.

'The Democratic convention,' said Longy quickly. 'Look, the guy who's going to get the nomination there is going to be president. There's no way Hoover could get elected today. When the Democrats get in, they'll kill Prohibition. We agreed three years ago in Atlantic City this was in the cards. That's why we built up this thing around here as a hedge. But we lose the hedge if they shut down the city. We can bring them over to Jersey if worst comes to worst, but we still need New York if this is going to pay big.'

'What's that got to do with picking a president?' whined Lansky.

'That's not the point,' said Longy coolly. 'The point is, one of two guys is going to get the nomination in Chicago, Smith or Roosevelt.'

'They're neck-and-neck right now,' chipped in Costello, 'from what I hear downtown.'

'That's where we come in,' said Longy. 'New York has 47 votes. Each guy needs those 47 to go over the top. Who controls most of the 47 votes? Tammany Hall. Who controls Tammany Hall? Jimmy Hines, and he's one of your boys, Frank.' Longy nodded to Costello.

'That's right,' said Costello, 'but you forget, Jimmy only controls Manhattan. How we gonna reach the others. Al Marinelli in Brooklyn, for instance? He's all for Smith.'

'I don't care,' answered Longy, 'who's for who. What we need is an angle to be able to call in our chips. We got to let them know we don't care who gets the nomination, as long as it's the guy who promises to call off Seabury.'

Frank Costello, the most astute political brain among the

New York boys, got the idea first. He exploded with laughter, applauding. The others in the room stared at Costello.

'I gotta hand it to you, Abe.'

'Hey, Frank,' said Luciano, 'don' keep it a secret. What's it all about?'

'It's simple,' explained Costello. 'The two guys who want to be president so bad they can taste it, they know they don't have all the votes they need. The key is New York's 47 votes. The city controls most of them votes, so these two guys, they need the city. Now, all we gotta do is find out which one of these two jokers promises to kill the Seabury investigation.'

'That's right,' chimed in Meyer Lansky, a quick mind. 'We wait until the last minute. We don't offer any help to anybody until the last minute. Whichever guy says no more Seabury, we give him our delegates.'

'You got it,' said Longy, smiling. 'If we play it right, we own the convention, and we get the nomination for the guy who calls off Seabury. How's that for an edge? Our guy in the White House.'

'Let's go to Chicago,' said Luciano.

The combination rented a series of suites at the fashionable Drake Hotel on Chicago's North Side. Luciano settled into one. Using Costello's influence, he got Brooklyn boss Al Marinelli, a staunch Smith man, to share the suite with him. Costello was on the floor below in an equally posh suite. With him was an old pal, Tammany Hall boss Jimmy Hines. Lansky was given the job of dealing with the upstate delegations, especially those from Rockland, Orange, and Sullivan counties.

For the sake of appearances, Longy Zwillman stayed on the same floor with people he knew better than anyone else, the New Jersey delegation. He wasn't there to influence their votes; he knew they'd vote his way. Longy remained with the New Jersey delegation because he wanted to give the New York delegates an appearance of neutrality. That would make it easier to deal with them. He also wanted to be free to wheel and deal away from the eyes of the New Yorkers, and be able to dash unobtrusively from the hotel to the convention hall floor in the Chicago stockyards across town.

It took Longy only a day to get to the upstate New York delegation leaders. The message he had was simple. We – he mentioned the city bosses – control the swing vote. Whichever way we go, do you go with us? It's okay if you go your own way, but don't come to us after the nomination is locked up for our man and expect any favors. They listened, and indicated they would go the way Longy wanted.

Then Longy tackled his biggest job. The first step was a meeting with Roosevelt. He had Costello send word to Louis Howe, who was FDR's aide, shadow, and appointments chief. All Longy needed was 10 minutes with the governor. All he wanted was a yes or no answer.

The answer was no meeting with the governor. It was too risky for FDR to be seen anywhere near a racketeer. Instead of Roosevelt, Longy could meet – if he wanted to – with one of FDR's trusted aides. The man was a neighbor of Roosevelt's in Dutchess County, Howe said. He would be speaking for the governor.

Longy met the Roosevelt assistant – until the day he died, Longy would never reveal his name – in the small restaurant in the basement of the Drake. Longy didn't fear meeting in the open. Few of the political reporters covering the convention in Chicago knew anyone on the crime beat except Al Capone, and Capone was in jail on an income-tax rap. Most New York reporters, especially, wouldn't know the tall, good-looking, well-groomed, expensively tailored Abner Zwillman of Newark, sitting in a crowded restaurant, talking to another erect, well-dressed fellow. To all appearances, they could be two well-heeled tycoons having a quiet business lunch.

The Roosevelt aide opened the discussion. He stuck to finances at first, asking whether Longy's group was ready to contribute to the governer's campaign.

'If your man is nominated,' said Longy quietly.

'What help are you prepared to offer?' was the next question.

'We offer the nomination, all wrapped up,' shot back Longy. He was tired of indirect discussion.

'That sure, are you?'

'Yes,' said Longy, speaking softly. 'We have the votes to put your man over the two-thirds majority he needs for the nomination.'

'I don't buy that,' said the FDR aide.

Longy smiled. 'Then, why,' he asked silkily, 'are we meeting?'

The aide stared. In front of him, he saw a supremely confident young man, someone who could pass muster as a member at his own patrician club on Fifth Avenue. The aide had been prepared to encounter a wiseguy gangster with a Lower East Side accent. This fellow was unexpectedly quite different. The aide decided to drop all pretence.

'What's your price?'

'Your man has to call off Judge Seabury.'

'That's impossible! The scandal would ruin my candidate before he even got started on the campaign trail.'

'Your man is smarter than that. We don't expect him to fire the judge. There are other ways to accomplish what we need. I'm sure your man is wise enough to know how to get the nomination for president without compromising himself.'

A long pause. The Roosevelt aide pursed his lips, sensing he was out of his depth.

'I'll have to get back to you,' he said.

'I understand,' answered Longy. 'But time is short. The delegates are getting restless. They smell the presidency is going to go to the Democrat this year.'

The signal came from FDR himself. He denounced crime in his home state to a group of reporters gathered in his suite. He supported Judge Seabury's attempt to clean up the city. But – and this was the key Longy was looking for – FDR said he couldn't see that the case against Jimmy Walker or Jimmy Hines was strong enough for him to be able to act. He'd rather leave it to the courts.

Longy brought the word to his allies. Roosevelt was going to play ball with them. He wanted the nomination that badly. It was up to Costello to ask Smith the same had question. Smith was aghast. He wanted the presidency, but the Happy Warrior told Jimmy Hines he wouldn't call off Judge Seabury, couldn't if he had wanted to. He wasn't the governor. Roosevelt was.

In his book, *The Last Testament of Lucky Luciano*, the tough little Sicilian gangster describes Al Smith's reaction when he was told that the boys were switching their delegates to Roosevelt, and why.

'He looked me square in the face,' wrote Luciano, 'and shook his head real sad. "Charlie," he said. "Frank Roosevelt'll break his word to you. This is the biggest mistake you ever made in your entire life, by trustin' him. He'll kill you." When I walked out of Smith's suite, my knees were shakin'. My bones told me that we'd walked into a trap – that Smith was right.'

Lucky Luciano's bones foretold the truth. Franklin Delano Roosevelt got the nomination because of the New York delegation's swing, engineered by Longy Zwillman. Right after his acceptance speech to the convention, Roosevelt unleashed Judge Seabury with a fury that toppled Jimmy Walker and his henchmen.

Chapter 10

Benevolent Racketeer

Plumbing the soul of the real Abner Zwillman would tax the powers of an expert psychoanalyst. The man was a mass of contradictions. He could be a reserved, austere, and coldly distant business executive when dealing with racketeers and killers. He could also be kind, warm-hearted, and extremely loyal in dealing with family, friends, even slight acquaintances. Some of his charitable acts were still being recalled with warmth more than 15 years after his death. At the same time, some of his former associates actually blanch when asked about his ruthless behavior.

Zwillman had charisma. His ability to inspire loyalty was incredible. Those prepared to dislike him found themselves, after spending some time in his company, virtually unable to resist his charm.

Longy never finished the eighth grade. Yet cultivated people with whom he came in contact considered him urbane, an intense, avid student of music and literature. In social gatherings, Zwillman could often pass for a poised, affable, articulate companion. Guests would spend an entire evening in Zwillman's company and, unless the host or hostess revealed the truth, would never guess they were consorting with one of America's top mobsters, the man responsible for organizing crime in America along traditional business lines.

In the early days of the bootlegging era, Longy already had the knack of disarming the unwary. In 1926, Zwillman's picture appeared in the *Newark News* after he was picked up by the police on an assault charge. The wife of the judge who was hearing his case saw the photo. She turned to her husband. 'I can't believe,' she said, 'that such a perfect gentleman could do such a nasty thing. Why, he always holds the door open for me.'

The judge and his wife were fellow-tenants of Longy's at the Riviera Hotel, yet she never suspected that the 'young gentleman' who always held the door for her was one of Newark's toughest gangsters.

Longy's ruthlessness in dealing with underworld figures was in sharp contrast to the graciousness and affability he exhibited to friends and family. The murder of Arthur Flegenheimer is one example. A flamboyant gangster who cut a large swath in New York Prohibition-era circles, Flegenheimer adopted the monicker of Dutch Schultz partly to conceal his Jewish origins. He was allowed by the Big Six – Longy, Lucky Luciano, Frank Costello, Joe Adonis, Meyer Lansky, and Ben Siegel – to control a restaurant protection racket in the Bronx after the repeal of Prohibition.

Schultz always had an appetite bigger than his connections – or natural ability – warranted. He was never satisfied with the territory he was assigned. His inevitable response was to use his muscle. He wasn't above killing one of his own men if the spirit or circumstances moved him.

One of Schultz's typical moves was an attempt to muscle in on Waxey Gordon, who was allowed by Zwillman to control beer distribution in New Jersey. Schultz tried gunning down Gordon in the Carterct Hotel in Elizabeth. Waxey escaped through a window, but two of his henchmen were killed.

Later Schultz killed one of his own enforcers, a man named Jules Mogelevsky, also known as Jules Martin and Julie the Commissar. It was this murder, coming at an inauspicious time for the Big Six, that settled Schultz's fate.

Governor Herbert H. Lehman of New York, trying to clean up corruption in the Big Apple, named an ambitious young lawyer, Thomas E. Dewey, as a special prosecutor. Dewey began to give the Big Six fits with his investigatory zeal. Using subpoenas, raids, and informers, Dewey picked off gangsters one at a time. The strategy became transparently obvious to Longy: Dewey was hoping to pick up a weakling who had been personally involved in a murder, then force him to talk about the total operation of the Big Six by using the death penalty as a threat.

Word went out that Dewey was going to indict Dutch Schultz for the murder of Jules Martin. Longy also got a tip that Schultz had tried to get Albert Anastasia to murder Dewey. Zwillman worried that Schultz's instability would lead to trouble for the Big Six.

Longy called a meeting of the group.

'The Dutchman,' Longy told his partners, 'worries me. I think he is way out of line. And he's giving us a lot of headaches. He's got Dewey on his tail, and we'll never know how he'll react to heat from that guy. Besides, I don't think he knows his place.'

The Big Six hashed over the Schultz problem. Finally, they agreed with Longy that Schultz had to die. Only Lucky Luciano was hesitant.

'If we get rid of the Dutchman,' Luciano told his pals, 'Dewey comes after me next. I can smell it.'

Longy placated Luciano.

'Dewey has nothing on you,' Zwillman told Luciano. Longy's quiet reassurance dampened Luciano's doubts. A contract was handed to Murder, Inc. This Brooklyn all-Jewish gang of killers was led by Louis 'Lepke' Buchalter and Jake 'Gurrah' Shapiro. They were the enforcing arm of the Big Six when reason failed and violence was necessary.

The gang was reluctant at first to take on Schultz – not out of fear, but because the Big Six hadn't put up enough cash. This, Lepke told Longy, was the biggest job they had ever handled. It deserved big money.

Longy used his persuasive powers, assuring Lepke that killing Schultz would be a simple job.

'You can do the job in Newark,' said Longy to Lepke. 'We'll get you the hardware and the protection.'

The Brooklyn gangster understood. Longy controlled the Newark City Commission, and that meant control of the local police. If Schultz were rubbed out in Newark, there'd be only a quiet investigation, and fewer questions would be raised.

On an October night in 1935, Dutch Schultz was lured to Newark on a pretext. He had agreed to come if the meeting were held in his favorite Newark eating place, the Palace Chop House. With him were two of his bodyguards. Abe Landau and Bernard Rosenkrantz, as well as his bookkeeper, a man known as Abba Dabba Berman.

Schultz spent more time enjoying his meal, then rose from the table to go to the men's room. Two men entered the restaurant just at that moment. One was Charley 'The Bug' Workman, a Murder, Inc. hit man. The other was never identified. Probably at a signal from someone in the restaurant, Workman went right into the toilet. Schultz was standing at a urinal. Workman pointed his gun and fired one shot at the Dutchman. The bullet entered Schultz's chest, and he fell, mortally wounded.

The unidentified second gunman, meanwhile, had methodically sprayed the people at Schultz's table. Rosenkrantz, Landau, and Berman were killed instantly. No one else in the restaurant was injured.

Schultz lingered in the hospital for a day, deliriously moaning out disconnected words. A police stenographer sat at his bedside the entire time, trying to pick up information from the delirious and dying man, but Schultz didn't reveal a single secret – according to the Newark police. A story went around after the Dutchman died that he had asked to be converted to Catholicism on his deathbed.

The New York district attorney, a man named Foley, told newsmen that Schultz had been assassinated by a hit man from Chicago, and that Lucky Luciano had ordered the job done to keep the Dutchman from interfering with the operations of the Big Six. He had the motive right, but the method wrong. Workman worked for Lepke, not for anyone in Chicago.

As soon as Schultz was dead, Longy was called in by the Newark police. Deputy Chief Haller let it be known that *he* didn't want Longy for questioning; pressure from New York forced Haller's hand.

Longy spent some time at headquarters, and the deputy

chief told newsmen that Zwillman had an ironclad alibi. Longy had made certain to be seen conspicuously miles away from the Palace Chop House when Schultz was being shot.

Then New York Police Commissioner Lewis Valentine said he wanted to talk to Zwillman. He sent three detectives to Newark. Longy didn't object. He showed up ready to be questioned. His lawyer, Harold Simandl, protested that he wasn't being allowed to be present while his client was being interrogated, but Longy told him to keep quiet. He had nothing to be afraid of, said Zwillman.

When the New York cops had finished with Longy, two agents from the FBI took over. They chased all the police, local and New York, from the room and questioned Longy for a solid hour.

The bullet that struck Schultz, according to Newark police, was too battered to be identified by ballistics efforts. It also turned out that the management of the Robert Treat Hotel, where Schultz maintained an apartment, had permitted an unidentified man to remove Schultz's luggage from the rooms after the Dutchman died. When questioned, hotel personnel said they had been instructed to get the bags out of the hotel as quickly as possible. They didn't explain who issued the orders. It was interesting, however, that a longtime resident of the same hotel was Richie 'The Boot' Boiardo, one of Longy's friends and his sometime partner.

Years later, one of Longy's bodyguards told an acquaintance he was given a bag full of pistols right after Schultz was shot. His orders were to get rid of them. He didn't doubt that these were the weapons used to kill Dutch Schultz and his pals.

A month after Schultz died, the Newark office of the FBI had a report from one of its local informants. Schultz had been killed with Longy's knowledge, said the report. Proof was the fact that, within an hour after the Dutchman was shot, every document in his hotel room had been photostated, then replaced. The copies were delivered to Longy, so he could examine them and determine which of the originals had to be destroyed.

Another sidelight in connection with the Schultz murder took place in New York. Wayne Listerman, special agent in charge of the New York City office of the FBI, sent a memorandum to J. Edgar Hoover, FBI director. Enclosed was a letter from William B. Wachenfeld, then Essex County prosecutor. The Wachenfeld letter asked the New York FBI office if all the information it had on gambling and vice in Newark could be turned over to the Essex County Grand Jury, then conducting an investigation into corruption in that city.

Hoover wrote back an emphatic note: 'Don't give Wachenfeld anything. He used to be Zwillman's attorney before he became prosecutor. But say it nicely, when you let him down,' Hoover wrote to Listerman. 'We don't want him to become suspicious.'

Hoover was on to Longy and his strength in the rackets. He had maintained a careful surveillance of the big man in Newark even before Schultz's murder. Reports kept filtering in to the FBI about Longy's prominence in the Big Six, and Hoover began paying close attention. He advised his Newark office that Longy was as big a racketeer as America could boast.

Hoover had good reason for watching Longy. In order to gain publicity for himself and the bureau, Hoover had set up a national 'Hoodlum Watch,' which he called (officially) the 'Crime Survey Program.'

Every agent in every major city in the country had been instructed to forward the least little scrap of information on the major hoods directly to Washington. Leading the list were Charlie Luciano, Frank Costello, Meyer Lansky, Joe Adonis, Ben Siegel, and Longy Zwillman. That was the Big Six, as Hoover called them, and he wanted careful attention paid to their activities.

In addition to the Big Six, Hoover asked for information on Louis 'Lepke' Buchalter; Jacob 'Gurrah' Shapiro; Morris Kleinman; Joseph 'Doc' Stacher; 'Trigger Mike' Coppola; Gerry Catena; Angelo 'Gyp' De Carlo, another Longy associate in New Jersey; Nick Delmore, who ran

Longy's Elizabeth breweries during Prohibition; Willie Moretti; Ben Kutlow; Frank Orsatti; Louis Stromberg, also known as Dutch Goldberg, and Hyman Stromberg, Philadelphia hoods, along with Niggy Rosen; William Weisman, a Longy henchman; Moe Wolensky; Moe Dalitz, the onetime Cleveland bootlegger; Morris Wolin; Frank Erickson, who ran the bookie operation for the Big Six in New York; Richie Boiardo; Mike Lascari, Longy's partner in the Public Service Tobacco Co., and a great friend of Lucky Luciano's; and Vincent Alo, known as 'Jimmy Blue Eyes.'

Hoover's interest in Longy, already strong, quickened immediately after Schultz died. He received a memo from one of his deputies in the FBI hierarchy in Washington, E.A. Tamm, who reported a telephone conversation with US District Court Judge William B. Clark. The judge was angry. Gangsters, he told Tamm, were all over Newark. They were tied up in local politics. The local police were very poor, and did nothing to halt gambling and loan-sharking.

Where was the FBI, Judge Clark wanted to know? Are you investigating here? If not, why not? The Internal Revenue Service has an intelligence unit in Newark, responsible for prosecuting income-tax evaders. It was doing nothing. These gangsters, went on Judge Clark, were coining money hand over fist and not reporting it. The IRS either didn't have enough agents to handle the work in Newark, or they weren't interested in cracking down on gangsters. And the FBI, Judge Clark felt, was neglecting Newark.

Tamm told Hoover that he had ordered Robert Whitley, special agent in charge of the Newark office, to see Judge Clark. He explained to the judge that the FBI had no jurisdiction in income-tax matters. The judge wasn't buying that.

'Don't rest on technicalities,' he told the FBI men. 'If the IRS can't do the job, you people go in and do it for them. The important thing is to prosecute these gangsters.'

Whitley wrote to Hoover right after his interview with

Judge Clark. The special agent in charge told the FBI director that Longy ran all the gambling, slot machine, numbers, and lottery rackets in New Jersey, and had a hand in night clubs as well.

The murder of Dutch Schultz in Newark also showed how powerful Longy had become, said Whitley. Judge Clark, in complaining to Whitley, pointed out that not only the Newark police but most of the city's higher officials had been corrupted by Zwillman, who wielded enormous political influence in the city. Longy, said Whitley, was allowed to operate with a free hand. His income was substantial, and growing larger now that he was tied into the New York mob through the Big Six.

Clark asked Whitley why New York wasn't going after the Big Six. Because, the agent told the judge, the racketeers in New York held the law in contempt. They didn't think Thomas Dewey, the New York district attorney, was strong enough to put a crimp into their operations.

Things in Newark were no better, said the FBI agent. We received a tip that a printing press in an apartment on South 11th Street and 13th Avenue in Newark was turning out thousands of illegal lottery tickets every day. The operation of this press was so open that the noise actually drove one of the tenants to move out of the building.

'We reported this to Police Commissioner Duffy,' said Whitley, 'and nothing was done about it. In Bayonne, Longy Zwillman is supposed to be handing out $1,000 a week in protection money to all kinds of people, including Jersey City Mayor Frank Hague and two guys named Abe Bressler and James Connolly. Again, nothing happened.'

There was another Abner Zwillman, a man as warm as a loving grandfather when his heart was touched by a personal tragedy or loss of hope.

Longy was a notorious soft touch. A horde of people were dependent on him for weekly and monthly handouts – his own immediate family (mother, brothers, sisters, and in-laws) and scores of others, and people who had touched him one way or another because of their abject poverty.

In Newark, Longy's charity was legendary. A bootblack whose stand was outside the Third Ward Political Club that Longy ran had a game he played almost every day. Longy would stop for a shine. The chore finished, Longy would toss a half dollar into the air. If the bootblack caught it, he could keep it. If the boy dropped it, the shine was free. Longy learned early on that the bootblack was adept, so the 50 cents for a shine that normally cost a dime became the boy's almost daily guarantee.

The week before he died in 1959, Longy read a newspaper article about some children in a Newark house who were sleeping on the floor because their parents were too poor to afford beds for all the large family. He called one of his henchmen and ordered him to buy two beds and mattresses to be sent to the family, anonymously.

Every Thanksgiving, Longy's trucks would spread out all over Newark delivering turkeys to churches and ward leaders, who were expected to give them to the poor.

'Longy used trucks from beer distributorships he owned, getting the turkeys and other food to these agencies,' said a member of his gang, 'because they knew where the poor lived. The same thing happened every Christmas and every Passover. Christmastime, he added toys to the baskets of food. I guess it cost him as much as $15,000 for Christmas, maybe $10,000 every Thanksgiving. He did this every year right up to the time he died.'

Longy also organized mammoth charity benefits in the Thirties and Forties. He would rent the Mosque, a huge 4,000-seat theater in Newark. Top talent from the Broadway stage, and from radio, would arrive to entertain. They never asked a penny in return, not even for expenses. Most of the entertainers owed Longy a favor, or they owed it to one of his friends in the Big Six. Proceeds from these benefits went to several Catholic charities and to the Hebrew Orphan Home in Newark. Each child in the orphanage would be taken to New York twice a year, before Passover and before the High olidays, and be outfitted with new clothing. A trip to a shoe store followed, where two pairs of shoes were bought for each child.

The Rev. Thomas J. Walsh was third bishop of Trenton when he was selected by the Vatican in 1929 to head the Newark Archdiocese. Bishop Walsh came to New Jersey's largest diocese with experience in dealing with poverty. As chancellor of the Buffalo Diocese, he had organized a guild whose major task was to aid the poor and assist the volunteers who took care of their needs.

No experience, however, could have prepared the bishop for the economic catastrophe that paralyzed the entire country beginning the year he took over the Newark Archdiocese. Bishop Walsh had called together all the clergy under his care. He wanted to establish a guild like the one in Buffalo to take care of the poor. A devastating series of stock-market crashes occurred just as the bishop called his first meeting. Widespread unemployment and sudden, grinding poverty engulfed the nation, and the Newark region was hit as hard as any.

To meet the challenge, Archbishop Walsh formed the Mount Carmel Guild, dividing his diocese into 26 units, each with its own moderator-general. Every unit worked in conjunction with government welfare agencies and Catholic Charities to distribute food and clothing to the poor.

The poor proliferated as the Great Depression deepened. In Newark, the situation became desperate, and the archbishop realized desperate measures were needed to deal with the most immediate problem – feeding the poor at least one hot meal a day. So began the Mt Carmel Guild's first soup kitchen, in the basement of St Patrick's Pro-cathedral on Mulberry Street.

Nearly 170 volunteers worked four-hour shifts to feed as many as 250 people at a time. The crush was so big that funds began running out. Then Longy Zwillman came to the rescue.

Longy became aware of the problem at the Mt Carmel Guild soup kitchen when one of his proteges, Newark City Commissioner Meyer Ellenstein, introduced him to a young priest, Msgr John Delaney. Delaney told Longy the soup kitchen was feeding so many that it was being overwhelmed with the need for cash.

While charitable, Longy was wary of requests for money unless he had firsthand knowledge of how it was being spent. He trusted John Delaney; still, Longy put on old clothes and stood in line behind St Patrick's to see for himself just what was being done for the poor of Newark at the soup kitchen. Longy sampled a meal, talked to a few of the people eating and working there, then went to call on Msgr Delaney. He handed the priest an envelope. Inside were ten crisp, new $100 bills. The money, Zwillman explained, was for the soup kitchen.

'An envelope just like this one,' Longy told the flabbergasted Delaney, 'will be given to you every week, as long as the kitchen stays open.'

Some time later, when word leaked out that the soup kitchen's benefactor was a notorious racketeer, a prominent Catholic layman approached Archbishop Walsh.

'Your excellency,' he sputtered, 'did you know we're getting money for the soup kitchen from Longy Zwillman, a gangster. That money is sinful!'

'Ah,' answered the archbishop, quickly adding in his own mind that a year's worth of Longy's envelopes would come to, 'but $50,000 of that money is blessed.'

The Mt Carmel Guild's soup kitchen lasted more than seven years. It didn't close down until 1939. And those 'blessed' envelopes were delivered from Abner Zwillman every week for as long as the soup kitchen was open.

The soup kitchen meeting was the beginning of a relationship between John Delaney and Abner Zwillman that lasted until Longy's death. It was a strange companionship that shaped Longy's bearing and character.

'What John Delaney got out of it is hard to say,' a relative said years later. 'Msgr Delaney was a prince of the church without ever having reached the real hierarchy. Other priests today still recall him with awe. He was a true intellectual. More, he had the aura of power around him always.

'On his deathbed, when the archbishop came to call on him, sick as he was, John Delaney looked up and said:

"You know, I should have had your job." He was that strong and respected throughout the diocese. Why didn't he become a bishop? Who knows. He was sick with diabetes.'

A few people who knew Msgr Delaney have another explanation. He was a heavy drinker. Although he was never seen drunk in public, the church hierarchy nevertheless felt that John Delaney had a curse he couldn't control.

John Delaney was one of two sons of a Paterson butcher who became priests. His brother, Joe, was a different type, ascetic and artistic, never reaching for power.

Even as a young man, John Delaney inspired respect and loyalty in parishioners and priests alike. When he demanded, people responded without hesitation, often dropping their own affairs to be at his beck and call. A broad man, six feet tall, Delaney had a brilliant intellect and was a shrewd judge of character – except for one blind spot. He could be handcuffed by flattery.

'Not too often,' said one of Delaney's relatives, 'but John could be taken in by people who kowtowed to him. I often felt he knew they were fakers, but tolerated them anyway. He understood power and how to use it.'

John Delaney was a bigger influence on Abner Zwillman than any other single individual. Because Delaney advised it, Longy hired a young priest, Hugh Mulcahy, to correct his speech pattern, improve his diction, get a better grasp on the language, learn English literature. Because of Delaney, Longy was inspired to hire music and art teachers from Seton Hall University to instruct him in the fine arts.

Msgr Delaney never shrank from his association with the gangster after the Kefauver hearings exposed Longy's doings to the entire country, even after Zwillman's trial for income-tax evasion revealed the fact that he had bribed members of the jury.

Every Thanksgiving Day and every Christmas from December 1939 until Longy's death, the priest had an honored place at the Zwillman table. Zwillman bought and stocked a farm in Chester, New Jersey, where Msgr

Delaney not only relaxed but ran a summer retreat for boys. The priest also spent two-week vacations at Longy's summer home at 109 Jerome Avenue in Deal. He was always present, for instance, when Longy had as his guests former Governor Harold Hoffman and his wife and daughter.

A member of the Delaney's family recalls being taken along to the Deal summer place.

'Abe – all the grownups called him Abe – always was impeccably dressed. He wore a well-tailored suit and shirt with a conservative tie. We never saw him sloppily dressed. He owned a huge motorboat, and when we went sailing he always had men around him. Come to think of it, he always had a couple of men with him, even onshore. The two of them, the priest and the gangster, were imposing figures, very dignified, never loud or boisterous. But they could have fun. I remember Abe's face breaking into smiles at the monsignor's stories. He was a gracious host.'

The boat the boy mentioned had been given to Zwillman by labor racketeer Joey Fay. Did the priest know about the people Zwillman had killed?

'It was something in the past, as far as Msgr Delaney was concerned. Abe's tough-guy days were over by that time, before John Delaney met him. By the time they became close friends, Abe was the mover and shaker type, not a thug. And I guess the priest felt about Abe as he would about any sinner who comes into the confessional. They can all be shriven. Don't forget Abe's charities. They were monumental, far greater than any layman's in the diocese.'

Chapter 11

Love and Marriage

Longy Zwillman stopped talking the moment she walked into the Chanticler Restaurant. He had been stressing a point to a dinner companion when his eyes flicked across the room for an instant, and he spotted the young woman. She was tall, about 5 feet 6 inches he guessed, blond, and had a poised, self-possessed, aristocratic air that caused eyes to turn her way.

'Toots Shor once said she is one of the most beautiful women ever to walk through the door of his restaurant,' said a friend who knew Mary Mendels as a young woman. And a lot of strikingly beautiful women used to eat at Toots's place.

'She was regal, not flashy,' said another youthful admirer of Mary's. 'She looked a lot like the young Ingrid Bergman, the one who starred with Cary Grant in all those foreign intrigue pictures. Except she had a finer nose than Bergman's.'

On this balmy June evening in 1937, Mary DeGroot Mendels Steinbach was 23 years old. When she walked into the Chanticler Restaurant in Millburn that Saturday night, she had never even heard of Abner 'Longy' Zwillman. The circles in which Mary Mendels moved were as far removed from Longy's as his immigrant mother's first American home in Newark's Central Ward was from the mansions of West Orange's Llewellyn Park, where the Dodges and Sloans mingled with the Edisons and Shanleys and the rest of New Jersey's high society.

Mary was the only daughter of Eugene Mendels, a stockbroker and one of the founders of the old Curb Exchange in New York, later to become the American Stock Exchange. Gene Mendels lost everything he owned but his self-respect in the stock market crash of 1929. That pride – and love – caused him to scrape together somehow the necessary funds to send his only daughter to Miss Beard's School in Orange. It was, without a doubt he was told, the finest private secondary school for girls in New Jersey.

In Mary's senior year, she met young John Steinbach, scion of a wealthy family. John's father, Arthur, was a member of the board at Hahnes's, one of New Jersey's finest department store chains, owned by the Steinbach family. Arthur Steinbach was also deeply involved in real estate. He had built and still owned the Berkeley-Carteret Hotel in Asbury Park, among other properties, when his son started dating lovely young Mary Mendels.

Mary Mendels and John Steinbach eloped to Elkton, Maryland, in 1933. She was barely 17. It had been a whirlwind courtship. Her father didn't approve. The young schoolgirl, brought up in luxury, had been forced to readjust her life style after her father lost his money. Mary Mendels was a spunky young woman. She realized early on that her years at the Beard School had taken all her father's remaining resources. By the time she was a senior, she was looking for ways to help him. Along came John Steinbach, young, rich, handsome, and eager for marriage. Mary Mendels didn't look upon marriage to John as an escape from genteel poverty. Still, she was young and impressionable. Her beau was not only rich; he was dashing. The young girl took the plunge.

The marriage lasted barely longer than the courtship, about a year and a half. Mary became pregnant soon after the wedding. The prospect of fatherhood was something John Steinbach hadn't bargained for. As for Mary, she soon learned that her new husband had problems of his own, not the least of which was an inability to stay away from other women.

'By the time Johnny, the kid, was born in 1934, his father was already out of his life,' said a friend of the family's. 'The boy's father rarely saw his son after the kid was born. As far as anyone knows, he wasn't interested in fatherhood, before or after the divorce.'

When it was all over and the divorce decree final, Mary took her baby and moved in with Gene Mendels, her father. She tried some modelling jobs in order to help build the family bank balance; it wasn't enough. Then she took a job as a salesgirl at Slater's, a fashionable shoe store on Central Avenue in East Orange. It was then the most prestigious shopping street in the Essex County suburbs, and working at Slater's, while a comedown for a Mendels, was no disgrace. The Depression hit more than one well-to-do family in New Jersey. Mary was working at Slater's when she went to dinner at the Chanticler with friends and met Longy Zwillman.

Longy Zwillman didn't wait too long before arranging an introduction to the statuesquely beautiful young woman sitting a few tables away from his. William Naue, owner of the Chanticler (as well as another excellent restaurant in Newark, The Roost), was a friend of Mary's as well as Longy's. A quick word to Bill Naue from Longy, a slight gesture of the head toward Mary, and the introductions were made.

That's all it was to Mary at first, an introduction to a tall, soft-spoken, well-groomed, distinguished-looking, handsome young man who seemed to have impeccable manners. She'd never heard of Abner Zwillman, and Bill Naue didn't tell her more than the simple fact that the young man wanted to meet her.

A dozen roses were delivered to Mary the next day. They were from Longy. Mary was intrigued. She asked around about Zwillman, was told he lived alone in a luxurious apartment at 32 South Munn Avenue, East Orange. That was an address Mary knew well. Some of her father's old friends – bankers, corporate executives, Wall Street tycoons – lived in that same apartment building.

Mary didn't date much. Going out to dinner with friends, mainly married couples, was the extent of her social life for some time after her divorce from John Steinbach. When Longy called and asked her for a date, she was hesitant. By that time, she'd learned a little more about Zwillman.

Longy, at the time, was riding high as a founding member of the Big Six combination in New York. The group – Longy, Meyer Lansky, Frank Costello, Lucky Luciano, Joe Adonis, and Benjamin 'Bugsy' Siegel – controlled the biggest gambling operations on the East Coast, as far down as Florida. They were involved in loan-sharking and the numbers racket, as well as a number of legitimate businesses.

On his own, Longy was branching out into any business that he believed would offer him a respectable income. He invested in Weston & Co., a New Jersey liquor-store chain. He owned with partner Mike Lascari the Public Service Tobacco Co. in Newark, New Jersey's largest cigarette vending machine operation. He had investments in films, in hotels (New York's posh Sherry Netherlands was one), and controlled the movie projectionists' union as well as some of the locals in the stagehands' union.

Longy was also involved with Moe Annenberg in a wire service that furnished the latest track information to just about every illegal betting parlor across the country.

Not everything Longy touched turned to gold. One of his biggest mistakes was about to go down the tubes when he met Mary Mendels Steinbach.

In 1936, a man named Herman Harr came to Longy with an interesting proposition. Harr said he had invented a beer-cooling system that would revolutionize keg-tapping in saloons. Bar-servicing was a business Longy knew at first hand; he had virtually cut his bootlegging teeth handling bartenders during Prohibition. Longy turned over some cash to Harr, and a company was formed called the Harr-Kegtap System Inc. Longy had a 50 percent interest.

Business was brisk once Harr began manufacturing his coolers. Harr was a good mechanic. Longy had the connections in the saloons. Few saloon owners would turn down an invitation to buy a new cooling system from a company in which Longy Zwillman had an interest. Besides, the cooler was no fluke; it really worked well.

In 1937, just about the time Longy met Mary, a resident of Florida named Herman E. Schulze showed up in a

Newark court and asked Judge William B. Clark to enjoin Harr-Kegtap Systems from further sales. Harr-Kegtap's cooler, according to Schulze, was a carbon copy of a kegtap on which Schulze held a patent. It was being manufactured at that moment in Belleville, New Jersey, by the Novadel-Agene Corporation.

Longy didn't really know his partner, Harr. He had met the inventor through another business connection, United Brewing Yeast Co., a natural business investment for a former bootlegger. The people at United told Longy about Harr and brought the two together. United Brewing also bought the first coolers produced by Harr. They were going to use them as premiums to boost yeast sales to brewers.

When Judge Clark decreed that Harr had indeed infringed on the Schulze patent, a settlement was reached. The judge allowed Harr-Kegtap to remain in business until it delivered the last cooler for which it held a contract. Deliveries had to end in 60 days, in any case.

Longy tried to separate himself from Harr-Kegtap before the hearing before Judge Clark began, but couldn't. So he tried to work out another deal. He arranged to meet Novadel-Agene's vice-president, William J. Orchard. The meeting was engineered by A.H. Rachlin, former superintendent of elections in Essex County.

Longy asked Orchard if one of Zwillman's companies could become an agent for Novadel-Agene's tap, now that Harr-Kegtap was giving up the ghost. Orchard, with one eye on the exit, said he'd have to 'ask his board of directors.' It was a polite way of saying Orchard was afraid of turning down an offer from Longy Zwillman right to his face. Longy never did get the rights to sell the Novadel tap, at least not under his own name.

This one business setback didn't keep Longy from concentrating his attention on Mary Mendels Steinbach. The young woman found the gangster fascinating company. Longy was urbane, polite, concerned with her welfare, and had a droll sense of humor. Best of all, Mary told her father, Longy was what she called 'an old-fashioned gentleman.' He was never loud or boorish. In general, Mary said,

Longy, a product of the Newark ghetto, behaved far better than did most of her old 'society' beaus.

Mary's description of Longy as an old-fashioned gentleman was borne out by his behavior during their courtship. He was prim, almost excessively prudish. When they were out on dinner dates, Longy made sure to bring Mary home by what was then deemed a 'respectable' hour. When Longy asked Mary to go for a ride in the daytime, invariably young John, Mary's son, was invited to go along. Johnny would sit in the back when his mother drove, or in the front seat if one of Longy's bodyguards took the wheel. Longy never drove. When the couple would take overnight trips – as they sometimes did to Atlantic City – young John would often be taken along, as were one of Mary's friends or her father. For Longy, Mary Mendels Steinbach was a woman to be protected, cherished, married.

The happiest person at the prospect of Longy finally settling down was his mother. She constantly worried – not about Longy's safety, but his seeming disregard for a settled domestic life. She knew about his affairs with movie stars and starlets, with dancehall girls and nightclub entertainers. They were trash to Anna Zwillman. They didn't deserve her Abie, as she always called Zwillman. She had seen her son transfer his affections from one woman to another, with no apparent thought of a permanent arrangement.

'She's not the marrying kind,' Longy would tell his mother when she asked about one of his woman friends. 'Or maybe I'm not.'

Longy's mother worried about him. He never failed to visit her in the grand new home he had bought for her in Newark's Weequahic section. One day, after Longy had gone upstairs to take care of some personal needs, Mrs Zwillman turned to Sam Katz, Longy's boyhood friend, sometime chauffeur, and bodyguard.

'Sammy, watch out for him. You hear, Sam? Take care of my Abe.' To her, Longy – gangster, businessman, bootlegger, lover of movie stars – was still a little boy, and she always called him 'Abe.' When she learned that Abner was to marry Mary Mendels, Longy's mother cried with joy. At least now, maybe with God's help, she could become a grandmother.

The wedding finally was set for July 7, 1939. Bill Naue, the man who had introduced the couple, was asked to make his place available at 10 A.M. The Chanticler was to be the site of the wedding and the reception to follow, and the entire restaurant was declared out of bounds to other diners for this particular Saturday afternoon affair.

The guest list for the wedding and reception was a melange of Wall Street financiers, government officials (including former Governor Harold Hoffman of New Jersey and every commissioner in the Newark and Jersey City local governments), bigwigs from both political parties (including Frank 'I Am the Law' Hague, boss of Hudson County) and well-heeled gangsters. Some 350 invitations were sent out. There was one oversight.

Doc Stacher had been delegated by Longy to oversee the guest list and the floral arrangements. He made a big 'mistake.' He didn't invite Ruggiero 'Richie The Boot' Boiardo, a Zwillman associate. Longy discovered this gaffe just before the wedding ceremony. He was livid. The affront to Boiardo was inexcusable, he told Stacher. Doc insisted it was a mistake, an oversight, and surely not a deliberate attempt to insult the Boot.

'I don't care what you say,' said Longy. 'You just don't do that to someone like the Boot. I'm going to have to explain this, tell him it was all your fault, and I don't know if he'll ever believe me.'

Longy didn't speak to Stacher for a month after this.

Boiardo later told Longy he realized the oversight was a mistake, but Longy never knew if deep in his heart, Boiardo hadn't believed it to be a deliberate slight.

The best man was Joseph Sisto, a Wall Street financier, head of J.A. Sisto & Co., chairman of the board of Barium Steel Corporation of Pittsburgh, a company in which Longy held a controlling stock interest. Sisto and his wife, Gladys, were old friends of Mary's. The young socialite didn't want one of Longy's 'boys' to be in the wedding party. Joe Sisto became best man; his wife, Gladys, was matron of honor.

The wedding ceremony itself was held in a small room off the main dining area. Guests for the ceremony were limited to 50 people. There was no bridal procession. The bride simply walked into the room on the arm of her father. Longy was waiting, walked over to stand beside her. Julius Krill, municipal judge of Caldwell, delivered the few necessary words, the couple kissed, then went out to join the 300 other guests waiting in the main room.

The number of hard-nosed gangsters in the reception crowd (every top mobster in the country was on hand) drew the attention, naturally, of the law. FBI agents, prosecutor's investigators, State troopers – all had a crack at checking the comings and goings of the guests. It was a scene to be repeated at many an underworld social function.

The honeymoon was a prolonged, leisurely trip west. A royal bungalow was set aside for the newlyweds at the Beverly Hills Hotel. The arrangements were made by Bugsy Siegel, and came complete with fresh flowers in the rooms every morning, champagne on ice all day, and special tours of the movie lots whenever the newlyweds felt like sightseeing.

Bugsy Siegel hauled Longy off to the golf course one day at the Hillcrest Country Club while Mary went on a shopping spree. Siegel was a good golfer; Longy, while not exactly a duffer, wasn't in Siegel's class.

The honeymooning bridegroom took a practice swing at the first hole. Unfortunately, Longy (still in the clouds after the wedding) didn't notice that the club pro had bent down to tee up. Longy's swing caught the pro on his right hand. Mortified, Zwillman apologized profusely. The pro's hand, after all, was the indispensable tool of his profession. Then, in a characteristic gesture, Longy reached into his pocket, pulled out $2,000 in cash, and stuffed it into the injured pro's back pocket. Money, to Longy, could fix anything.

There were side trips to the Grand Canyon, to San Francisco, and to Lake Tahoe. All told, the honeymoon lasted about three weeks, most of it spent in Hollywood. Longy had an unusual experience during his stay in Beverly Hills. He ran into Howard Hughes in the lobby of the hotel one morning. He hadn't seen Hughes in years, not since the time he had enticed Jean Harlow into leaving the Hughes stable of actors and go on to stardom on her own.

It could have been an awkward moment, for Mary was standing by when Hughes greeted Longy most affably. It was obvious he held no grudge, and didn't want to offend the newlyweds by bringing up old stories or recriminations. Longy, after introducing Mary, excused himself and held a short conference with the then still-young and handsome movie tycoon. The conversation was never recorded, and Mary knew enough not to pry into her new husband's business affairs at this early stage of their marriage. There is some evidence that Hughes and Longy discussed a possible partnership in a production company, for not too long after, Longy began investing more heavily in films – not necessarily produced by Hughes – than ever before.

Once back East, the newlyweds moved into 32 South Munn Avenue. Longy had arranged to rent a large apartment on the tenth floor of the luxury building. Before his marriage, he had occupied a smaller apartment on the seventh floor, with his partner, Gerry Catena, living on the fifth floor.

The tenth floor suite was more suitable for a married couple with a child (young John, naturally, had come to live with his mother and new stepfather). A couple who had been caring for Longy's household needs, Mattie and Wheeler, agreed to stay on now that their employer had wed.

The household, from all accounts, was harmonious. Longy, perhaps for the first time in his life, was content, at peace with himself, and deeply in love with his beautiful young wife. His relationship with Mary's son, John, which could have presented a problem, proved the most surprisingly felicitous of all.

The boy had never known a real father. He accepted Longy as the male role model he needed to follow. For a confirmed bachelor (until he met Mary), Longy proved to be an understanding, helpful father, even when having to deal with a stepson. The boy was only four years old. While his mother had been away from home at work, the boy had been spoiled somewhat by a doting grandfather. Longy provided the structure and discipline a bright, mischevious youngster needs. He made young John toe the line. At the same time, he showed the boy genuine love, an emotion the child quickly returned. The two were inseparable. Longy took John wherever he possibly could, including to business meetings. At home, when some of Longy's associates would call, the youngster was never sent out of the room.

'I always wondered about that,' a former bodyguard of Longy's said years later. 'The kid was always playing in a corner when the guys met to talk business. They paid no attention to him. But kids are smart. They pick up things we never realize at the time. They listen, and this kid listened, I'm sure, Longy didn't care. Only when John got older, about teen-age I guess, did he ask him to leave the room when a meeting began. And the guys would take care of the kid too. A couple of them, good golfers, took him out to teach him the game. He became a fine golfer. Other guys taught him to fish, although Longy was good at that himself. You could see that Longy loved the boy. And you could see the kid adored the big man.'

It was young John's good fortune to be brought up in a household that had structure and discipline. Longy was used to the tightly knit family units that characterized East European Jewry. In his own household, he had experienced the warmth and concern of both his parents. He had watched his own father strive to keep a family together while trying to earn a measly living, and his mother work from daybreak deep into the night to keep that home functioning.

In later years, when John got out of line (as young fellows will), Longy's reaction was sharp and quick. The young boy wasn't spoiled, as might have been the case with a stepfather who was anxious to buy the child's affection. Yet,

John recognized that Longy was treating him just the way he would a natural son.

One incident is revealing. John sneaked the family car out one night while his mother and Longy were out to dinner. He invited a few of his young friends to take a ride, even though John was too young to have a license. As luck would have it, the car was stopped by a Roseland policeman. The boys were hauled into police headquarters; the cop recognized John as soon as he saw the car's registration.

A call went to the Zwillman residence in West Orange. John's grandfather, Eugene Mendels, was the only one home. He didn't have a car, but called one of Longy's bodyguards and asked to be driven to the police station. There, Mendels put up a small bail and brought the youngster home. The grandfather hoped the incident would be kept from Longy. he didn't count on the relationship between most of the Essex County police authorities and Zwillman. Longy learned about the incident the next day.

'The kid really got it,' said Longy's bodyguard. 'A couple of good shots to the rear, a lecture that would have made a Marine drill sergeant green with envy, and confinement to his room for a week.

'Longy didn't just holler. He slapped him so hard that the boy almost shot across the room. He explained the facts of life to the boy. He had been put into a delicate position by the kid's foolish behavior, and he laid it all out, exactly how the kid could have hurt his father by his action, about all the newspaper publicity that could have resulted – if the cops hadn't kept the whole thing quiet. The boy never forgot the lesson.'

Despite the deep father-son relationship between Longy and his stepson, the boy was never legally adopted. Longy took the trouble to explain why so John could understand.

'If I adopt you, you'll carry my name,' he told the youngster. 'You'll be marked for life, and that won't be an advantage. No matter what you do, how well you behave, you'll be pointed out as a Zwillman. I've seen it happen to the rest of my family, and I don't want it to happen to you.'

The boy understood; the feeling he got from Longy was more than enough. He had never known his own father. For all intents and purposes, Longy was his father, and he treated him with the affection and respect he was taught a father was owed. He was proud of Longy, no matter what he read in the newspapers or heard on the street.

Longy and Mary had a child together in 1944, a daughter they named Lynn. She grew up to have an attitude toward her father that was the exact opposite of John's. Longy loved the girl passionately, but she never really returned that love.

Lynn Zwillman was a bright but hard-to-reach child with a deep distrust for most people. She could never accept her father for what he was, and her feelings became plainer as she grew older. They were exacerbated by her experience in applying for certain schools. Lynn had artistic talent. She had applied for a number of special schools in this country and was turned down – purely because she was a Zwillman.

Mary and Longy had an enduring marriage. It lasted until Longy's death in 1959.

Chapter 12

Gangs, Gambling, and Labor Goons

In 1939, Longy Zwillman had two brushes with a federal grand jury. Three assistant US attorneys – Matthias F. Correa, Jerome Doyle, and William Young – summoned Longy before a federal grand jury in New York. The three federal prosecutors were conducting an investigation into gambling on the Eastern seaboard. They wanted to ask Longy what he knew about the system used by the gambling combine known as the Big Six (Longy, Meyer Lansky, Frank Costello, Lucky Luciano, Joe Adonis, and Ben Siegel) of harboring fugitives seeking to avoid interrogation into gambling activities. Longy refused to say a word, letting his attorney plead the Fifth Amendment guarantees against self-incrimination in his behalf.

Longy's attorney was Arthur Garfield Hays, at the time the most prominent civil-rights advocate in America. Hays was the William Kunstler of his day. No unpopular cause escaped his attention, if in his eyes it entailed a violation of somcone's constitutional rights – or an opportunity for personal publicity. He also managed to make a good buck out of his devotion to the rights of the accused.

Hays assisted his friend, Clarence Darrow, in the famous Scopes 'Monkey Trial' in the Twenties, defending a Tennessee schoolteacher who was accused of teaching evolution in a school system that believed children should learn only the creationist theory of the world's origins. Hays was involved in every liberal cause he could find. At the same time, he had a lucrative law practice that paid him handsomely and which took on clients, whatever their cause, who could pay stiff fees.

Longy Zwillman had been one of those clients ever since his bootlegging days. Hays had served as a trustee for

Longy in numerous businesses. He could say, after Longy's unsavory past became public knowledge, that he had defended Longy to guarantee his basic rights. Actually, it was Longy's fat checks that guaranteed the appearance of Hays as Longy's counsel.

Longy, on the advice of Hays, refused to talk to the 1939 federal grand jury. This tactic proved successful – for Longy – after a secret hearing before a federal judge, Johnson J. Hayes. What took place in that hearing was never revealed, except that Hays emerged from the judge's chambers grinning like a Cheshire cat.

'My client,' Hays told a sprinkling of media people waiting in the corridor, 'knows nothing about harboring fugitives from justice. I told that to Judge Hayes. Get the spelling right, fellows. Judge Hayes and I are not related. My client stood on his fundamental constitutional rights in not answering any other questions.'

The next day, Longy was back before the same grand jury. This time, Prosecutor Correa took a different tack. He didn't ask Longy anything about harboring fugitives. Instead he went right to the heart of the matter on his agenda – gambling. What did Longy know about gambling in New Jersey? What did he know about the location of gambling houses? What did he know about the owners of such places? And what did he know about the patrons of these pleasure palaces?

Longy remained mum. With Hays at his side, he gazed at the ornate ceiling in the federal courthouse on Foley Square in downtown Manhattan, while Hays uttered the monotonous phrase about his client refusing to answer on the grounds of self-incrimination.

This time, Judge Hayes wasn't as forgiving as he had been the day before. Answer the questions, he told Longy, or face contempt charges. Longy sat mute.

Judge Hayes sentenced Zwillman to six months in federal prison. Longy left the courtroom and headed home to East Orange. Hays appealed the judge's ruling almost immediately. The contempt sentence was reversed. The Fifth Amendment guarantee held. Later, Correa said he could have forced Longy to talk by offering him immunity from prosecution on matters in which he was personally involved. He didn't want to do that, said Correa, for it would have kept him from some day prosecuting the man he felt was ohe of the chief architects of high-stakes, illegal gambling in the country.

Correa was right. In the days before Las Vegas became the legal gambling capital of the nation, the really big games were held in a variety of locations, most of them in New Jersey's Bergen, Hudson, and Passaic counties. In the Thirties and Forties, everynight saw a seemingly unending parade of rented black limousines coming through the toll gates of the George Washington Bridge and the Holland Tunnel, spreading out to take the high-rolling players to gambling casinos hat were as elaborate as the most elegant hotels on the boardwalk of Atlantic City today, or as mean as a shantytown barn on the seamiest stretch of Route 46 in Lodi, NJ. In the places where Park Avenue clientele with impeccable credit-ratings could play roulette, chemin de fer, and high-stake crap games, the players sat in beautifully appointed, carpeted rooms while sipping champagne and nibbling on caviar provided by the house. In Lodi, Garfield, Paterson, and Cliffside Park, the less-affluent customers were packed shoulder-to-shoulder in joints with sawdust on the floor and a green army blanket as the craps-table or card-game cover. These dingy joints and their more luxurious counterparts produced about $500,000 a month in profits for the Big Six – all tax-free.

This monthly hoard of gambling receipts was all in cash, mainly in small bills. It had to be converted into larger bills and kept safe. Longy had about six safe places to keep his own share. One was a fireproof movie-film reel container kept in the attic of a house in West Orange owned by one of his bodyguards, Sam 'Big Sue' Katz. Big Sue was one of Longy's most trusted aides. The two had grown up together in Newark's Third Ward slums. They had played basketball together in the schoolyards of Charlton Street. Katz had become a member of Longy's first street gang, and later went along as one of Longy's strongarm aides in the days when the bootlegging trucks carrying whiskey throughout the East had to be protected from hijackers.

Katz was a tall, solidly built, tough customer who was particularly adept with a stiletto. For that skill, he earned the nickname 'Sammy the Shochet.' A shochet is a ritual slaughterer who supplies kosher meat and chickens to orthodox Jewish families. Katz was Longy's protector-shadow. He served as Longy's driver, bodyguard, gofer-companion, and buffer against unwanted visitors.

Longy trusted Big Sue implicitly, so it was easy to see why cash left with him was safe. He wasn't so fortunate with other close friends or relatives. He gave about $150,000 to the husband of one of his sisters. The guy took off with the money. Longy found out; the brother-in-law was never seen again.

Part of that $150,000 belonged to the other members of the Big Six. Longy replaced the lost funds from his own pocket.

The big sums that belonged to the entire organization had to be banked. But how do you keep hundreds of thousands of dollars in bank accounts without bringing suspicious law-enforcement agents into the picture?'

The intricate scheme has never been uncovered by government agents. According to people in Longy's pay, the smaller bills were converted into large ones by bank employees who had been bribed. Then, with the connivance of friendly, well-paid-off branch bank managers, legitimate accounts were opened using fictitious names. It was a simple scheme that should have been spotted easily. Somehow, neither the Internal Revenue Service's intelligence division, nor the FBI, nor bank examiners ever spotted the trick. And Treasury agents took the time, for some reason, to set a trap in any of the banks used by the Big Six.

One man was assigned to keep track of all the money taken in by the Big Six. George Goldstein, a certified public accountant from Newark, was given this job. The fact that a math wizard like Meyer Lansky, a seasoned gambling genius like Frank Costello, and strongarm men like Lucky Luciano and Bugsy Siegel would all agree on Goldstein as the choice for bookkeeper says more about the respect and regard these men had for Longy Zwillman's acumen and honesty than it does about Goldstein's reputation. If Longy vouched for Goldstein, that was good enough for the other members of the Big Six.

Goldstein was another of the neighborhood kids who had grown up with Longy. He was a nervous, mousy little man who was a Hollywood casting agent's version of what an accountant should look like. He was a whiz at figures. Most important, Longy had learned early in the Prohibition days that Goldstein could do as much bookkeeping in his head as most CPA's could do on paper.

In the bootlegging era the ability to keep accounts accurately by memory was a priceless trait. After Repeal, when the Big Six organized gambling and combined it with legitimate business enterprises, Goldstein had to learn all over again how to put numbers down on paper – but continue to keep certain facts in his head.

The Big Six were adamant about keeping good records of certain legal activities, and paying their fair share of taxes on these business earnings. That assured them of taxable incomes to show the IRS, either for their own activities or through the stock held by their wives, mistresses, or relatives. They fell afoul of the government only when George Goldstein slipped – or was pushed by the federal government – into remembering numbers the Big Six had urged him to forget.

Gambling was the mother lode of Longy's fortune in the Thirties and early Forties. He was doing so well in this bigtime racket ($20,000 to $30,000 a week) that, after his marriage, he turned his Newark numbers business over to some of his lieutenants. One was Billy Tiplitz. The other was Danny Zwillman, a cousin (Longy was always taking care of relatives, especially his brothers and brothers-in-law).

Longy also became involved in labor unions. This stemmed as much from a need to find jobs for his army of relatives as to his desire to further the cause of labor. Longy had been supporting close relatives since he was 14. As he got older and more affluent, their demands on him grew. He began by handing out large sums of money as so-called loans he knew would never be repaid.

Along with the relatives and friends who periodically hit him for money, Longy was used to giving to charity. A newspaper story relating a heartrending case would bring a message from Longy to one of his aides:

'Send a couple of hundred to this kid's family.'

There were other, more regular contributions. A number of young people in Newark, New York, Cleveland, and Chicago owed their college educations to Longy's largesse. Some five or six were sent through medical school and five or six others through law school by Longy. In this group were two sons of waiters at Toots Shor's restaurant, one of Longy's favorite hangouts in New York. Shor was a great friend of Longy's right to the end.

After his marriage to Mary Mendels, the handouts to relatives became an embarrassment. Longy decided finding jobs for them would be preferable, getting this army of hangers-on off his back. For people without gainful employment this meant sinecures in some of Longy's legitimate businesses. If these people couldn't cut the mustard in a vending machine or motor-truck sales organization, for instance, there remained the labor organizations that Longy or his close friends controlled.

A natural involvement for Longy was in the unions that were organized in the liquor industry when the manufacture and sale of whiskey and beer was legalized. In New Jersey, Longy quickly took control of the liquor salesmen's union, as was to be expected, considering his connections to the industry during Prohibition. Through his friends in the Big Six, Longy quickly moved into the liquor unions on a national scale.

Longy got to know a union official, Sol Cilento, who had once been a member of Al Capone's organization. Cilento began his union career as secretary-treasurer of the Allied Workers International Union, a catch-all organized as soon as Prohibition died. From that vantage point, he moved to the secretaryship of the Distillers Rectifying and Wine Workers Union, an AFL affiliate.

With the end of Prohibition, Longy quickly cashed in on his connections in the liquor industry. He began by organizing a union, Local 19 of the Wine and Liquor Salesmen of New Jersey. He didn't do any of the organizing work himself; all he had to do was put up the money and the muscle.

Controlling a union wasn't Longy's idea of fun and games. It had to mean something more – making money, for instance. The chance to cash in came via Cilento and a couple of his associates – George Scalise and Little Augie Pisano.

They began by using a tactic they had developed in New York – shaking down employers in the distillery business. They were collecting money for 'labor peace,' they explained. The idea was neat: If you pay us, Cilento told the owners of distilleries, you'll never have any trouble with the union. No wildcat strikes plus good, honest contracts.

'We'll keep the workers happy by giving them a finger,' one of Cilento's men explained to a distiller. 'We won't let them take your hand. You do business with us, and you'll never have any problems.'

It was Longy who added an extra touch – using the union's health and welfare benefits fund as a source of ready cash.

The conduit for this scheme was a Newark insurance agent, Louis B. Saperstein. His agency, HarLaw, handled all the union's insurance, including accident, health, and life, to the tune of about $1.5 million a year. His commissions most years came to more than 10 percent of this sum.

The commissions had to be split with Longy, as were kickbacks from insurance companies who accepted business from Saperstein's agency. Handling the details – collections and muscle – were Cilento, Scalise, and Pisano.

In 1948, records of the Distillery Workers Union were subpoenaed by a New York Grand Jury investigating the murder of a union official. What the grand jury found induced it to ask for the records of HarLaw, Saperstein's agency.

Saperstein was called before a New York court and asked to testify about his work as agent for the union. He refused to talk, and was sentenced to serve five years for contempt. He was shipped to Riker's Island, where he spent four months being harassed by fellow prisoners who were told that he was a wealthy union official.

Four months was all Saperstein could stand before notifying the court he was ready to talk. He was freed on low bail of $5,000, and sang like a bird. As a result of his testimony, Cilento, Scalise, and Pisano were indicted.

Saperstein never implicated the real mastermind of the kickback scheme – Longy Zwillman. The reason isn't hard to find. Saperstein was walking down Newark's Broad Street one day after he had testified against the New York trio involved in the insurance racket. Four shots rang out; Saperstein fell. The shots, the police said, had been skillfully placed from about a foot from the victim.

'They could have killed him, but didn't,' was the way one police officer put the attack. 'They were intended to scare the guy, but good.'

Scare Saperstein they did. He never said one word to the grand jury about Longy's involvement in his agency – or the union. The indicted trio – Cilento, Scalise, and Pisano – never spent a day in jail on any of the charges placed against them.

Local 244 of the Motion Picture Machine Operators Union was under the thumb of business agent Louis Kaufman, who later went to jail for extorting money from theater owners. Two of Longy's brothers, Barney and Irving, were given jobs as projectionists in this union, as was a brother-in-law, Dan Oliner.

Zwillman's hold on the movie projectionists' local was so strong that when convicted racketeer Willie Bioff tried to horn in on East Coast film and theater labor groups, Al

Capone's strong-arm lieutenant, Frank Nitti, sent him a warning.

Don't fuck with those guys in New York and New Jersey, Nitti warned Bioff. You'll get your head blown off by Longy's people.

In certain racket circles where Longy had personal attachments, Zwillman was known by pet names like Shorty, George Long, or Abe Fitzell. Only close associates, including the police, called him Shorty.

Another Zwillman labor fiefdom was the International Union of Operating Engineers (AFL), whose headquarters were in Newark. Boss of this union was Joe Fay, a tough bird who also spent some time in jail for labor racketeering later in his career. And who was the strong arm behind Fay? Longy Zwillman, of course.

After Fay went to jail, Longy would visit his wife and children at their Newark home on Lake Street, and leave money, of course.

After Joe Fay was released from prison, Longy continued to take care of him. He arranged for Fay to become a salesman at De Cozen Chrysler-Plymouth, a car agency in East Orange. The first two sales Fay made were to Abe Zwillman, a Chrysler Imperial and a smaller Chrysler. He also sold an Imperial to Gerry Catena.

Longy's power in labor relations was exhibited in a threatened strike against Bamberger's, New Jersey's largest department store chain. A strike was averted when the Retail Clerk's Union, then a fledgling outfit with little real strength, managed to secure a contract with the store's owners.

Executives at Bamberger's were lavish in their praise of Joey Fay's efforts at avoiding a strike. He had popped up at the bargaining table as the key negotiator, a sort of unbiased mediator. No one seemed to know how Fay injected himself into the talks at Bamberger's. But there he was, bringing the two sides together with cajolery, tough talk, and threats.

Fay's achievement in negotiating an agreement between

a rich and powerful store management and a fresh, newly created union of clerks was easy to explain once you were aware of the background. Negotiating for Bamberger's was a Newark city commissioner, Meyer C. Ellenstein, who had a labor-relations and public relations consulting business on the side.

The head of the Retail Clerks' Newark local was a man named Abe Lew, who let Fay do the talking at the negotiating table. Lew, it turned out, was a Zwillman cousin, installed as head of the local on orders from Longy.

Abe Lew performed other services for Longy that were only tangentially connected to labor unions. One involved an outfit called the Newark Window Cleaning Contractors Association.

In 1944, the Newark office of the FBI was notified by an informant that the association was trying to monopolize the window-cleaning market in the city. The system used was as simple as it was time-honored. Clients of window cleaning companies that didn't belong to the association were visited by goons – in most cases Abe Lew and Ira Berkowitz – with a message. Either change your window cleaner to a company we recommend, or face a strike by your employees. The message was underlined, if a company official demurred, by using the name 'Longy' in the menacing message.

In another case, Howard Mann, a member of Longy's 'labor peace' army, tried to convince the Continental Paper Company in Ridgefield Park, New Jersey, that he could settle a long and bitter strike, insuring labor amity for years to come. In return, the company would only have to switch its pension insurance business to an agency controlled by Longy.

Meyer Ellenstein, of course, had been in Longy's back pocket ever since he left dentistry for politics. A tall, good-looking, eloquent man, Ellenstein held a law degree besides being trained as a dentist. He deserted dentistry for politics on Longy's advice.

You'll make more money in politics in one month, Longy

told Ellenstein, than you'll make in a year as a dentist. And it'll be less work.

Longy was prophetic. Ellenstein's earnings as a dentist were fair to middling, never higher than $20,000 a year. His salary as a city commissioner was $8,500 a year. The first year after entering politics at Longy's urgings, Ellenstein reported earnings of $70,000.

After being elected to the Newark City Commission, Ellenstein, a boyhood friend of Longy's, became a regular Saturday morning visitor to Longy's home. On these visits, he delivered the news from City Hall, then got orders to transmit to his fellow commissioners.

The Bamberger negotiations, it therefore turned out, took place between two parties, each under the protection of Longy Zwillman.

Local 1247 of the International Longshoremen's Association (AFL) was organized by a waterfront racketeer named Charlie Yanowsky. Tough Charlie, who later died on the docks with an ice pick through his chest, was supposed to be so mean that he never bowed down to anyone else on the waterfront. Yet police eavesdroppers had recordings of Yanowsky phoning Longy's office at a cigarette vending company. In the conversations, he constantly referred to 'The Boss,' and it took little imagination to figure out who Yanowsky meant – Longy Zwillman.

Another waterfront labor leader, Peter Panto, got into trouble with some of his own union members. The intra-union battle spilled over on to the docks in the type of labor fracas later captured so graphically by the film *On the Waterfront.* First, a waterfront figure named Albert Silvers was discovered shot to death in his car alongside a Connecticut gas station. Silvers was known to be acquainted with Longy. In one union local, Silvers was the man to see if an election was to be held. It was common knowledge that Silvers would visit Longy to find out which side to favor.

After Silvers was found dead, his arch-rival, Peter Panto, suddenly disappeared. New York District Attorney William O'Dwyer stepped into the picture. It was rumored that he was after Longy in order to question him about Panto's disappearance. O'Dwyer made a special point of calling an unusual press conference.

'I never said I wanted to talk to Zwillman,' O'Dwyer told the media. 'I did say I wanted to talk to Albert Anastasia about Mr Panto's disappearance.'

This demurer didn't fool knowledgeable New York newsmen. They were aware that Al Anastasia was a hit man for the Big Six. They realized that, if Panto was dead, Anastasia surely had something to do with it. They also knew Anastasia's connection to Zwillman. And they wondered why O'Dwyer didn't ask his questions about Panto's disappearance directly at the source.

When a teamsters' strike hit New York and New Jersey with particular fury, stalling shipments of food and other necessities, a wise trucking company executive unclogged the jam in his warehouses with one phone call – to Longy Zwillman. Longy got in touch with friends in Local 478 of the Teamsters Union. The wise executive's trucks were soon rolling to their delivery destinations; everyone else's were stalled in their garages.

Longy's power in the labor movement surfaced in a 1949 knockdown fight for leadership of the New Jersey building trades council. Sal Maso, head of the council, was trying to fight off a challenge to his leadership. Maso wanted to support one candidate in the 1949 gubernatorial election. The dissidents wanted to support another. The fight became so bitter that it looked as if Maso would lose his job. He appealed to Joey Fay, who was in prison. Fay asked Longy to intervene.

If Maso was bothered (killed or maimed, that is), it could hurt Fay's chances for a parole or a pardon. Longy sent out the word – lay off Maso. The labor leaders did exactly as Longy said; Maso kept his job.

Longy's power in the Teamsters Union was demonstrated when the Port Authority of New York and New Jersey opened a multimillion-dollar truck terminal in Newark. Local 478 officials insisted on contract terms that all but barred efficient use of the terminal.

Up stepped the newly appointed vice-president of People's Express, a trucking company. He could settle the Port Authority's problems in one day, said Gerardo Catena. His fee; a lease on the trucking terminal for People's Express – at an extremely favorable rental, of course.

Port Authority officials notified the Senate Crime Committee, asked it to look in to the power play. The committee examined Mr Catena's record. He had a police dossier going back to 1922. That was the year he met his benefactor – and boss – Longy Zwillman. Clever, smooth, and utterly devoted to Zwillman, Gerry Catena was one of the few non-Jews in Longy's early Newark mob. Longy discerned in Catena a man without religious prejudice, who was trustworthy, who could carry out orders with precision and skill.

Catena rose quickly in Longy's esteem and his organization. Eventually, a strong bond was forged between these two quiet but efficient gangsters. Catena moved into 32 South Munn Avenue, Longy's apartment building in East Orange. They socialized, entertained visiting gangland figures from out of town, did business together in legitimate fields. When Longy bought into the Public Service Tobacco Company in 1936. Catena was put into the business as a front for Longy, who held a 50-50 share. The other partner was Michael Lascari, an intimate friend of Charlie Luciano's.

Public Service Tobacco, the largest cigarette-vending machine business in the East, was started by a pair of brothers named Lillian. Al and Bill Lillian were old bootleggers operating along the Jersey Shore in the days when Longy Zwillman controlled most of the whiskey coming down from Canada.

Al Lillian was murdered in the course of his rum-running activities. Bill Lillian got the message and chucked bootlegging as a career. Instead, he went into the cigarette-vending machine business. Public Service Tobacco's headquarters were on Broad Street in Hillside, a community hard by the southwest corner of Newark.

In 1936, looking to expand his legal activities, Longy cast a covetous eye at Bill Lillian's cigarette vending operation, it had prospered beyond Lillian's expectations, making almost as much money for him legally as he had been able to earn as a bootlegger.

A series of business discussions ensued. Bill Lillian, reluctant to sell, finally got an offer he couldn't refuse – he was taken out one night and given the beating of his life. After Lillian recovered sufficiently to be able to sign his name to legal papers, the Public Service Tobacco Company became a corporation. The incorporators were Gerardo Cateno, Joseph Rosen (also known by his real name, Doc Stacher), and Abner Zwillman.

After 1939, Zwillman's stock was transferred to his wife, Mary, Catena's stock had already been transferred to Michael Lascari. Business became even brisker, for Longy had his own sales methods, developed from the lessons he had learned selling whiskey to recalcitrant saloonkeepers.

Longy managed to keep his name out of the crime news in the years just before World War II. The O'Dwyer incident caused a slight ruffle of interest in the Zwillman career, but it was quickly lost as the war news from abroad grew grimmer. O'Dwyer helped, of course, by switching attention from Longy to the magic name Anastasia. The cruel enforcer for the Big Six was a favorite figure for any reporter anxious to get a rise out of his Sunday feature editor.

Longy did break down and give an interview to Helen Worden, star reporter for the *New York World-Telegram.* He agreed because Worden was a good friend of Toots Shor, and Shor vouched for her. Sitting in a Shor's restaurant over ham and eggs, Longy played the shy country boy trying to shake off all the labels pinned on him by slick city district attorneys and federal crime fighters.

'To understand me,' Longy said to the reporter, 'you have to understand my past. Sure, I was a bootlegger. I didn't consider that a sin in the old days. I'd be one again, given the same setup. My father was dead. My kid brothers and sisters were hungry. There was no food in the house.

We had bills to meet. In the same circumstances today, I might even do worse than sell bootleg whiskey.'

What about your conviction for assault, Worden wanted to know. She had done her homework.

'I got in wrong politically,' Longy told her. 'I got caught in a political whirlpool. Judge Brennan, who sentenced me, is still a judge. That shows how much political clout I have. I didn't make much sense in those days. I was a Republican then. I'm a Democrat now.'

Longy denied he had anything to do with Dutch Schultz's death. He denied he had ever machine-gunned anyone. He denied he had anything to do with political shenanigans in Newark. Told he was considered the leading gangster in America by certain law-enforcement officials, Longy smiled.

'If that were true,' he told the reporter, 'I wouldn't be here now. I would be where no one could find me.'

An interesting sidelight to Longy Zwillman's career involves J. Edgar Hoover, who headed the FBI during the years Longy was at the height of his powers.

In October 1948, Peyton Ford, assistant to the US Attorney General, sent a request to the FBI for all the data it had on Longy and his career. The information was to be made available, said Ford, to the Internal Revenue Service. The IRS was already considering prosecution of Zwillman for income-tax evasion.

The request went through FBI channels all the way to the top. Every bureaucrat in the FBI knew that trading information with any other government department had to be cleared by his superiors.

Eventually, the request reached Hoover's desk. A letter went out to Peyton Ford.

'Pleased be advised,' wrote Hoover, 'that a search of the records of this Bureau fails to reflect that Zwillman has ever been the subject of an investigation conducted by the Federal Bureau of Investigation.'

This at a time when the bureau's files contained at least 600 pages of information on Zwillman's illegal activities. A later memorandum from Hoover's office reiterates his policy on interdepartmental sharing of information on figures involved in crime.

The Director's instructors were explicit, though. Tell him (the Attorney General, Hoover's nominal boss) nothing. We must never let them know that we have a confidential investigation (the Crime Survey Program, called 'Hoodlum Watch') going.

'It will be recalled,' said a later memo to the same FBI officer, 'that Zwillman is one of the most prominent underworld characters in the country and has been engaged in racketeering and criminal activities in New Jersey for many years.'

Chapter 13

Business Is Business

Criminal pursuits, to Abner Zwillman, were just another form of business activity. He got into crime in his youth because it was a quick path to instant cash. His large family, without a father, was destitute; responsibility for their care fell naturally on Abner, the oldest son.

The ease with which he made lots of money illegally surprised and appealed to Longy. He became aware that he was a clever gangster, not just a hood. This realization was a major reason why Zwillman remained in the rackets throughout his life. At the same time, Longy's hankering for respectability, for the chance to come out of the shadows of his criminal career, kept tugging at him with ever-increasing force as he grew older.

Longy was still relatively young – just 29 – when Prohibition ended and he switched to gambling as his major source of income. His first tentative ventures into legitimate businesses were connected, naturally, to liquor. He put his money – and/or his muscle – into wholesale liquor firms like J & J Distributors, Galsworthy Wine and Liquors and Browne Vintners. The last was a large liquor importing firm created by Joseph Reinfeld almost on the day Repeal arrived.

The next step, just as naturally, was to invest in the liquor stores, night clubs, and hotels that sold liquor. Longy's money went into a liquor store chain known as Weston & Co., into the Tavern Restaurant in Newark, the Blue Mirror night club, and the Casablanca Club, all in Newark. At the Casablanca, he offered patrons the pleasures of high-stakes gambling along with the solace of liquor.

As he began to expand his activities, Longy invested in bigger hotel projects: the Club Greenacres in Miami Beach (where the gambling casino was the major attraction), the Hotel Versailles in Long Branch, New Jersey, the Colony Surf Club in West End, New Jersey, the Sherry Netherland Hotel in New York, the Dempsey-Vanderbilt Hotel plus a number of smaller hotels in Miami Beach, and eventually four major Las Vegas palaces, beginning with the original gambling mecca, the Flamingo.

Not every venture in the liquor and hotel field was successful. The Harr-Kegtap beer-cooler fiasco cost Longy, as did the US Yeast Company and the US Brewing Company. He learned from his mistakes, however, and his investments became shrewder and more sophisticated. One reason was his connection with Joseph A. Sisto, Wall Street financier, whose firm, J.A. Sisto & Co., served as Longy's investment vehicle.

Joe Sisto and his wife, Gladys, were patricians, members of the class to which Mary Zwillman belonged, she by birth, and her father, Eugene Mendels, (once a stockbroker) by profession. Whenever Longy was asked to invest in a proposition in the years from 1939 on, his first move was to consult Joe Sisto.

That's the way it worked with Longy's interest in the Barium Steel Company, in the Hudson & Manhattan Railroad (later renamed PATH by the Port Authority of New York and New Jersey when it bought the New Jersey commuter line), in Kermouth Manufacturing Co. of Detroit, which made auto parts, in the GMC and Diamond T Truck Sales franchises in Newark. The GMC Truck company held the Newark franchise for all General Motors truck sales in the city, Longy's new reach in the investment field also surfaced in a land deal in Louisville, Kentucky, and in a housing development at Barnegat Light, a New Jersey Shore community.

One of Longy's legitimate investments had a shady beginning. It was a clever project dreamed up by an old friend of his bootlegging days. Manny Kimmel had grown up with Longy on Prince Street. He acquired a small garage business in the neighborhood and, with the help of Longy, developed it into a large and highly successful venture.

Kimmel had bought up a bunch of old warehouses in the Third Ward, intending to convert them into garages. The timing was right; the auto was becoming more and more popular with the masses as a result of Henry Ford's Model T, sold at a price almost every workingman could afford. Owning a car created a new problem for those who lived in apartment houses or in modest private homes built on small lots without any room for a driveway.

This gave Manny Kimmel his chance to go legitimate in a shrewd move – converting his warehouses into neighborhood garages where the general public could store their vehicles, in return for a small monthly fee.

Kimmel soon had a string of such garages in the Third Ward. They also had a second use, for which Longy paid Kimmel a pretty penny. They served as warehouses for Zwillman's bootleg whiskey. Some of their basements offered Longy floor space where his men could fill kegs with illegally brewed beer.

The money Manny Kimmel made from renting his garages to Longy Zwillman enabled him to buy real estate in downtown Newark, empty lots he later converted to parking spaces. They were designed for those who were coming by car in increasing numbers to the city's growing skyline of office buildings. These commuters had no place to leave their vehicles.

The first such parking lots (as Manny dubbed them) was on Newark's West Kinney Street. The name appealed to Kimmel. When he later formed a corporation and expanded his parking-lot empire into New York, he called it Kinney Parking Systems. That corporation grew, and later combined to form a huge conglomerate that included Warner Communications and New Jersey's Garden State National Bank.

According to the FBI, Longy also had an investment in another bank, the Columbus Trust Company of Newark. His connection to this bank was noted by federal authorities after a Newark Police Court judge named P. James Pellecchia gave himself up. Pellecchia admitted to embezzling some $675,000 from the bank. He had lost the money,

Pellecchia said shamefacedly, gambling in the Bergen County casinos owned by Longy and his Big Six partners.

Before he turned himself in, according to agents in the Newark FBI office, Judge Pellecchia went to visit Longy. The purpose: to get instructions on what to say to federal authorities so that Longy's name wouldn't be connected with the case. Longy had nothing to do with the embezzlement, but he didn't want the fact that he was an investor in the bank made public.

'Always, when they pick a guy up for some swindle,' Longy told a friend later, 'they try to frame me, even though my only connection with the deal is that I was stupid enough to invest in a proposition that could be ripped off by someone so easily.'

When it came to shadier investments, Longy didn't need Joe Sisto's advice. He was his own expert. So it was with the Public Service Tobacco Company, acquired by Longy, his top aide, Gerry Catena, and Mike Lascari from its former owner, Bill Lillian. Longy helped build this firm to a point where it was selling 650,000 packs of smokes a month in about 1,000 machines. Locations were acquired without much effort; Longy's name and reputation were the best sales pitch. No other vendor would attempt to replace Longy's machines with any of his own.

A number of other projects like the cigarette vending company, including the Las Vegas hotels, offered Longy a chance to use his reputation to acquire and manipulate an apparently legitimate enterprise. It was natural, for instance, for Longy to move his cigarette-vending business into New York.

So came into being the Manhattan Cigarette Service Company at 1485 York Avenue in New York. And the Runyon Sales Company, originally called the Royal Music Company, with headquarters at 123 West Runyon Street, Newark. Runyon's line was the juke box, then appearing in restaurants, bars, even small candy stores, wherever Americans gathered. The New York office of Runyon Sales was at 593 Tenth Avenue, where Longy's buddy Doc Stacher was listed as owner of record.

Distributing juke boxes was made especially easy for Runyon Sales because of its cosy relationship with the union that covered the industry. The union's boss was one Joseph Heimberg, who owed his post to Longy Zwillman.

In 1954, the Chicago Crime Commission reported that a company whose name had become an American household word – Muzak – was controlled by Longy Zwillman. Longy insisted he had nothing but a stock investment in this company, which sent soothing music by wire into thousands of offices across the country.

Even when Longy was trying to do business legitimately, his old associates would sometimes bring a whiff of gangsterdom into a project. A case in point was the time Longy heard that US Steel was going to sell some of its open-hearth furnaces. He could use them for his Barium Steel Company, which was stretched to capacity because it was growing so quickly as the result of steel shortages during and just after World War II. Longy sent an old pal, Phil Weiss, to dicker for the furnaces. Along the way, Weiss stopped off in Detroit.

'I went out there because I heard you needed parts for the General Motors place in Newark,' Weiss told Longy. 'I also heard that the Willys Motor Company was selling parts.'

That wasn't exactly the sequence of events. Weiss's negotiations with US Steel fell through. He didn't want to return to Newark empty-handed. When he heard about the Willys parts being available, Weiss figured he could pick them up cheaply and return to Newark with a smile.

Once in Detroit, Weiss fell in with some of his old pals in the Purple Gang.

'I met Abe Bernstein in Detroit,' Weiss told Longy as they sat in Peacock Alley. (Longy always used this lobby-floor lounge at the Waldorf Astoria Hotel in New York when discussing business with his friends. Its buzz of voices from other patrons was a perfect counterfoil for any eavesdroppers.) 'Abe said I was crazy to buy the parts. He knew for sure they could be picked up for nothing. I couldn't pass up a deal like that.'

Weiss was accused of stealing the parts. He was never brought to trial. His indictment was dismissed, and he high-tailed it to New York to report to Longy.

Two of Longy's legitimate enterprises in Newark – GMC Truck Sales and its Parts and Service Inc. affiliate – did $1 million worth of business with the city in the years between 1947 and 1951. GMC Truck Sales did half of this, involving sales of trucks, fire apparatus, and parts. The second company did another $500,000 in repair of trucks and equipment.

The US Senate Crime Committee, led by Senator Estes Kefauver of Tennessee, painted this as a crooked deal by Longy's control of the city's politicians. Actually, all the purchases from Longy's company were done by contract after public bidding in accordance with state laws. That Longy's firms won the contracts had as much to do with the lack of competitive bidders as it did with the bid prices. Few rival contractors were bold enough to compete with a firm known to be controlled by a feared individual named Abner Zwillman.

In Hollywood, Longy at first dabbled in motion-picture production more as a sideline to his amorous adventures than for money-making purposes. His investments in films began with his romance with Jean Harlow. They continued as he met other women – starlets like Blanche Williams, Alice Irene Sheppard, and Suzie Donner, none of whom achieved either the fame or fortune of Harlow. It continued with his association with Howard Hughes after Harlow's death.

Control of Longy's film investments was exercised by Manhattan Productions and Greentree Productions, headed by old friend Jules Endler. One producer with whom Longy dealt was Sol Wurtzel, who became Zwillman's connection with 20th Century-Fox after the Harlow affair was over. Wurtzel eventually wound up as executive producer of the 20th Century-Fox B-picture unit, turning out films like *Charlie Chan in Panama, Life Begins at 40,* a slew of Mr Moto pictures, and four minor Laurel and Hardy comedies. Wurtzel's best-known film was the classic

Ramona, remembered best for its haunting musical score.

In some of these film ventures, Longy made as much as 100 percent profit. In others, he dropped a bundle. He considered his Hollywood losses a lark, the cost of giving him the pleasure of hobnobbing with film stars, writers, and directors.

Jules Endler, who ran Manhattan Productions, was a trusted and close associate, one who held Longy's interests above his own right up to the day he died. It was Endler, for instance, who was sent by Longy to Louisville, Kentucky, to work on a complicated deal that involved the purchase of a square block of the city's downtown real estate. The $1.8 million project included purchase of a large federal post office building, a proposal that stirred rumors that Longy's influence reached into the halls of Congress.

For a number of reasons, the Louisville deal never made as much money as Endler – or Longy – had hoped. Yet the amount of money involved revealed how much Endler was trusted.

The Browne Vintners Company deal was a hangover from Prohibition. The importing firm was owned by Joe Reinfeld, with Longy holding a minority interest. It controlled all the Seagram whiskeys imported into this country from the Bronfman family, owners of the giant Montreal distillery.

Longy's share was carefully hidden. As late as 1940, when the Bronfmans acquired control of Browne Vintners, Sam Bronfman told *The Wall Street Journal* that he had no idea who owned stock in the American importing firm. All the firm's assets, said Bronfman, were bought for cash.

The sale of Browne Vintners caused a rupture in Longy's relationship with Joe Reinfeld. After the sale (price $7.5 million), profits were divided up in a number of ways. About $900,000 went to Longy. Varying lesser amounts went to Doc Stacher and Niggy Rutkin.

Rutkin, a killer but a lower-ranking member of Longy's old Prohibition gang, received less for his shares than did either Longy or Stacher. He stewed about this for three years. Finally, in 1943, he acted.

Joe Reinfeld received a message. Rutkin wanted an additional $250,000 from the Browne Vintner proceeds, or he'd blow Reinfeld's head off. Reinfeld later testified that he went down to his bank vault in Newark and withdrew $608,000 in $1,000 bills. He stuffed them into two cardboard boxes that he brought to a law office on Market Street. There he handed the money to Doc Stacher. Why Stacher?

'Reinfeld would never have shown up if Rutkin was there,' said a law-enforcement official. 'He was afraid Jimmy [Rutkin's real first name was James] would take the money, then kill him. He did trust Doc Stacher.'

Why $608,000, if all Rutkin had asked for was $250,000? The answer was simple. The rest of the money went to Longy and Doc Stacher, a form of protection payoff to ensure Reinfeld's continued survival. Stacher and Longy divided the remaining $358,000 equally.

They also kept their promise to protect Reinfeld, who died in bed in Canada as a knight of the realm, Sir Joseph Renfield. Niggy Rutkin, indicted for income-tax evasion, died in a cell in the Hudson County Jail. Jail authorities called it a suicide.

Zwillman had a nice nose for slightly esoteric business deals. One of the best examples was the way he recognized that a small mineral-water well almost hidden on an Essex County picnic ground could be turned into a fountain of dollars.

John Munkacsy was still a young man when he arrived in the United States from Hungary some years before World War I. A skilled woodworker, he soon made enough money to buy – very cheaply – a large, beautiful chunk of land along the Passaic River in what is now Fairfield, New Jersey.

'My father loved this area,' said his son, also named John, many years later, 'because it reminded him so much of the old country.'

That beauty is still evident today, when development is encroaching closer and closer to this idyllic bucolic setting.

Interstate Highway 80 runs close to the Munkacsy property, but the plot of land is so hidden, that you'd need precise instructions to find it. Snow-white herons still wheel and soar close to the river whose shoreline doesn't look much different today than it did when Mad Anthony Wayne was maneuvering his Colonial troops in the area.

John Munkacsy made a living creating models for inventors who required them to help obtain a US patent. He worked in a little shed on the property, one that still stands today. To make ends meet, John Munkacsy ran a picnic grove.

The Munkacsy property was clean and well-tended. Because of that or because it reminded them of the old country, it was enormously popular with immigrant families living in the squalid tenements of Paterson, Passaic, and Newark. They reveled beneath the tall willows swaying in the wind, played beside the placid river, which rolled by makeshift barbecue pits on which these hard-working people could roast lamb and veal, meat they could never have afforded in Europe. They came to Munkacsy's grove the rugged way – by trolley from Newark to Caldwell, after which they'd have to trudge a couple of miles on foot, carrying their baskets of food and blankets. From Paterson and Passaic, it was a little easier, for the trolley ran to Grandview Park, only a short walk to the Munkacsy grove.

'They were rugged people,' said John Munkacsy, Jr. 'They'd walk in here late on a Saturday after work, pick their spots, lay out the food and drink, play with the children, or take boat rides on the river (I rented boats out at 10 cents an hour). My father had a makeshift bar set up near the house, and he put out about 150 tables on the grounds. We'd sell about 20 half-kegs of beer and a lot of wine on a weekend. My father used to make the wine himself, about 600 gallons every winter. We'd sell out before the summer was over.

'Many of the families would sleep over Saturday night, on benches, tables, on the ground, wherever they could find a comfortable place. Whole groups of them would stay here until late on Sunday, as if they hated to leave the country to go back to the stinking cities.'

The Munkacsy grove became popular enough for the local Board of Health officer to pay it a visit.

'You don't have enough water here to serve all these people,' he told John Munkacsy. The remedy was easy; dig another well.

Munkacsy chose a spot about 50 yards from his house, far enough back from the river so he'd be sure of getting pure artesian-well water. The drillers had to go deep to find the water, but the new gusher spewed out 3,000 gallons an hour.

'The water was very hard,' recalls John Munkacsy, Jr, 'so hard that it took my mother up to ten hours to boil some potatoes. My father consulted a water chemist. The water was so hard, he said, because it contained large amounts of calcium and magnesium sulphate. It didn't taste bad, however.'

Word soon began filtering back that people who drank the water reported it had marvelous curative powers. The aches and pains of rheumatism and arthritis seemed to melt away, and constipation was easily relieved. Once the good news got out, John Munkacsy's well was swamped with customers.

'We began by selling the water for two cents a glass,' said John Jr. 'Then we went to jugs, ten cents a jug. In 1936, in one day, we sold 1,000 gallon jugs of water. The crowds began to get bigger and bigger. People would come over at three A.M., to stand in line. Big shots in New York sent their chauffeurs over. It got too much for us.'

The solution appeared one day in a 12-cylinder Cadillac. A tall, good-looking young fellow dressed in an expensive suit got out of the car. With him was another tall, bulky, round-faced young man who introduced himself as plain Sam and said he lived half a mile away. He didn't introduce his companion. Sam said he had a business deal to propose.

The crowds around the well were so thick that Munkacsy asked the visitors to come into the house. They sat in the woodworker's modest living room as the visitors presented their proposition.

'We'll take over selling the water for you,' said Sam, 'do all the work, and pay you $1,000 a week in royalties, whether we sell any water or not.'

'You know what $1,000 a week meant in the Great Depression?' John Munkascy, Jr, asked. 'My father felt like he was dreaming. We worked like dogs selling that water day and night and never made that much money. After he shook hands on the deal, and was told that some lawyers would come out to sign the papers, my father walked around with this big smile on his face all day. Imagine, he kept telling my mother, $1,000 a week free and clear, and we don't have to do anything for it.'

The lawyers came, the papers were signed, and the new operators took over. First they put up a large bottling plant that ran seven days a week, 24 hours a day. It employed 45 people who worked in what was then the largest building in the town.

Soon, they were shipping the water all over the East; 1,200 cases a day went to New York City alone. The Munkacsy Fountain, as they called it, became a household word. Actresses on the Broadway stage sent over for the water so they could bathe in it. Bernarr Macfadden, the eccentric publisher and health faddist, sent his chauffeur up from his Englewood home to buy cases of it.

The Newark entrepreneurs loved the action. They had made a sweetheart of a deal. Paying Munkacsy $1,000 a week was peanuts. They were raking in $90,000 a month – most of it in cash.

For Abner Zwillman – yes, he was the tall, silent young man who had arrived with Sam Katz at the Munkacsy grove that day – this kind of cash business was a bit of nostalgia. It reminded him of the good old Prohibition days.

'We wondered about all that cash,' said John Munkascy. 'They didn't appear to care for banks. They kept it stuffed in cardboard boxes for days. And they didn't trust anybody but my wife, Betty, to watch it.'

The Munkacsy Fountain deal illustrates, partially, Longy Zwillman's basic business philosophy: Try and be good to others. Do it because it's the right thing to do for those who are less fortunate through no fault of their own. If, at the same time, you just happen to make a good buck out of your charity, don't be squeamish; pocket the money.

A good example of this mixing of philanthropy and investment involved the Newark Housing Authority. Longy watched as the sons and daughters of his old immigrant neighbors, Jewish and Irish alike, prospered and moved out of the old neighborhood. They were being replaced by poor blacks from the South and Hispanics from the Caribbean. The homes he and his buddies had grown up in, never too prepossessing in the first place, became dilapidated eyesores.

Longy's impulse was to do something. The Newark Housing Authority was a natural conduit for his concern. It was just beginning, after World War II, a program of public housing in the city's center. But a shortage of funds – and a sloppy, often crooked administration – kept the promise of better housing for the poor far from fulfillment.

Longy came up with a suggestion. Why not, he asked a group of civic leaders, form a nonprofit redevelopment corporation that would put up seed money for new housing? The federal government was encouraging such local groups to help push programs of housing for the poor. He, said Longy, would put up $250,000 of his own money to get such a redevelopment effort going.

This was a noteworthy offer – with its own angle: Longy had a controlling interest in several brickyards. He also had a special 'in' with Louis Danzig, executive director of the city's housing authority. If any housing was built, Danzig would make sure that only Longy's bricks would go into them.

Another altruistic housing offer involved an old city-owned ballpark that had once been the home of the Jersey City International League baseball team. In 1947, long after the team had deserted the venerable stadium, the city decided to demolish the park and construct public housing on the site.

The proposal eventually was translated into a contract with the giant Prudential Life Insurance Company to erect the housing. With Longy's connections in the Jersey City government, it didn't take long for the city commissioners to recognize they couldn't really do business with the strait-laced people whose company logo was the Rock of Gibraltar. Somehow, the contract was switched from Prudential to one Leslie Weber, who dabbled in realty using the resources of Longy Zwillman.

Some years later, Weber testified before the Larner Commission, set up by state authorities in New Jersey to investigate skullduggery in Jersey City. Yes, he had put in a bid to buy the old ball park from the city for $90,000, Weber admitted, so he could fulfill the contract to build housing for the poor. Where did he get the money for the purchase? Weber was asked. Squirming in his chair, the real estate expert had to admit that $20,000 of it came from Abner Zwillman.

Weber – and presumably his moneyman, Longy – made only a small profit on that deal. The purchase price of $90,000 was translated into a $94,000 award for damages garnered by Weber from the city when it reneged on the contract he had.

It's not quite certain that Jersey City's commissioners had ever intended building the 1,100 units of housing that was supposed to go up on the site of the ballpark. It *is* certain that it was Longy's influence that had the original contract switched from Prudential to Weber. The $94,000 that Weber – and Longy – received in damages from the city was a minor sop to the anguish of not being able to build housing for the poor. As it worked out, a $4,000 profit for tying up that much money for months wasn't such a hot deal, after all. In many ways, it was similar to the Harr-Kegtap fiasco yaars before, in which Longy lost a chance to monopolize the beer-cooling business when the man he backed turned out to have infringed on another's patent.

Longy's desire for rendering public service – mixed with a propensity for making money on his benevolence – came to the fore during World War II. Longy contributed heavily to war relief agencies. He ran benefits for the USO. He also secured talent for New York's Stage Door Canteen, where the big stage and screen stars not only entertained servicemen and women but actually got on to the floor and danced with them. Many of the stars owed Longy favors for the boosts he had given their careers, either in Hollywood or on Broadway.

At the same time, Longy was making a bundle on war work for the military. He had financed a small aircraft parts plant called Alkuno & Co. The owner of record was an engineer named Kuno Hayman. The real owners were Longy and Mike Lascari, his partner in the Public Service Tobacco Company.

Eugene Mendels, Longy's father-in-law, was listed as secretary-treasurer of the company. Mendels drew $75,000 in salary from Alkuno over a three-year period, although he did little but sign checks. His high position in the company was later justified on the basis of an investment of capital. Later, it turned out, Mendels' investment was a measly $500. It was also revealed that Mendels, who had lost all his own money in the 1929 Crash, turned over $35,000 of his $75,000 salary to his daughter Mary (Longy's wife), 'to do with as she pleases,' he said.

Alkuno's expertise in manufacturing aircraft parts, it also turned out, was the result of accumulated experience in repairing cigarette-vending machines.

Chapter 14

Strange Bedfellows: Longy and the Politicians

When Joseph G. Bozzo died in 1969, his obituary never made *The New York Times*. Yet in life, Joe Bozzo (better known and feared as plain J.B.) controlled much of Republican politics in New Jersey, and all of GOP affairs in Passaic County.

Small and round in appearance, Joe Bozzo held audience every Friday at lunch. His court was in the dining room of the Alexander Hamilton Hotel in Paterson. He would sit at a corner table, his back to the wall. Waving his ever-present gold cigarette-holder imperiously, J.B. would eat well in the company of a few sycophants that included lawyers, judges, and office-holders, petty politicians all. Then J.B. would settle back comfortably and await the petitioners.

They came, old and young, the immigrants bowing low as they once did to the *padrones* at home, the native-born standing straighter, but maintaining a strict deference and distance. They would all tell their stories and await J.B.'s favor.

Popping pills (in later years, Bozzo suffered from heart and kidney problems), J.B. would dispense favors, promise jobs, and settle disputes, his voice rising only high enough to be heard by those closest to him.

J.B. at those sessions reminded onlookers of a jovial Hasidic rabbi, his faithful followers gathered round and clamoring for a morsel of wisdom from his lips. The luncheon levee over, J.B. would heave himself up from the table, walk out to his sky-blue Cadillac, and be driven to his estate at Erskine Lakes. His manor house sat on a hilltop overlooking the North Jersey District's reservoir system in Ringwood. The setting reminded one visitor of the Scottish highlands, a comment that pleased J.B. no end.

J.B. would walk around his estate admiring the scenery, the greener than green lawns, and the lush garden foliage. Indoors, he would escort a visitor around the spacious home, pointing casually but proudly to the antique furniture, some of which had been brought over at great expense from his native village in Sicily. When visitors weren't present, he would spend time conversing with his 'house guest,' Betty Van Dine Smith. Then he would check the mail, and see to his dogs. His chores finished, J.B. would plump himself into an easy chair on his flagstone patio and conduct his real business – deciding who would run for political office, who would be bypassed. In his later years (after the Kefauver Crime Committee had ripped off his cover of respectability), Bozzo confined himself to the politics of Passaic County. Before that, his domain extended to the entire state – and both political parties.

Joe Bozzo, whose hold on state GOP affairs was partially the result of 'loans' to the state committee, had a political partner named Abner 'Longy' Zwillman, who had a similar hold on Democratic political affairs. Between the two, they virtually ran politics in New Jersey in the late Thirties through the Forties.

The Zwillman-Bozzo combination had its genesis in booze and gambling. During Prohibition, if you wanted to buy and sell illegal liquor, you had to control the politicians who could not only put a crimp in your business, but aid it immeasurably if they were cooperative. The same rules applied to gambling.

Longy, of course, was the biggest rum-runner on the East Coast. His education in politics began in Newark when he was 14 and already immersed in neighborhood petty gambling. As he grew older and expanded his illegal business horizons, Longy also increased his political influence. The two businesses – rum-running and illegal gambling – required constant watering of political plants to be successful. The bigger the game, the higher you had to reach to corrupt.

Longy's first advance into the politics beyond his immediate neighborhood came during Prohibition, when he had to buy the favors of citywide officeholders. This was accomplished via two old friends. One was William J. Egan, who rose from Newark City Clerk in 1916 to the city commission in 1930. He later moved up to become a member of a triumvirate that ran Essex County Democratic Party affairs, and went on to be named an assistant state attorney general.

It was when Egan was a city commissioner that one of the most bizarre incidents in New Jersey political history took place.

The election of 1932 was a Roosevelt runaway on a national scale. In few places were the local results more astonishing than in Newark's Third Ward, Longy's home base. There the GOP registered just eight votes for every Republican candidate, local and national. Except Herbert Hoover. He got nine. The Democrats got exactly 587 votes registered and cast for every one of their candidates, including F.D.R.

These results astounded the local GOP hierarchy. They were used to losing the Third Ward, but with a greater variety of numbers coming out of the poll booths. They asked that the ballot boxes be impounded.

Longy Zwillman went into his magic act. First, the poll books of Newark's six wards were stolen from the office of the commissioner of registration. When court officers came for the ballot boxes kept in the city clerk's office, they found that somehow the boxes had managed to walk off by themselves, right past a phalanx of police guards and right out of the City Hall basement.

A clamor arose. How could all of this have taken place? GOP leaders roared they wanted the ballot boxes and registration books found, and the thieves punished. Everyone in the city knew who was responsible for the caper. The city's public safety director, whose police were supposed to be watching the ballot boxes, was Commissioner Bill Egan, a friend of Longy's. The city clerk, from whose care the boxes were snatched, was Peter J. O'Toole, a friend of Longy's. And, said an FBI report, the theft had been planned in Longy Zwillman's suite at the Riviera Hotel.

Longy supplied the men who picked up the boxes, and the trucks that carted them away.

A few minor individuals were finally indicted for the theft. None were ever convicted. The man who suffered most – only temporarily – was Bill Egan. The stench of the theft lingered long enough to smoke him out of office at the next election. That didn't mean too much. Egan merely joined Charles P. Gillen and Colonel William H. Kelly to make up the troika that ran the Democratic Party in Essex County and helped A. Harry Moore, another friend, run the state as governor.

Through the late Forties, the mayor and at least three of Newark's five city commissioners owed their jobs to Longy. One was Meyer C. Ellenstein, an old and trusted Longy ally.

Ellenstein's rise in Newark politics began with the death of a commissioner in 1932. Ellenstein was a candidate to replace him, but the remaining four commissioners couldn't agree on a successor. Then Longy went to work.

Suddenly, Jesse Salmon, who headed the GOP in the county, sent word to a Republican commissioner to switch his vote to Ellenstein. The move was unexpected only by those who didn't know that Longy – through his buddy Joe Bozzo – had contributed substantially to Salmon's campaign chest. When it came to politicians, Longy, too, played no party favorites.

Ellenstein's selection was by no means unpopular. When he ran for office on his own in 1933, he garnered a record number of votes for a commission candidate. Much of the total came from Longy's Third Ward, where Ellenstein pulled twice as many votes as the nearest competitor.

In 1949, Longy brought the state CIO organization into Newark politics through the back door. It began with a pact between the Italian vote-getters in the First Ward, led by Ralph Villani, and the Longy-led Jewish group in the Third Ward, fronted by Meyer Ellenstein.

If Villani's people supported Ellenstein, the Third Ward would support Villani. When both were elected, they could divide up the patronage they controlled at City Hall.

Msgr. John Delaney.
(Newark Archdiocese Archives)

Mayor Meyer Ellenstein of Newark (left) with Archbishop Walsh and Msgr. Delaney. The Archbishop is accepting a check for the soup kitchen. (Newark Archdiocese Archives)

The Mount Carmel Guild Service Kitchen, with the men partaking of its bounty. (Newark Archdiocese Archives)

Joe Bozzo. *(The Record)*

Angelo "Gyp" De Carlo (AP)

James "Niggy" Rutkin. (AP)

Willie Moretti. Alive. (AP)

Willie Moretti. Dead *(The Record)*

94-65 LAS VEGAS OFFICE
BANK OF NEVADA
102 FREMONT STREET
LAS VEGAS, NEVADA

THE Flamingo
NEVADA PROJECTS CORPORATION
LAS VEGAS, NEVADA

No 920

May 6 1947

PAYMENT STOPPED

ONE HUNDRED THOUSAND AND NO/100 DOLLARS $ 100000.00

THE FLAMINGO OPERATING ACCOUNT

PAY TO THE ORDER OF DEL E. WEBB CONSTRUCTION CO.

PAYMENT STOPPED

PAYMENT STOPPED

BY Ben Siegel

94-65 LAS VEGAS OFFICE
BANK OF NEVADA
102 FREMONT STREET
LAS VEGAS, NEVADA

THE Flamingo
NEVADA PROJECTS' CORPORATION
LAS VEGAS, NEVADA

No 1384

June 16, 1947

FLAMING 50000 DOLS 00 CTS DOLLARS $ 50,000.00

THE FLAMINGO OPERATING ACCOUNT

PAY TO THE ORDER OF
Del E. Webb Const. Co.
5101 San Fernando Road
Los Angeles, Calif.

BY Ben Siegel

Ben Siegel's famous bounced checks to the Del E. Webb Construction Company (AP)

The end of Ben "Bugsy" Siegel. (AP)

Senator Estes Kefauver, preparing a campaign for national office. With (from left) David Wilentz, William Egan and Mayor John V. Kenny of Jersey City. (AP)

Longy with his attorney Arthur Garfield Hays, preparing for appearance before the Kefauver Crime Investigating Committee in Washington.

Frank Costello, flanked by his attorneys, Joseph L. Delaney (left) and Morris Shilensky. (AP)

Gerry Catena. (AP)

Longy (at right), appearing in Federal Court in Newark in January, 1956. With him is his counsel, John E. Toolan. The charge: income tax evasion. (AP)

Longy' funeral on February 27, 1959. John Steinbach, assists his mother, Mary, as an unidentified friend assists Longy's daughter, Lynn Kathryn. Longy's attorney, Morris Shilensky, walks in front. (AP)

Longy, always one to hedge his bets, called on some of his union friends at the state level. He would agree to back the CIO's candidate for city commission, Stephen Moran, in exchange for support for Ellenstein and Villani.

This deal was strengthened even further. Moran chose Charles Handler as his campaign manager. Handler was Longy's lawyer, and his agent in a number of corporations.

The ticket fashioned by Zwillman won handily. All three – Ellenstein, Villani, and Moran – were elected.

Under Newark's commission government, the five commissioners chose a mayor after the election. It was customary for the commissioner winning the largest number of votes to be selected mayor. This time, it was different. The Zwillman-backed trio combined to select Villani, who had run behind Ellenstein. In return, Handler was named city attorney, and another old Zwillman pal from the Newark Housing Authority, David Kent, was chosen to be deputy mayor.

Another Zwillman hanger-on named Ira Goodman was appointed Commissioner Moran's aide. Goodman proved to be a turkey, too greedy and stupid for his own good. He tried to shake down milk dealers in Newark, was caught and convicted. None of that scandal rubbed off on Commissioner Moran.

The Zwillman-Bozzo combine really hit pay dirt in 1946. One of the candidates in the GOP gubernatorial primary was Harold G. Hoffman, who had been governor of the state from 1935 to 1938. Hoffman needed money to run his campaign, and he went to Bozzo. He was too late. J.B. had been tapped by the Republican state committee, which was broke. Bozzo's first contribution was a check for $25,000 as a contribution.

J.B. forked over a second check. It was, he considered, a good investment in the future. Some day, he'd get his $25,000 loan back. The second $25,000 would be his hook into the state party organization. For J.B. had a secret hankering. He never cared for public office – except one post. He was dying to become a member of the state racing commission.

Some 20 years later, Bozzo confided to a newspaperman that the GOP state committee had swindled him.

'They took my $50,000,' said Joe Bozzo. 'They used it and my friends to re-elect Al Driscoll governor when he didn't stand a chance. They never returned my other $25,000, that loan I gave them. And they never made me a racing commissioner. It was the only job I ever wanted from those bums in all the years I worked for them.'

The Driscoll re-election was a classic example of the power that Bozzo and Zwillman would wield in state politics when they combined forces. Driscoll, an honest official, had been an excellent governor in his first term. It was Driscoll who pushed through a new state constitution and court reform, an objective even the popular Woodrow Wilson couldn't achieve as governor.

Driscoll, however, made political enemies galore in doing so, and the scramble to depose him began in a bitter primary fight. He won the primary, but knew he'd have an uphill battle in the general election. That didn't faze Al Driscoll. He had won tough fights before.

The tight race shaping up gave Longy an idea. He hopped into his car and asked George Haber, his chauffeur-bodyguard, to take the back roads to Erskine Lakes. The car headed up the Newark-Pompton Turnpike through Bloomingdale and Riverdale into Ringwood, then climbed the steep hill to Joe Bozzo's mansion.

'What can I do for you, Abe?' asked J.B. after they were comfortably ensconced on the patio. Zwillman's close friends and associates always called him Abe, not Longy.

'This election,' said Longy. 'It gives me an idea, Joe. You know I always said if we can get a good attorney general here, it would make things a lot easier for all of us. This is our chance to put somebody we think is good into office.'

Bozzo listened. He was sharp enough, having worked with Longy before, to get the point of a conversation without having all the details spelled out.

'I have a list of five reputable guys who would make fine men for that job,' said Longy. 'No governor in his right mind could say they're not. We show the list to the candidates. I'll take it to Elmer Wene [the Democratic candidate], you take it to Driscoll. Whoever says okay, we give him enough votes to become governor.'

'I get the picture, Abe,' said Bozzo. 'But this guy Driscoll, he has a hard head, know what I mean. You can't talk to the man.'

'Does he want the job or not?' asked Longy. 'You know he's going to need Hudson and Essex for even a ghost of a chance of winning.'

'I know that, Abe. You know that. But Driscoll, he has faith. You know how hard it is to talk to man who has faith?' Bozzo started to cough, snuffed out his cigarette. 'Tell you what, Abe. Why don't you try Wene first? If he says no, we'll talk again. Then it'll be my turn, Okay?'

'We'll do it your way, Joe,' said Zwillman. He trusted Bozzo. The man had offered to cut Longy in on a lucrative black-market operation during World War II, in tires and gas ration stamps. Longy turned him down – he had a stubborn patriotic streak – but he dampened his patriotism long enough to accept Bozzo's offer of ration stamps for food.

Longy's interest in the attorney general's spot stemmed from the new state constitution. It gave the attorney general power to remove county prosecutors he deemed to be laying down on their jobs. This had happened in Bergen County, where Driscoll's attorney-general, Theodore Parsons, named a special prosecutor, Nelson Stamler, who promptly put Joe Adonis, one of the Big Six, in jail.

Longy sent Meyer Ellenstein to see Elmer Wene, the Democratic candidate.

'Show me,' said Ellenstein, 'the names of the guys you might tap for attorney-general. If they're the right names, I have $40,000 to put into your campaign fund right now, and more later.'

Wene vacillated, then shrugged off Ellenstein's offer. A shrewd chicken farmer, Wene had a good idea who sent Ellenstein on this mission; he feared that any connection with Longy would give Zwillman too much power in the State House. He, Wene, would have to take the rap if word got out.

The rejection cost Wene the election. Longy didn't even wait to see which way Driscoll would respond. He told Bozzo Wene was out, as far as he was concerned. Whether Bozzo carried this information to Driscoll is problematical. Joe probably figured that, as long as Wene was dead, he could tell Driscoll he'd win the election without bothering him with details about attorneys general.

Wene carried Hudson County by a measly 3,000 votes, far too few to offset the heavy GOP downstate vote. He actually lost Jersey City to Driscoll, the first time a Democratic gubernatorial contestant had failed to carry the city in modern history. The story was similar in Essex, where Longy mobilized the machine against Wene. The state CIO, in debt to Longy, lined up with Driscoll.

The election over, Driscoll had to quiet the rumors that he had been bought by Longy.

'If I had known Zwillman was working in this campaign for me,' said the governor, 'I would have repudiated him publicly.'

Driscoll was so adamantly honest that when one of Longy's friends, a power in GOP politics, tried to see the governor to talk about a pardon for labor racketeer Joey Fay, he told Zwillman: 'I can't even get in to see the governor.'

When Joe Bozzo appeared before the Kefauver crime hearings, he identified himself as a Paterson clothing manufacturer who 'dabbled in local politics.' He admitted knowing Longy, but said Zwillman had only asked him to help out in a political matter once – when Harold Hoffman was running in the GOP primary for governor against Alfred Driscoll. He couldn't help much, Bozzo said, because, after all, he was only a rank-and-file party worker. The committee dropped the subject.

Chapter 15

The Kefauver Shadow

In 1951, Longy Zwillman was at the height of his power, financially, politically, and in gangsterdom's hierarchy. He was rich, raking in a minimum of $30,000 a week from all his enterprises, legal and illegal. His political power had expanded. In New Jersey, it reached right into the governor's office, where a clerk, Harold John Adonis (no relation to Joe Adonis, whose real name was Doto), had been paid $228,000 over a 19-month period for protection from state law-enforcement harassment. It stretched beyond New Jersey to Washington, through Longy's connections with organized labor, and to the West Coast and Las Vegas through his investments in films and in gambling casinos.

In criminal activities, the original Big Six (now reduced to five with Luciano's exile) still ruled the roost. Its spokesman now was Frank Costello. Lucky Luciano had held that post, but he had been deported in 1946 after serving a stiff sentence as the result of prosecution by an ambitious prosecutor, Thomas E. Dewey.

Luciano was paroled in 1946 at the behest of Dewey, the man who had put him in jail. Two versions exist of why Luciano was released. Dewey let it be known that he was supporting Luciano's request for release in gratitude for Lucky's assistance to the American armed forces in World War II. Rumor had it that Lucky, through his connections in Sicily, had eased the way for American troops invading the island in 1943.

That was all it was – rumor. The fact was that Lucky and Longy, through their connections on the waterfront, had enlisted the help of the longshoremen's union in protecting war goods on the piers from sabotage, freeing military personnel for other chores.

Luciano's own version is more interesting. He had promised to deliver the New York City vote to Dewey in the 1942 gubernatorial campaign.

'Dewey had to win the governorship of New York,' wrote Luciano in his *Last Testament*, a book compiled by Martin Gosch and Richard Hammer, 'in order to get in line for another shot at the presidential nominaion.'

The job of engineering the necessary votes to make this possible was handed to Longy. His work at the 1932 convention which nominated FDR put Longy close to many of the New York county leaders. The idea was for Dewey to win the governorship, then pardon or parole Luciano. The deal went through – with one hitch. Lucky had to agree to deportation on Dewey's insistance. That meant waiting in jail until the war was over. Luciano had to accept. He had no other choice.

Lucky's portion of the Big Six income was safeguarded – and transmitted to Italy – by Meyer Lansky. The rule in the partnership was simple: death put an end to a stockholder's interests; shares could not be passed down to relatives. Exile didn't matter; you still were entitled to your illicit earnings from those enterprises – mainly gambling – that were held cooperatively.

The Big Six had a unique method of operating. Each member could invest in individual enterprises in his own bailiwick – legitimate businesses, for instance, such as Longy's cigarette-vending business. They could also bring in another member as a partner. Competition in any staked-out region was forbidden. When it came to larger interests, such as Las Vegas gambling or interstate horse- and professional sports-betting, share and share alike was the rule.

Luciano was a gregarious type who enjoyed the limelight, even if it meant being a constant target for scrutiny by law-enforcement agencies. He was born Salvatore Lucania in 1897 in the tiny sulphur-mining town of Lercara Friddi in Sicily. He came to this country in 1906 with his father, Antonio, and his mother, Rosalie. They lived in the Little

Italy section of New York. His name, Charlie, came from Meyer Lansky's Jewish friends who had trouble pronouncing his real name. Later, he became known as Charlie Lucky. Luciano was a name he picked for himself after he was forced to move out of his home because of a row with his father.

Luciano's desire to hog the limelight gave him the chance to be the spokesman for the Big Six. In the privacy of their meetings, however, Luciano – although he loved the clever Meyer Lansky like a brother – recognized Zwillman as the brains of the outfit.

Lansky, a little man, tough and overly ambitious, was a brilliant gambling executive. He didn't need a computer to calculate the house's take in any operation, and he could figure odds in his head on bets running into the millions of dollars. He and Luciano had excellent rapport; they grew up together and helped each other survive in the tough criminal world of the Lower East Side.

Lansky was also notoriously cheap. He hated to spend money, even on himself, and was the sloppiest dresser of the Big Six combine. One story of Lansky's miserliness told by a bodyguard for one of the Big Six involved the honeymoon of Longy Zwillman's stepson, John Steinbach, Jr.

Longy was dead when the young man married, and his father's old associates made it a point to be especially kind to him and his new wife when the honeymoon began in Miami Beach. The newlyweds were given a lavish suite in one of the posh hostelries along the famed Hotel Row on the beach. Everything was on the house – food, liquor, entertainment.

In addition, each of his stepfather's old friends came to pay his respects to young John. As each man left the meetings after offering his condolences, Steinbach was handed a wedding gift, usually a large bundle of cash running into the thousands. Then it was Lansky's turn.

'Meyer spent a long time with the boy,' said the bodyguard, 'reminiscing about the old days, commiserating with Johnny over Longy's death, all the right things. Then Meyer got up to leave. The other guys had brought fat envelopes with the money bulging in them. Meyer came without one. As he said goodbye, Meyer clasped John's hand. In his handshake he had some bills. Meyer left, after patting the boy's cheek, and John opened his hand. In it were three bills, two hundreds and a fifty.'

Lansky lasted in big-time crime circles through the Seventies, when he was constantly being harassed by a series of law-enforcement agencies. To escape, he fled to Israel, where he parceled out large gifts – although it hurt him – in order to get public support for his request for Israeli citizenship. As a Jew, he was entitled to an Israeli passport under Israel's Law of Return, written originally to allow refugees to settle in the new country without the formality of applying for citizenship or asylum.

It didn't work in Lansky's case. The notoriety surrounding his gangland past cost him. Lansky lost his bid to remain in Israel after taking his case to the highest court in that land.

Joe Adonis, slick, smooth, hair greased back, expensively tailored, one of the handsomest men in the Big Six, was also one of the least attractive. He had small, weak eyes but was too vain to wear glasses. His original base of operations had been Brooklyn, where Adonis had a speakeasy. Local politicians began beating a path to his saloon door when they found out that Adonis, born Joseph Doto, could swing elections, either legitimately or by force of arms.

Adonis was born in a tiny town near Naples in 1902, and came to the US when he was three years old. By the time he was 18, Adonis had acquired a reputation as a fearless thief. He also had picked up the name Adonis. This was, at first, a nickname of disdain, born of poking fun at Adonis's habit of looking in the mirror and slicking back his hair about ten times a day. He later came to bask in the name, for he was a vain man who loved women of all shapes and sizes.

Adonis came into the Big Six because of his friendship with Luciano, Lansky, and Siegel. Adonis and Siegel had been two of the four gunmen who murdered gangland boss

Guiseppe Masseria in 1931, an act that catapulted Luciano into the forefront of the New York racket scene.

By the late Thirties, Adonis had moved his family to a large brick house on Dearborn Road in Fort Lee, New Jersey, hard by the George Washington Bridge. By this time, Adonis also was into legitimate business endeavors. Among other interests, he was a majority stockholder in Automotive Conveying Company, which transported Fords from the company's Edgewater, New Jersey, assembly plant.

Adonis's business address was at Duke's Restaurant in Cliffside Park. FBI and IRS agents used to try and hang around Duke's. They had a tough time, because local police would harass them. The restaurant closed before Adonis was deported to Italy in 1956. He lived in Milan until his death in 1971. His body was brought back to be buried in Fort Lee.

Frank Costello was born Francesco Castiglia in Italy in 1890 and came to this country two years later with his parents. The Castiglia family settled in East Harlem among their countrymen.

Young Frank learned early on that he had to be tougher than tough to survive. He was convicted in 1915 of carrying an unlicensed pistol. He used his mother's maiden name, Severio, as an alias when he was arrested.

It was Frank's first experience in jail, and he didn't like it. It made him determined to switch to white-collar crime. He went into business making counterfeit Kewpie dolls that were used as prizes in punchboard gambling. From that humble beginning, Costello (as he soon called himself) rose to the top ranks of gangsterdom.

Always well-groomed and dapper, Costello learned early in life that corrupting politicians was easy, cheap, and useful. In time, he came to control the people who ran Tammany Hall, Manhattan's Democratic headquarters.

An articulate man, Costello spoke in a raspy voice. It was the result, he said, of mistreatment by throat doctors. He lived in quiet splendor at the Majestic Apartments, a luxurious high-rise on the corner of 72nd Street and Central Park

West in New York. His personal friends included some of the top people in government, in the courts, in the entertainment world, and in gangsterdom.

In New York, Costello (through Frank Erickson) ran the biggest bookmaking operation in America. Together with Longy, he had a hand in Moe Annenberg's wire service, an indispensable element in horserace betting. He also was the owner of a number of legitimate businesses, among them Tropical Park racetrack and the Wofford Hotel, both in Florida. The latter he used as the southern center for his business meetings with other racketeers.

The missing member of the original Big Six was Ben Siegel. Bugsy, a name he hated, was born in the Williamsburgh section of Brooklyn, but at an early age moved to the Lower East Side, where his father had a tiny tailor shop. There he met Meyer Lansky. Barely in their teens, the two buddies formed the Bugs and Meyer Gang, as it was called. Bugsy, four years younger than Meyer, got his nickname from the fact that he was fearless enough to make people believe he had to be crazy.

The early crime specialties of the Bugs and Meyer Gang included petty theft, robberies, and extortion. As they grew older, the two friends realized that the real money was in gambling. Along with another buddy, Lucky Luciano, the trio began a climb into the rackets hierarchy while still in their teens. Bootlegging – as it had with Longy Zwillman – brought them the cash that greased the climb.

Handsome as a movie star, a sharp dresser who loved hand-crafted shoes, silk shirts with long pointed collars, tailor-made suits, and fur-lined overcoats, Siegel lived in the Waldorf Astoria Towers before heading West. He was married to Esther Krakower, and had two daughters, Millicent and Barbara. Ben ensconced them in a beautiful home in Scarsdale, New York, at one of Westchester County's fanciest addresses, while he raced around the country with a collection of beautiful women as his escort.

Siegel's best brainstorm was his selection of a dry desert hamlet in Nevada as the site of a new approach to gambling. He had moved west to Lost Angeles because he was in love. Bugsy was always in love with one woman or another, including Esther, his wife. This time, it was with a little French-born actress who was sent from Broadway to Hollywood by a producer who thought she had star qualities but needed more polished English. She never made it big in the film capital. Bugsy did.

Introduced into film society through Longy's old girlfriend, Jean Harlow, Ben Siegel was soon making as big a splash along the boulevards of Hollywood and Beverly Hills as the richest movie mogul. He bought a house once owned by Lawrence Tibbett, an opera star turned film hero. His earnings from the Big Six gambling activities were equal to those of the biggest box-office draw in the business. His good looks and easy repartee soon had Siegel hobnobbing with real royalty as well as the film variety.

Siegel originally arrived in Las Vegas from Hollywood to oversee the Big Six's investment in a bookmaking wire-service operation. The tiny town had been chosen as the service's headquarters because gambling was legal in Nevada. Casino gambling, however, was big only in Reno to the north. Las Vegas had only the horse rooms, a few sawdust joint casinos downtown, fewer, more polished casinos on the Clark County-Las Vegas 'strip,' the direct route to Los Angeles, and some whores.

Siegel had driven out to Las Vegas from Hollywood. He remarked to Virginia Hill, his latest paramour who accompanied him, how easy a ride it had been. The California state line was less than 50 miles from Las Vegas; the road was as straight as a surveyor's chain. A good driver could do 70 mph all the way without fear of bends or patrol cars. There just weren't any.

Siegel bought a small casino called the Northern Club and put a henchman, Moe Sedway, in as manager. The money started rolling in. It was wartime, and California had a slew of defense plants strung up and down the state within easy driving distance of the Nevada line.

Siegel called his partners back home in New York.

'I want to build the biggest goddam hotel and casino in the world,' he announced to Lansky. 'I can get the land for pennies. Construction costs out here are peanuts. I can do the whole job for less than a million.'

Lansky listened patiently. He never let emotion get the best of him, at least outwardly. What makes you think, he asked Siegel, that a casino in that fly-infested rathole will make any money?

Siegal gave Lansky a quick summary of his earnings in the tiny Northern Club in less than six months. Meyer whistled. The little computer in his brain began extrapolating the possibilities. He called his partners, Costello, Adonis, and Zwillman. He outlined Siegel's ideas.

'Tell Ben,' said Longy, 'we'll call him back.'

A discussion followed. Longy wanted all the answers. Was it a worthwhile investment? Woluld it pay off big enough to risk putting in a lot of cash? Where was Siegel going to get scarce building materials? Lansky called back in a matter of hours.

'Benny,' he said, 'has all the answers. Benny says he has a US senator from out there named Pat McCarran who's ready to expedite the construction materials. I say we go,' said Lansky.

Adonis and Costello held back. They looked at Longy. The big man put his finger alongside his nose. Then he smiled.

'I'll take a few points of Benny's casino. He may be on to something big.'

And so was born the Flamingo, the first big casino-hotel on a strip of sand that had known nothing grander than a few fleabitten casinos. It was to be followed by a score of others, including some, like the Sands, in which the Big Six held controlling interest. None of the later deals gave the Big Six as much pleasure – or anguish – as that first investment in the Flamingo.

Trouble began almost as soon as Siegel had ordered the first shovel into the ground. Despite Bugsy's reputation as a killer, construction supplies and equipment were being stolen constantly. In at least one case, Siegel's construction supervisors, the Del E. Webb Corporation of Phoenix, Arizona, paid twice for the same load of supplies, once when it was delivered and a second time after it had been stolen and redelivered.

Siegel overpaid construction help, overpaid architects, over-prescribed the thickness of walls and floors. In a climate that required plasterboard and thin strips of steel, he ordered plaster walls of double thickness. Each of the hotel's 92 rooms had its own sewer system. The plumbing bill alone – $1 million – exceeded Siegel's original estimate for total construction costs.

Siegel kept begging his partners back home for money, more money. At first, grumbling, they sent it to him. Then, grumbling even louder, they began to question him. Siegel, a man possessed by his dream, cried for more. He would open on time, he promised, and the money would start rolling in.

The hotel opened the day after Christmas, 1946, still unfinished. The casino, wonder of wonders, lost money. Siegel, beside himself with anxiety, closed the hotel two months later, vowing to keep it closed until the entire structure was complete. He fired Moe Sedway, his hotel manager.

The hotel reopened in March. Instead of Moe Sedway, the combination back East had shipped Doc Stacher out to run the casino. Stacher was a gambling wizard on a par with Lansky. He had other attributes, including a pleasing manner with customers, something the dour Lansky lacked. Lansky, with his bookkeeper's mind outraged by the Flamingo's soaring costs – now $6 million – insisted on accompanying Stacher. The word went out that Las Vegas as a gambling resort was Benny Siegel's dream gone sour.

Doc Stacher, whose real first name was Joseph, was from the start one of Longy's closest associates. They were boyhood friends, and became partners in crime while still in their early teens.

Stacher had a feel for gambling – the art, as well as the business. Zwillman never ceased marveling at how quickly Stacher could size up a roadblock in a gambling operation, prescribe a remedy, and see to it that his prescription was accepted – or else. This knack was the basic reason, for example, for Zwillman's insistence that Stacher go to Las Vegas to take charge of the Flamingo after Bugsy Siegel's excesses cost the combine $6 million.

Stacher's connection to Zwillman went back long before the day they quit school together after Longy's father died. When Longy was still helping his father in the chicken market, Stacher sold newspapers, then got a job in a fur-processing plant. He didn't like the filthy, humdrum work.

Once Zwillman became involved in his own numbers racket, Doc left the fur plant and went to work for Longy full-time. Doc had a long police record in Newark, something Longy had studiously avoided compiling. That record, and the threat of violence it advertised, helped Stacher keep numbers runners and bankers in line. His reputation as a tough guy was enhanced during Prohibition, when he helped Longy police shipments of illegal whiskey, knocking off attempted hijackers.

As he got older, Stacher liked violence less and less. He became addicted to the social life of a successful gambling man. A portly, bald-headed fellow who looked more like a banker than a gunman, Stacher married a pretty former model named Miriam Youngerman. They had two children.

Once the heat hit Longy's old gang (after the Kefauver hearings, Zwillman's tax troubles, and his death), and the IRS started looking into Stacher's affairs, Doc thought it best to get out of the country. In 1966, Stacher headed for Israel. His wife left him and moved to Italy, where she later died of cancer. Stacher lived quietly in Tel Aviv, appearing in the public eye for the first time when he showed up at Ben Gurion Airport to greet the newly arrived Meyer Lansky.

Stacher's name came up in the Israeli press one other time. Like so many gangland people, Stacher seldom thought legitimate rights could be obtained legitimately. He could never do much without hedging his bets. He wanted to apply for Israeli citizenship, a status to which he felt entitled under the Law of Return. Just to be sure there'd be no hitch, Stacher sought the help of a prominent member of the Israeli Knesset, or parliament.

A comedy of errors ensued. The politician agreed to spur Stacher's quest for citizenship. He induced Doc to give lavishly to charity, suggesting Stacher could enhance his case by contributing liberally.

Doc opened his Swiss bank vault and started passing money around. He also offered to invest $100,000 in a plan dreamed up by the Knesset member – a housing development open only to young people just out of the army who had to postpone wedding plans because they couldn't find living quarters.

The politician took Stacher's $100,000 and used it to build a hotel for tourists instead. Stacher complained. He wanted his investment back. The politician countered with a claim that the $100,000 wasn't a loan, but a gift.

In the old days, this double cross would have been settled simply. Stacher would have put a gun to the politician's head and made him an offer he couldn't refuse. But Stacher was anxious to present a new image in his new country. He took his case to court, and the Israeli public discovered how a supposed big man in the Mob in America had been skinned by a country politician in Israel.

Stacher received justice. He won the case; his money was refunded. He also was given citizenship.

In the late Seventies, Stacher met a young German actress who had come to Israel to shoot a film. Bewitched, the aging Stacher spent all his time in the girl's company, trying to bedazzle her with gifts and money.

Stacher stayed glued to the young German girl's side. When she returned to Frankfurt, Stacher followed. The girl, by this time annoyed by Stacher's attentions and convinced he had run out of money, gave him the gate. Doc died of a heart attack in 1981 in a German hotel room, alone and unmourned.

Meyer Lansky saw for himself what was going on at the Flamingo, and went back to New York with his report. Things were quiet for two months. Siegel hied himself off to Beverly Hills to compose himself.

On the night of June 20, 1947, Ben Siegel and a friend, Al

Smiley, were sitting in the living room of the home Bugsy and Virginia Hill shared on North Linden Drive in Beverly Hills. Bugsy had the sports pages of the *Los Angeles Times* spread on his lap. The floral print on the couch on which Bugsy sat was a mite too gaudy for good taste. The large French window leading to the well-shrubbed front lawn was closed, but the curtains were drawn back.

A shot rang out. The first bullet buried Ben Siegel's right eye in a mantelpiece 15 feet away. A second drove into his neck and shredded it into sliced beef. Nine shots in all were fired. One caught Allen Smiley's coat sleeve. Others hit furniture or paintings, shattering the decor of the living room. Benny Siegel didn't care; he was dead.

When Siegel died, his estranged wife mourned for him as deeply as if they were still living together. Interestingly enough, her mourning period was spent with her two children at the Jersey Shore. Longy rented a house for her near his own large structure surrounded by spacious lawns on Jerome Avenue in Deal.

The word was on the street almost as soon as Ben Siegel died. Not all of those millions had gone into bricks and mortar, curtains and casino tables at the Flamingo, said the wise boys. Bugs had crossed his partners, skimmed off some of their money, and stashed it in a Swiss bank account. The buzz was everywhere, from Los Angeles through Kansas City, St Louis, Chicago, Cleveland, and into New York. The big guys had struck again at someone who doublecrossed them.

The Beverly Hills police were not used to homicides. They never uncovered Siegel's killers. This is known, however. In the days before he died, Ben Siegel made lots of trips to Los Angeles. He was trying to raise money, said Virginia Hill.

He also made several trips to South Munn Avenue in East Orange. That's where Longy lived. The word went out that Bugsy was trying to get Longy to talk to the other partners. Was it for more money? Or was it Bugsy's plea that Longy help him stay alive?

The members of the Big Six would want Ben Siegel dead

only if he stole from them. If he had mismanaged the construction of the Flamingo honestly, they would have shrugged and absorbed the loss.

If, on the other hand, Siegel had skimmed off some of the $6 million they gave him, he'd have to hide it in Switzerland. Or give it to Virginia Hill, the woman he lived with, to hide for him. She had a big mouth. She was living with Bugsy, but still sleeping with other mob figures – in Chicago and elsewhere. That's the kind of a broad she was. If, in a moment of passion, she bragged about the money to one of the guys she was in bed with, he would have sent word back to the Big Six. That would mean Bugsy's end, for sure. His partners could forgive stupidity, but not theft.

There's another theory, held by one of Longy's old bodyguards. Bugsy found out that Virginia talked about the money. He manhandled her. She complained to someone, possibly a relative. The relation did the job out of revenge, doing the Big Six an unwitting favor. Longy's man maintained all through the years that's the real way Bugsy Siegel met his end.

Virginia Hill was never punished, except indirectly. She never lived high off the hog again. In 1966, she walked out to a pond behind the modest house where she lived in Switzerland and killed herself.

The beginning of the end of Longy's reign at the top of gangsterdom actually began before that raw day in 1951 when the Kefauver Committee, as it came to be called, reached out and pulled him into the national limelight.

Intimations of trouble began early in 1950. The Big Six then were still at the top of the heap in gambling and loan-sharking. They were just beginning to penetrate the uppermost strata of the legitimate business world when Estes Kefauver, a folksy lawyer from Chattanooga who wasn't nearly as much of a rube as he sounded, became chairman of the Senate Crime Investigating Committee. The Big Six, with all their connections, had no idea how quickly and deeply Kefauver would attack.

Kefauver had proposed a committee to investigate

organized crime's infiltration of American business almost as soon as he was elected to the Senate for the first time in 1948. His suggestion was authorized with a relatively tiny appropriation of $150,000. None of Longy's friends recognized how far that initial appropriation would stretch.

Carey Estes Kefauver (he dropped his first name soon after entering college) was born in Madisonville, Tennessee, a small town near Chattanooga, just a few months before Zwillman entered the world in Newark. The two men arrived at their confrontation in the US Senate by totally different routes.

Kefauver's grandfather was a Baptist preacher in Madisonville, a small farming community. Estes was working on his father's and grandfather's Tennessee farm while Longy was hustling humbers from a fruit and vegetable wagon in Newark.

Kefauver's exposure to his grandfather's rousing sermons awakened in him an interest in oratory. He spent his spare time as a youth attending trials in the Madisonville courthouse, while Longy was convoying trucks loaded with illegal booze from the docks at Port Newark.

Kefauver's first political victory – election as president of the student body at the University of Tennessee – was won at the time Zwillman was bribing police commissioners and Treasury agents to look the other way as his bootleg beer was being brewed.

The two men were almost the same height; Zwillman was six feet two inches tall, Kefauver six-three. Kefauver played right guard and tackle on the Vols' varsity football team while Longy was collecting his share of the take from a gaggle of numbers bankers in Essex County.

Estes Kefauver taught mathematics to a group of fresh-faced high school kids in Hot Springs, Arkansas, while Longy Zwillman was teaching a group of immigrant candy store and tailor-shop owners how to pass on their policy slips and cash to his collectors.

Estes Kefauver entered Yale Law School in 1927, a few years before Abner Zwillman lost his first case to legal justice and was sentenced to six months in the Essex

County hoosegow. Kefauver was graduated from law school in New Haven *cum laude.* Zwillman was allowed out of the Caldwell county jail a month early because of good behavior.

Kefauver met his wife-to-be on a blind date; she was Nancy Patterson Pigott, a Scottish girl, daughter of an American-born knight of the British Empire. Zwillman met Mary Mendels, daughter of an impoverished American stockbroker, in a restaurant. The Kefauvers were married in 1935; the Zwillmans wed in 1939.

Kefauver started up the ladder in politics through a reform party organization in Chattanooga. Longy was given his first leg-up in the world of criminal high finance by joining with a topflight bootlegger, Joe Reinfeld.

In 1939, Kefauver was elected to the House of Representatives from Hamilton County, Tennessee. Nine years later, he decided to run for the Senate. He was opposed by the Democratic boss of Memphis, Edward H. Crump.

No Democratic candidate in Tennessee, the conventional wisdom went, could get nominated for the post of dog catcher without Boss Crumps's okay.

To stave off Kefauver, Crump labeled him a stupid pet coon trying desperately to cover up a bad record in Congress. Kefauver turned the epithet into an asset. He began wearing a coonskin cap, creating a warm personal symbol that stuck to Kefauver throughout his political career. He also used the coon theme against Crump.

'I may be a pet coon,' Kefauver retorted, 'but I'm not Mr Crump's pet coon. A coon may have rings around his tail, but *this* coon will never have a ring through his nose.'

Kefauver won the nomination by 40,000 votes, the first setback suffered by Crump in 20 years.

It's easy to forget the impact the Kefauver Crime Committee's hearings had on the American people. The hearings were seen on television, then a brand-new medium. Millions sat transfixed in front of their tiny screens, watching a parade of criminals, the hierarchy of America's hoodlum world, twitching, sweating, rolling their eyes, wringing their hands as they tried to answer – or avoid answering – the insistent questions of the senators on the panel and their sharp-tongued, caustically witty special counsel, Rudolph Halley.

To hear an investigator ask public enemies embarrassing questions on radio wasn't nearly as riveting as seeing them squirm before your eyes, as if you were sitting right down front at the counsel's table.

Also, for the first time, people watching the hearings became conscious of how searching the relentless eye of the TV camera could be, how it could pick up every pore on a person's skin, every glint of anger in the eye, every nuance of expression. Nothing could be disguised. The camera reached into the very soul of those being questioned, and laid it bare.

Kefauver and his comrades dragged into the blinding lights of television a passel of gangsters who had, up to that moment, taken every precaution to shield their lives and their activities from public scrutiny. Those who relished their tough guy image (in criminal circles) and those who had adopted respectable fronts to hide their activities were treated alike by the camera – exposed for what they were and how they did their work.

Killers like Albert Anastasia and slick, behind-the-scenes operators like Meyer Lansky and Longy Zwillman received equal treatment from the camera. Some – like Longy – came away from the experience outwardly calm. They appeared almost smugly pleased with their performance at the hearings. Others – like Frank Costello – seethed at the way they were harrassed and exposed.

Of the original Big Six, Bugsy Siegel was dead. Charlie Luciano was in exile, viewing the hearings in a darkened movie theater in Rome, biting his nails in frustration as he watched cow-country senators tearing apart the organization he had helped to expand, and to which he still proudly belonged.

Johnny Roselli's appearance before the Kefauver Committee was a surprise to everyone who didn't know his relationship to Longy Zwillman.

His real name was Filippo Sacco when he was born in Italy in 1905. His mother brought him to this country when he was six.

His stepfather asked young Filippo to burn down the family home so he could collect the insurance. He was then in the seventh grade. Filippo took off to escape the authorities, who had become suspicious. He ended up in Chicago, where he changed his name to Johnny Roselli when he joined the Al Capone gang during Prohibition.

When the Capone mob broke up, Roselli hooked up with Longy, who needed a man in Hollywood he could trust. Roselli's reputation as a tough guy who also had brains appealed to Longy. Johnny did well, guarding Longy's interests in the movie capital until Las Vegas loomed large in Zwillman's plans. Roselli was moved to Nevada as a muscle man to keep an eye on operations at the Sands.

Roselli was called to Chicago to testify before the Kefauver committee. He said nothing that could compromise any of his friends.

The next time Roselli hit the headlines was after the assassination of John F. Kennedy. The FBI investigation led to the surfacing of stories how the president's death was actually Cuba's answer to a CIA attempt to murder Fidel Castro.

Roselli was called to Washington to testify about the so-called Castro plot. He didn't tell his interrogators anything. Shortly after, he disappeared while he was in Ft Lauderdale, Florida, visiting his sister. His car was found later at Miami International Airport. Two weeks later, fishermen in Biscayne Bay spotted an oil drum wrapped in chains floating along. Inside, police found Roselli's body, the legs sawed off to make it fit into the drum.

Costello, Lansky, Adonis, and finally Zwillman all made their command performances before the committee. When it was all over, the question of stardom arose. Who – by the committee's vote – was the Number One gangster in America?

Senator Charles W. Tobey, innocent-faced, voted for the

absent Lucky Luciano. His vote was approved by the majority of the public watching. Halley, the committee's counsel, voted for Costello. Two other panel members decided Meyer Lansky was the evil mastermind of the Big Six.

Only Estes Kefauver refused to be fooled. He toyed with the testifying members of the gang that controlled crime in America. He probed, pumped, dug with a heavy hand, sliced with a scalpel. When it was all over, he signed the committee's report to the United States Senate.

Then he voted for the man he believed was the leader of the Big Six – Abner 'Longy' Zwillman.

The hearings moved like a traveling circus, from Miami to Chicago, from New York to New Jersey, and finally to Washington for the windup. Kefauver, a consummate showman as well as an excellent politician, showed his own preference for leader of the Big Six. His 'invitation' to Longy to appear before the Special Committee to investigate Organized Crime in Interstate Commerce of the United States Senate in the 82nd Congress, as it was known officially, ordered Zwillman to appear in the nation's capital, the core of federal power.

William O'Dwyer, former district attorney, former Mayor of New York City, now ambassador to Mexico, had taken the stand on March 10. He squirmed too, for the committee began to expose a pattern of cooperation between O'Dwyer, the 'fearless prosecutor,' as he liked to label himself, and some of the people he was supposed to be prosecuting.

It was Bill O'Dwyer that day who first named the combination the 'Big Six.' He gave their names to the committee: Longy Zwillman, Lucky Luciano, Meyer Lansky, Bugsy Siegel, Joe Adonis. And the sixth? Why, Willie Moretti, of course, said the ambassador.

Finally, officially, it was out. Longy Zwillman, who had kept his name under a bushel everywhere but in the top ranks of America's gangsters, had been exposed.

There was one glitsch in O'Dwyer's testimony – the sixth name in the list of the Big Six.

'Why not Frank Costello?' The question came from Rudolph Halley, who already knew the answer.

'His name,' replied a sweating Bill O'Dwyer, 'never came up to me.'

The reason for this lapse of memory was simple. Costello's connection in New York was Bill O'Dwyer, and had been ever since the ambassador's political career began as a Brooklyn judge.

Speculation began immediately. Would this Longy character be called before the committee? The senators would begin the metropolitan New York area only two more days. Reporters began buzzing around the counsel's table. They discovered an interesting fact. Halley wasn't planning to call Longy.

Why? The committee just didn't have enough material on hand about him. That's how well Longy had escaped scrutiny of the law and the public ever since his only jail sentence, way back when he'd almost killed Preston Buzzard, the Newark pimp, in 1928.

Longy was asked to show up at the Federal Building on Foley Square, just for an interview, Halley said. Zwillman didn't appear; his lawyer, Arthur Garfield Hays, did.

The next day, in a closed hearing, Frank C. Bals testified. He had been the police captain in charge of the detail guarding Abe 'Kid Twist' Reles in the Half Moon Hotel on the Coney Island boardwalk. Reles was being hidden from the mob's vengeance because it was his testimony that was supposed to send Al Anastasia to the electric chair for murder. Reles never made it; he died in a 'fall' from the upper floors of the hotel, 'trying to escape,' the cops guarding him said.

Bals testified that Reles told him that it was Longy Zwillman who chaired a meeting of Murder Inc., the gang to which Reles belonged. Longy was there representing the Big Six, said Bals.

Longy was called to Washington in secret. He and his lawyer met with members of the Kefauver committee for four hours.

When the story about the secret testimony broke, one

member of the committee discounted its importance.

'It wasn't a very productive meeting,' said Senator Tobey.

Longy had his own public answer.

'The state and federal governments,' he announced to a group of reporters, 'spend millions of dollars a year in an effort to rehabilitate murderers, drug addicts, and others. Yet a man who sold whiskey during Prohibition is constantly hounded while he is trying to rehabilitate himself.'

Something, however, had been uncovered in those four hours in Washington. Two days after Longy walked out of the committee room, its investigators were looking for him again. They had come five times to Longy's new home, a 22-room mansion at 50 Beverly Road, in the most fashionable section of West Orange, New Jersey. Longy had disappeared.

He did call the *Newark News.*

'I'm not running,' Longy told a reporter. 'I'm not hiding. I'm out of the state on business, and I don't know when I'm coming back.'

The Kefauver committee still wanted Longy to come and testify, its chief counsel kept saying. Interest in Zwillman had been marginal until Ambassador O'Dwyer named him as one of the original Big Six.

O'Dwyer, under fire on the stand, asked the committee to call John Murtagh, chief magistrate of New York City. Judge Murtagh, said O'Dwyer, would clear him of any suspicion that as district attorney in New York, Bill O'Dwyer hadn't done all he could to break up gambling in the city.

Murtagh's testimony was another eye-opener. He lashed out at Walter Van Riper, New Jersey's attorney-general in 1947. I called Mr Van Riper in 1947, Murtagh said in essence, and told him that Frank Erickson had moved his bokmaking operations from the city to Adonis's and Moretti's headquarters at Duke's Restaurant in Cliffside Park, New Jersey. Van Riper, said Murtagh, did nothing about it.

The committee kept issuing statements that it wanted

Longy to testify, but that it couldn't find him. Longy's attorney, Arthur Garfield Hays, told the committee that they could have Zwillman on the stand any time they wanted.

Sure enough, Longy walked into the Hays law office at 120 Broadway in New York and met reporters, who crowded around to see the new glamour boy, the man who had suddenly been pointed out as one of America's top gangsters. Asked to comment on Ambassador O'Dwyer's testimony naming him one of the Big Six, Longy smiled:

'That's so ridiculous that I don't feel called upon to say anything about it. That was, however, a real bombshell. I haven't been engaged in any illegitimate businesses for at least 12 years.'

What about Frank Costello's testimony, asked a reporter, that he and you were very close friends for at least the last 12 years? What about all those telephone calls from Costello to your house?

Zwillman stared at the questioner, but didn't answer.

After dinner on March 27, Abner 'Longy' Zwillman finally took the stand in the Senate hearing room in Washington.

Critics later said that Longy was the 'most polite' bootlegger they ever saw. Self-assured yet deferential, wearing a perpetually puzzled, hurt expression, he seemed to be saying: Why am I here? What do I have in common with these slimy people you've been hearing?

Longy was a consummate performer. His demeanor contrasted sharply with that of Frank Costello, for example, who appeared frightened, and with that of William O'Dwyer, who was extremely nervous.

Longy 'sirred' the committee to death. He was particularly respectful of Rudolph Halley, the chief counsel. He even apologized to news photographers when he had to ask them to stop taking pictures during his testimony. As the flash bulbs kept exploding, Longy turned to Senator Kefauver.

'I feel,' he told the senator, 'like I'm getting shot.'

The room exploded in laughter.

Before Longy was sworn, Morris Shilensky, his attorney, made it a point to have the committee agree that Longy hadn't been hiding, that he had offered to testify. Shilensky was a junior member of the Arthur Garfield Hays law firm. He was sent down to Washington by Hays to represent Longy at the hearing. Hays, usually a publicity hound, didn't want to appear himself until he could find out how the wind was blowing, how Longy would be treated. Hays had his own reputation to safeguard.

Kefauver began by asking Longy to recite the circumstances of his 1927 conviction for assaulting Preston Buzzard. Then Halley swept into the Prohibition days. Zwillman, still deferential, asked to be allowed to read a statement.

'I have a feeling that his committee, or in any event, one or more enforcement agencies of the government, is seeking to implicate me in some federal offense. I know that many enforcement agencies of the government have for a long time been engaged in an extensive investigation of my affairs and those of my business associates, and even my friends and relatives for many years.

'My attorneys have been told, directly by responsible officers of the government, that they have a suspicion and feeling that I have committed federal crimes, and that they seek . . . to prosecute me.'

That statement was prompted by the secret-session questioning Longy had undergone in New York in January. He had asked his lawyers to check into what and how much he could talk about his Prohibition activities. They drew this lengthy statement as a preliminary to his taking the Fifth Amendment. Longy wasn't about to give the Kefauver committee anything the IRS, the US Attorney-General, or state law-enforcement agencies could use against him.

'In my business,' he told the committee, 'I use the mails and other means of interstate commerce and communications. My income-tax matters are in the hands of the Intelligence Unit, which is the Penalty Division of the Treasury Department. I think the Treasury Department officials have attended these hearings, are in attendance now.'

Longy was right. Edwin Baldwin, chief of the IRS Intelligence Unit in Newark, had not only been taking notes in the back of the hearing room; he had been an active witness himself.

'This committee,' continued Longy, 'has obtained copies of my tax returns, and has made inquiries concerning the same. These and other factors contribute to my fear that the answers to some of the questions which may be put to me may tend to incriminate me. I also have the fear that in answering some of the questions that may be put to me that in themselves appear harmless, I may be waiving my constitutional rights.'

Longy then declined to answer any questions about his bootlegging days. But, protested Halley, I'm asking about stuff prior to 1932. I don't care, answered Longy.

'That's in an area which involves taxes,' said Longy. 'And I understand the Tax Department is still investigating that period as well as this. I may say, Mr Senator, that I have tried to sit down with the tax people for a number of years to effectuate a settlement, and for reasons of their own, probably good reasons, they have refused to make a settlement.'

Longy was right. The IRS had declined an offer to settle all his Prohibition-days tax liabilities for a lump-sum payment. They had been given a chance to hang Longy on other matters, and the IRS wasn't about to let him off the hook. At the time of the Kefauver hearings, neither Longy nor his lawyers actually knew this.

After this lengthy statement, Longy suddenly admitted to the committee that he had been a bootlegger, but he wouldn't name any of his associates. He admitted he got his illicit liquor in Canada, but refused to say from whom.

Longy admitted he knew Frank Costello and Willie Moretti, the latter only casually. He admitted he knew Joe Reinfeld, but declined to tell whether any of these people were in business with him.

The questions turned to Longy's involvement in legitimate businesses after Repeal. He admitted he dropped a bundle in the US Yeast Company, but wouldn't tell how much he had invested. He pointed out that by answering such a question, he would have to account for the source of his money.

'But,' protested Halley, 'I have been trying to keep away from your current income-tax situation, but I hardly see where 1935 would enter into the picture,' Shilensky interrupted.

'When you say current income-tax, the tax picture – the income-tax people have the tax returns under scrutiny all the way back, and what is more, they say there is a tie-in between the Prohibition money and the current business investments which Mr Zwillman has. It is their contention, not ours.'

Longy then told the committee that he lost a bundle not only in yeast but in the Harr-Kegtap affair. Then he talked about Public Service Tobacco. He didn't own the company, he said. His wife and two kids had half the firm and Mike Lascari's wife and two children had the other half.

Longy admitted he knew Doc Stacher and Gerry Catena, that they had sold him and Lascari the cigarette-vending business. He also pointed out that Mike Lascari had worked 20 hours a day to build the business, and that didn't sound like he was a gangster, did it?

Longy admitted he knew Lucky Luciano as well as Frank Costello, Meyer Lansky, Leslie Weber, and Phil Weiss. Then the questions got around to the Hudson and Manhattan Railroad (now PATH). Yes, he did own shares in it, once. He never had any influence in its management, although Bill Egan, his friend and onetime attorney, was the road's president.

Longy was toying with the committee, and only Senator Tobey of New Hampshire recognized it.

'Why do you not come clean with us here?' Tobey asked. 'Here is a Senate committee asking honest questions, and you come before us as an individual citizen. You have your rights, of course. We are looking for justice and to get the truth about these things. And so you cover up all the time. That is not the typical action of a real American citizen.

Frankly, it is not. Help the committee out and come through. You will feel better tomorrow morning for doing it.'

'I hope so, sir,' was Longy's answer, with as sincere a look as he could muster.

The questioning went back to the Hudson Tubes. Were your shares in the railroad in your name or someone else's, Halley wanted to know. Longy fenced again, then explained why he was being coy.

'When I talk about a trust,' he explained, 'it is not a case of concealing a situation. It is just a case where sometimes my name, with all this going on, kills a deal instead of helping out, and that is why I am in an unfortunate position as trustee.'

Longy went on to explain why he had bought Hudson and Manhattan shares. Someone told him he could make money in the company by installing juice machines on all the stations. It never happened, however.

The question of Bill Egan's appointment as president came up again, and Longy denied he had anything to do with it. Later, Egan flatly denied any connection between Longy and himself in the railroad post. He said he had become involved in the road at the request of ten of the stockholders fighting the old management for control.

Then Egan threw a jab at Halley. The only reason you're trying to connect me with Longy is the fact that I had been the sole member of the board of directors who had been against hiring your law firm as counsel for the railroad, Egan told Halley.

Longy went on to admit he knew I. George Goldstein, his accountant, and knew that Goldstein was the accountant for gambling interests.

'I found it all out later,' was the way Longy put it.

He admitted he hired Charles Handler, Newark city counsel, to do legal work. He said Handler had acted on his behalf in buying the GMC Truck franchise in Newark. He admitted knowing Abe Reles and a bunch of other unsavory characters. How do you meet these fellows,

Halley wanted to know?

'In the old days, I met everybody. Every place you went, you met somebody.'

Longy also answered questions about why he went to Duke's Restaurant in Cliffside Park, New Jersey, by saying he went there to eat. He used to meet other people there, who also came to eat, he presumed, and people like Willie Moretti, Joe Adonis, and Joe Bozzo 'because they hung out there.'

The name of former Governor Harold Hoffman came up. He didn't call Hoffman, explained Longy. It was 'a guy around my office, Joe Rosenbaum, who used to call the governor often.'

'Who do you think called him from your home?' asked Halley.

'It could be me,' admitted Longy. 'Nothing illegal, I am sure. Maybe something about Social Security.'

After this testimony, Hoffman sent the committee a telegram. He was then head of New Jersey's Employment Security office. When he had testified earlier, Hoffman said, he could recall no telephone conversation with Longy. Suddenly, he recalled two.

It was at the time, said Hoffman, he was stationed at the Brooklyn Port of Embarkation during World War II. He had been introduced to Longy by Joe Rosenbaum, a former state employee who later worked for Public Service Tobacco.

'I met Zwillman since then on a number of occasions,' said Hoffman. 'I was his guest at Madison Square Garden boxing events. He is a pleasant and interesting person who appeared to me to be sincerely interested in legitimate business enterprises, and devoted to his family. I can assure you that he has never made of me in any public office any request that in the slightest degree could be considered improper.

'I can recall two phone calls. One was in connection with Rosenbaum's son, who was later killed in the Pacific, and the other was a request made on behalf of a labor organization for my services as toastmaster at a testimonial dinner.

'As he testified, Zwillman has a large political club in Newark, and very frankly, I asked for his help in 1946 when I was an unsuccessful candidate for the Republican nomination for governor. He made me no promises, and if he did give me any aid, I think a perusal of the Primary election returns in Newark will completely destroy the myth that he wields great political power in that city.'

With this telegram, Hoffman was trying to distance himself from Longy, yet covering his tracks by trying to show that Longy wasn't the political big shot he was cracked up to be.

The questioning of Longy turned to politics. What officers in the city of Newark, asked Halley, did Longy know?

'I am 47 years old,' said Longy. 'I was born and raised in that city, and I have never left it. It is a small city. After 47 years, you get to know pretty near everybody in the city, in all walks of life. So,' continued Longy gallantly, 'I don't think it would be fair to let anybody get hurt who might know me, because of this stuff that is going on.'

Halley said he had no more questions. That didn't end Longy's ordeal. Senator Tobey wanted to know if Longy was the Al Capone of New Jersey.

'That is a myth,' answered Longy, laughing, 'that has been developing, Mr Senator, for a good many years . . . I should have had the sense to stop it, or get out of the state. I don't belong here today, but I am here . . . But these rumors go around. They accuse me of owning places. I walk into a restaurant, and I own the restaurant. I walk into a hotel, and I own the hotel. I take a shine twice, and I own the bootblack, too.'

'Well,' said Senator Tobey, 'those are the penalties of greatness.'

Do you know Virginia Hill, pressed on Tobey? She had testified she knew Longy.

'If what she says is true,' answered Longy, 'I don't recall the incident. He [gambler Swifty Morgan] introduced her to me once on a sidewalk in Florida. Well, if you call that knowing somebody, okay, although she looks too hard-looking to know. My wife is listening in, too.'

A roar of laughter caused Kefauver to rap for order.

Senator Alexander Wiley took up the questioning.

'Did I understand from your testimony,' asked Wiley, 'that since Prohibition days you claim you have gone legitimate in your business?'

'From that period of 1935 or 1936 up, I have been trying, Mr Senator.'

'What has been your business?' asked Wiley. 'First you tell us yeast, and then brewing beer. Now, what is it?'

'Well,' answered Longy, 'the cigarette business, washing-machine business, trucking, I am trying – trying hard.'

'And during that period,' pressed on Wiley, 'do you feel that you have not violated any of the laws of the land?'

'I have tried very hard not to,' answered Longy. 'Only by this here, you cannot tell when you are in business with an associate. I am not breaking the law insofar as gambling, narcotics, wire services, or anything of that nature; absolutely not.'

'Have you any interest whatever in any gambling establishments?' asked Wiley, still pressing.

'I am under oath and I am saying no,' answered Longy.

'Have you had any?'

'In 20 years?'

'Yes.'

'No,' said Longy, with emphasis.

'Do you know . . . there are four gambling syndicates operating in our country today?' asked Wiley.

'Well,' answered Longy, looking guilelessly at Wiley, 'you hear all kinds of rumors, but the only thing I know, in the county where I live you can't even place a $2 bet for the last 15 years, maybe 20 years.'

'How do you place your bets?' asked Wiley.

'Call the next county,' answered Longy. The hearing room broke into laughter.

'How old are your children?' asked Wiley, switching subjects.

'The boy is going to be 17 and the girl is going to be eight,' said Longy.

'What are you raising them to be?' asked Wiley.

'They will never be like this.'

'Why?' Wiley kept pressing.

'Because I'm paying for it now. I wouldn't do it again for $10 million.'

Longy went on to say he never had an interest in the Bronfman distilleries in Montreal. Maybe Joe Reinfeld and Niggy Rutkin did, not me, said Longy.

Longy also laughed off charges that he backed Walter Van Riper for state attorney general or Walter Winne for Bergen County prosecutor.

'Between you and me, Mr Senator,' Longy told Kefauver, 'if I support somebody, they lose. So, if he had my blessing, he wouldn't be attorney-general.'

That same day, Leo Carlin, then Newark's public works director and later its reform mayor, called on the Newark City Commission to have Corporation Counsel Charley Handler explain his association with Longy.

Longy's buddies on the city commission circled their wagons.

Said Mayor Ralph Villani: 'I see nothing wrong with Mr Handler representing anyone in connection with legitimate business matters. I see no reason why an able lawyer like Mr Handler should not represent a client, no matter who he is, in a legitimate enterprise which is not connected with city business. The position of corporation counsel is not a full-time job and does not carry tenure. He is permitted to engage in private practice.'

Commissioner Meyer Ellenstein chimed in: 'This is the first time I knew that Handler was Zwillman's lawyer in any business transaction. There is nothing irregular for any lawyer to be employed by Zwillman who, as far as I know, is engaged in only legitimate businesses. Many lawyers in Newark would be only too glad to get such business.'

The night after Longy finished testifying, calls poured into his suite at his Washington hotel. The phone kept ringing until two A.M. Longy left instructions at the desk not to cut them off. He was basking in the congratulations he heard. Strangers called to let him know they saw him on television, and that they felt he had vindicated himself before the committee.

'Maybe you were a bad boy once,' said the grandmotherly caller, 'but every sinner has a chance to repent.'

Zwillman told newsmen the next day that the callers were from all walks of life – clergymen, doctors, and plain people he had met in his travels.

On April 1, Longy took a calculated step; he decided to answer certain questions he had been skittish about. Yes, he had held $20,000 in Hudson and Manhattan bonds, and a share in Browne Vintners. He sold that share to Seagram's (the Bronfman family firm) in 1940. He had owned one-sixth of the company together with Doc Stacher through Joseph Davis, secretary of Browne Vintners.

On April 18, despite the publicity Longy's GMC Truck Sales at 570 Belmont Avenue, Newark, sold the city a sanitation truck for $2,317. GMC Truck Sales was the only bidder. Said Mayor Villani: 'The truck was bought from GMC Sales because the engineer in charge of the Bureau of Sanitation said it was the same type of equipment the bureau had been using.'

On May 1, Kefauver went public with his vote for the top gangster in America. His stinging report said that Longy Zwillman illustrates better than any one else how gangsters use illegally acquired resources to obtain economic and political influence.

'It may be more than coincidence that the registered agent for Zwillman's trucking company is also the corporation counsel for the City of Newark,' wrote Kefauver. 'It is also significant that Zwillman's control of the truck company is exercised through I. George Goldstein, who testified that he fronted for Zwillman, that Zwillman was afraid he would not obtain the General Motors franchise if his name appeared.'

The report went on to detail Longy's relationship with Joe Reinfeld and Niggy Rutkin, illustrating how Prohibition racketeers transferred their illicit enterprises into legitimate businesses. It was significant to Kefauver that Reinfeld had a New Jersey liquor license although he couldn't get one in New York.

Going on to gambling, Kefauver spelled out the vast riches the Big Six managed to obtain from this illegal exercise.

'Although the various gambling houses reported profits of from $100,000 to $250,000 annually for icome tax purposes,' said Kefauver, 'it was obvious that was a foolishly low figure.'

In one month, for example, the New Jersey gambling houses – the so-called Sawdust Trail – cashed customers' checks in a New York City bank (Kefauver delicately withheld the name) to the tune of $1 million.

It's obvious, said Kefauver, that if $1 million a month was cashed in check form, the profits must have been much greater, because most gambling is done with cash.

And, said the report, those whose names appeared as nominal owners of these gambling houses were actually dummies for the Big Six.

'The committee,' wrote Kefauver, 'places no stock in the professed inability of many law-enforcement officials to detect violations of the law apparent to any informed citizen. The blindness which afflicts many law-enforcement officials in wide-open communities is for the record only. There can be little question that these officials know perfectly well what is going on, nor can there be any doubt in the mind of the committee that vigorous, honest law enforcement can put an end to wide-open conditions in a very short time.'

Chapter 16

The IRS Hits

The Longy Zwillman who came home to his 20-room mansion in West Orange after the Kefauver committee appearance was – subtly – a different man from the one the public saw on the stand. To the camera's eye, Zwillman was a polished, polite, superbly self-confident professional. A gangster, yes. The evidence produced by the committee and the testimony of Longy himself had unveiled his underworld activities as well as his legitimate interests. But a new type of gangster, one who had made most of his money in bootlegging (which the American public never really considered a sin) and had taken his profits and invested in businesses just like any other American who had discretionary funds at his disposal.

Yes, this Longy the public saw had consorted with known killers, had been the partner of some, the friend of others. But he was of a different class, somehow. His exposure as an important gangster had the impact of a Hollywood film star's being caught smuggling rare art works from some impoverished European village into this country. It was wrong, to be sure, but understandable.

His lawyers told Longy he had nothing to worry about. His answers had been skillful. He had evaded contempt of Congress charges while avoiding revealing his real secrets. He had been, they assured him, a star witness.

The phone calls Longy received in his Washington hotel room the night he was excused from further questioning seemed to confirm the judgment of his attorneys. Longy was a realist, however. The opinion of his attorneys and the public were flattering. They gave him a feeling of euphoria, but it was short lived. Longy began to understand a few things, little signs that only he could recognize.

First was the nagging feeling that exposure had compromised his standing at the top of the Big Six. The first member of the group to cavort in the public's eye had been Lucky Luciano, and his reign had been cut short by exile. The banishment, Longy knew, was as much punishment for Luciano's brashness, for his self-projected 'public image,' as for his activities in crime.

Now, even banishment didn't mean peace for Luciano. Longy had received word of stirrings in the ranks. Just as Luciano had ridden to stardom by removing the old Moustache Pete gang leaders, a new crop of young Turks were edging toward the top. One of the pushier youngsters was Vito Genovese.

Genovese, born in Naples, had come into the Luciano-Lansky-Siegel gang in the 1920's as a simple hit-man. Small, unattractive, and overly ambitious, Genovese would have done well during the Renaissance among the Borgias and Macchiavelli.

Here's one example. On March 16, 1932, the body of Gerardo Vernotico, 29, of 191 Prince Street, New York City, was found on the roof of a building at 124 Thompson Street, in the city's Little Italy section. Another body, that of Antonio Lonzo, 33, of 305 East 28th Street, New York, was found in an alley below this same roof. Both men had been garroted. A police investigation was conducted without any solution to the crime, except the conjecture by detectives that Lonzo died solely because he happened to see Vernotico's murderers.

Two weeks later, Anna Petillo Vernotico, the widow of the dead man on the roof, married Vito Genovese. The couple went to Italy for their honeymoon.

Everyone even remotely close to the city's crime circles knew the real story of Vernotico's murder, and the swiftness with which his widow remarried. Vito Genovese was a widower when he spotted Anna Vernotico. It was love – real love that lasted a lifetime – for Vito. Anna, some said, was merely infatuated.

Genovese solved the problem of Anna's marriage by simply having her husband murdered. Anna didn't learn how she became a widow until some years later. When she did, her love for Vito turned to bitter hatred. Her revenge was straight out of an Elizabethan revenge play. Anna slept with every man brave enough to crawl into Vito's marriage bed, and some others who didn't realize who her husband was. And she boasted about it.

For some unfathomable reason, Vito didn't throttle Anna. Lansky and Luciano agreed that she was the only person they knew who could get away with that kind of behavior where Genovese was concerned.

Anna, burning because her promiscuous behavior didn't get under Vito's skin, finally asked for a divorce in 1950. At the trial, she revealed all of Genovese's rackets and the sources of his income. Still she wasn't punished. Years later, gang members would tell of tears running down Vito's cheeks when he talked about his lost love.

Vito Genovese was also a bigot, a trait that often irritated Lucky Luciano and Frank Costello. Once, the Big Six were discussing the absorption of some of Dutch Schultz's henchmen into the organization at a meeting in New York. They were going over the names, overwhelmingly Jewish, when Genovese – present only as Luciano's coat-carrier – burst out impetuously: 'What the hell you trying to do, load us up with a bunch of Hebes?'

Genovese was lucky that Zwillman and Lansky respected their partner, Luciano. Vito was his gunsel, and they expected Lucky to discipline his own people. Otherwise, Vito would have received a visitor that night who would have maimed if not killed him.

But before Luciano could berate his lieutenant, Frank Costello lashed out at Genovese. His cutting remarks were based on Genovese's origins as a poor Neapolitan.

'You're nothing but a fuckin' foreigner yourself, Don Vitone,' was Costello's shot. That cut two ways. One, it placed the pushy Genovese outside the closed Sicilian society. And the derisive use of the title 'Don' warned Genovese that he had gone beyond his station.

Genovese never forgave Costello, because word about

the put-down spread swiftly. Whenever a mob member wanted to rankle Genovese, he'd call him 'Don Vitone.' How long Genovese could carry a grudge was revealed 30 years later, when Vito felt powerful enough to repay the insult. He dispatched one of his button-men, Vincent 'Vinny the Chin' Gigante, to kill Costello. The bullet intended for Costello's eyes only grazed Frank's ear.

Genovese was itching for room at the top when the Kefauver committee hearings took place. He saw the public exposure of the Big Six as his chance to inch into the top ranks. His ticket of entry, Genovese decided, would be the daring elimination of Luciano in his Italian exile home.

It would be up to Longy to prevent Luciano's murder. Frank Costello was too absorbed in his own troubles with federal officials to recognize something was wrong. It wasn't until his close friend and partner, Willie Moretti, was murdered that Costello realized Genovese meant trouble.

Moretti's appearance before the Kefauver Committee gave Genovese a chance to get at Willie. Moretti, usually a jolly figure, used his committee appearance to try out his comic act. He played the fool, joked with the senators and the staff, and made himself the butt of the media. Those who really knew Moretti recognized this as his defense against having to answer too many embarrassing questions. Genovese, however, used Willie's garrulousness as evidence Moretti was going off his rocker.

'Willie got Al Capone's sickness,' was the word Genovese dispensed. The meaning was clear. Capone had died of paresis, the result of tertiary syphillis, which attacks the brain. Moretti had it too, Genovese was saying, and someone better take care of him before he spills his guts. Genovese didn't wait too long.

On the morning of October 4, 1951, Moretti walked into Joe's Elbow Room in Cliffside Park, New Jersey, for his usual coffee and sweet rolls. This restaurant had become Willie's unofficial headquarters after Duke's, up the street a bit, closed. Four men followed Willie in, went to his table, and greeted him deferentially. It was obvious Moretti knew the men, for he asked them to sit down after shaking hands all around.

A waitress came over and asked the visitors if they wanted to see a menu, since it was getting close to lunchtime. One man said he'd like to order lunch, but wanted a glass of water first. The waitress walked into the nearby kitchen to oblige him.

Almost as soon as the swinging door to the kitchen closed behind her, the waitress heard several shots. She was wise enough not to stick her head into matters that didn't concern her, so she stayed in the kitchen well after all the noise stopped. Then she cautiously peeked out.

On the floor, his head toward the kitchen, one leg bent as if he were trying to rise, was Willie Moretti. One hand clutched his chest. A pool of blood was collecting on the floor, flowing from Moretti's bloody head.

Willie Moretti's death concerned but did not frighten Costello. He was still too powerful. But his troubles with the government – not only the Kefauver hearings but a new threat from the IRS – were too much on Frank's mind for him to warn Luciano about Genovese's ambitions.

It was Longy who sent word to Rome that Don Vitone was getting too big for his hat. He urged Luciano to take precautions, reminding him that Genovese had cultivated a friendship with Mussolini before World War II, and probably still had connections in Italy. Attempts on Luciano's life were made, but he kept mum about them. He preferred to handle these matters discreetly, for he still hoped to be allowed back into the United States. In any case, Lucky wasn't harmed. Later, he had his revenge on Genovese.

In November 1957, Genovese called a meeting of gang leaders in the tiny upstate New York town of Appalachin. It was his first try at developing his reputation as a big power in gangland.

Luciano got wind of the invitations being sent to gangsters from all over the country. Mysteriously, the New York State Police were tipped off to the fact that a number of big-shot mobsters were guests at the summer home of a Buffalo businessman named Joseph Barbara.

The police surrounded the house. One of those inside spotted a few troopers and gave the alarm. Newspapaer stories the next day carried the ludicrous story of dozens of gangsters fleeing into the woods, pursued by shouting, sweating state policemen. Sixty mobsters were picked up. No charges ever stuck to them, but the humiliation for Genovese was complete.

Lansky's Israeli biographers, Dennis Eisenberg, Uri Dan, and Eli Landau, insist that Meyer also got his revenge, as much for Genovese's anti-Semitic mouthings as for his crude attempts to rise higher than the original Big Six.

Meyer's method was simple – plant evidence that Vito was running narcotics, and an aroused public would almost guarantee his conviction. The messenger carrying the evidence was one Nelson Cantellops, a former Lansky gofer.

Cantellops had been arrested on a narcotics charge. Lansky sent word that Nelson and his family would be guaranteed a life pension, as well as protection, if Cantellops would do a small favor. Cantellops agreed.

Soon after, a federal narcotics agent, George Gaffney, was told that Nelson Cantellops wanted to see him. The story Nelson had for the agent made him itch with anticipation. One of the most feared mobsters in the East, Vito Genovese, was a drug smuggler, and Nelson Cantellops had the evidence.

Genovese was arrested. Cantellops took the stand and named names, dates, and details of just how Genovese brought drugs in from Europe and distributed them here. Genovese was sent away with a 15-year sentence. Despite being coddled in prison, Genovese died in the Atlanta federal penitentiary in 1969.

Longy took stock of his troubles with the government's tax officials right after the Kefauver hearings ended. He began by listing his legitimate business holdings: shares in A.M.

Byers, a Pittsburgh steel company; half-ownership, in his wife's name, of the Public Service Tobacco Company; 100 percent ownership of Federal Automatic Company coin-operated laundry machines placed in apartment houses; in the GMC truck franchise in Newark; in E & S Trading Company, a scrap iron firm; in A & S Trading Company, engaged in buying and selling used machinery; in Diamond T Parsons, an auto and truck repair firm; and shares in a number of race tracks around the country.

Silently, Longy held shares with his Big Six buddies in three Las Vegas hotel casinos, and in a number of wholesale liquor companies in New York and New Jersey. Then there were the extensive illegal gambling connections: high-stakes crap games in New York and New Jersey; and roulette and poker along the Sawdust Trail, as well as in a variety of locations in Florida. They didn't figure in his taxable income calculations.

Longy rented a suite in a hotel in Saratoga Springs, New York, and sent his accountant, I. George Goldstein, to the resort with instructions to comb his books. Longy would have preferred not using Goldstein. He was livid at the way the little accountant had spilled so much information to the Kefauver Committee. But he needed Goldstein at this point. It would take another accountant – even if Longy could find one he could trust – months to get the hang of the Zwillman involvement in various business enterprises, how they were run, and how payoffs into Zwillman's pocket were steered through a variety of dummies.

'Look for every possible penny of taxable income,' Longy instructed Goldstein. 'I want to know exactly how much I should pay the government, how much I already paid, and what I owe. Sweat,' he told Goldstein, 'because your head is on the line. I don't want the IRS to catch me in a single mistake.'

Longy didn't realize it then, but he'd already made his big mistake. The top people in the IRS office in Newark had an instrument – in Longy's own handwriting – that they were going to use against him.

In 1947, Longy had gone to the IRS with his lawyers and accountant in tow. He wanted a settlement on all his tax liabilities. He had seen the tax people get Al Capone, and this had worried him more than he let on. For the first time in his long career, he was dealing with a law-enforcement agency that couldn't be cajoled or corrupted.

Longy offered the IRS a compromise. He would pay up all his back-tax liabilities, if the tax agency would arrive at a reasonable figure. His accountant had advised him, Longy told the IRS agents, that $110,000 should be sufficient to take care of any back taxes he owed. His current tax liabilities were already taken care of, Longy said.

The agent in charge of the IRS Intelligence Unit in Newark was Edwin Baldwin. His chief assistant was James Bonnano. Neither man could give Longy any assurances, either that the amount he offered would clear his previous tax liabilities or that their superiors would even agree to any compromise. They had, Baldwin said, to take up the case with New York. Before he could even ask New York's opinion, Baldwin told Longy, he needed a net-worth statement from the Zwillmans, Abner and Mary.

Longy fell for the trap. Rather, his lawyers and accountant never saw the danger in having Longy and Mary sign a net-worth statement. Without it, the IRS would have had to spend years digging into records, interviewing and bullying witnesses, and backtracking the Zwillman expenditures in order to build a case. With it, they had a Rosetta stone as the key to Longy's tax liabilities. And it was signed by both Longy and his wife, Mary.

New York turned down Longy's request for a compromise. The top IRS tax officials wanted to assess Longy on a year-by-year basis, as his income came to light. Longy had refused to give the Newark office any income disclosure. That was his part of the compromise. You tell me how much you want, he told Uncle Sam, but I won't tell you where the income comes from.

Longy's reasoning was perfectly logical. He had a lot of cash on hand from his bootlegging days. He didn't want to account for it, or for his current gambling income. He was ready to pay for all the income the IRS could find, but not a penny more.

Longy and Mary signed the net-worth statement, but wouldn't go an inch farther. New York wouldn't move. That's the way the situation lay as the Kefauver hearings began.

After the hearings, the IRS hierarchy in Washington decided to start investigating the incomes of five men who had been called to testify – Zwillman, Costello, Moretti, Joe Adonis, and Joseph Profaci. The last had been exposed as one of the leaders of the new crop of gangland leaders in New York.

Letters went out to all five on June 10, 1952. We're investigating your tax liabilities for 1951 and all previous years in which you were gainfully employed, it said. What about the statute of limitations under which the IRS was supposed to operate? If we can show a continuing conspiracy to avoid paying taxes, said the IRS, the statute of limitations doesn't apply.

Ed Baldwin was ordered to prepare the case against Longy. Baldwin had not only sat through the days when Longy was testifying before the Kefauver Committee. He had testified himself, on August 16, 1951.

Baldwin seemed to know more about Longy's business activities than anyone else in law enforcement. Longy, he told the committee, was Joseph Reinfeld's partner in a bootlegging operation that imported more than 40 percent of all the illegal liquor coming into this country during Prohibition. He estimated the Reinfeld-Zwillman income over a six-year period to be as much as $50 million. No taxes had been paid on that sum. (At that point, Longy's lawyers recognized where the continuing conspiracy element came in.)

Baldwin told the committee that his first lead into the Reinfeld-Zwillman combine came after the failure of the West Orange Trust Company, during the Depression. This bank was run by Walter Van Riper, once attorney general of New Jersey. After the bank failed, Baldwin was able to unearth records that revealed the masked accounts under which Longy kept his money. (As a sidelight, Baldwin told the committee that the bank's records showed that Longy had actually overpaid on his 1931 income taxes. That was the year Al Capone had been nabbed by the IRS, and Longy told his accountant that, if Capone could be nabbed, anyone could.)

Baldwin also told the committee how, during Prohibition, Longy would telegraph money to the Bank of Montreal in the name of the mayor of a Canadian port city, where the Canadian liquor was transhipped to this country. He also used shipments of gold to pay for the liquor, sometimes as much as $100,000 worth in one shipment. The gold was shipped to Canada in armored cars.

To do the actual spadework for an assault on Longy's tax liabilities, the IRS transferred John O'Hara, one of its brightest agents in New York, to the Newark office. Once in Newark, O'Hara was told his chief responsibility was to investigate Longy.

John O'Hara, tall, bulky, and shy was a new kind of crime-fighter. He never carried a gun. His weapon was a pencil, and a determination that taxpayers shouldn't have to carry the burden of crooked public officials. Years later, after O'Hara had been promoted to Ed Baldwin's job and had retired, he was hailed by a federal judge in Newark, Herbert Stern, as the man who helped put more hoodlums, corrupt public officials, and crooked businessmen in jail than any law-enforcement officer in the recent history of New Jersey.

'And he did all this,' said Judge Stern, 'without wiretaps, without surveillance, without informers, only through the scientific and methodical analysis of books and records.'

O'Hara's techniques alone didn't impress the New Jersey federal law-enforcement establishment – judges, prosecutors, and investigators. It was his zeal that made them sit up and take notice. Judge Stern again:

'When I had a problem with the bureaucracy here and in Washington as US Attorney,' said Judge Stern, 'I turned to John O'Hara, and suddenly I didn't have a problem anymore. He could always find a regulation that permitted us to do what we wanted to do rather than a regulation preventing it. It would have been easier for him to do nothing, especially when Washington was looking over his shoulder. But he did everything he could to help us because he thought it was the right thing to do.'

O'Hara was born and raised in Jersey City. He attended Fordham University, majoring in accounting. After World War II service in the infantry, O'Hara joined the IRS by chance.

His first case as an agent involved the conviction of the owner of an electroplating firm who cheated the government out of $200,000 in taxes. Later, he bagged a freezerful of butchers who had been hiding excess profits under their meat hooks. O'Hara broke the case in typical fashion.

'One of the butchers,' said O'Hara, 'liked to think of himself as the dean of the local sports crowd. When two former New York Giants football players, Frank Filchok and Merle Hapes, were involved in a betting investigation, this guy offered to go bail for the two players.

'We wondered about that. This butcher didn't even know the two players. And he made the bail in cash! A little checking by us revealed he was a tax cheater.'

O'Hara also was the agent who nabbed Ruggiero 'Richie the Boot' Boiardo, once Longy's enemy, later his bosom buddy.

'We tracked the Boot and 18 of his men for months,' said O'Hara. 'Then one day, when we thought we had all the evidence we needed, we raided a place where we knew we'd find them. They hadn't bought gambling stamps.'

Boiardo and his 18 henchmen were never brought to trial. The US Supreme Court declared unconstitutional a federal law requiring gamblers to buy a gambling stamp. The O'Hara raid wasn't wasted, however. All the evidence he had painstakingly gathered was turned over to the Essex County prosecutor, and Boiardo and his gang went to jail for violating state laws.

John O'Hara, IRS Intelligence Unit Agent 2003, arrived in Newark on June 11, 1952. He went immediately into the first conference on the tax-evasion case of Abner 'Longy' Zwillman. At the meeting with O'Hara were agents Stan Cangelosi, Herman Kuhel, and Thomas Quirk.

'It was decided at that meeting,' said O'Hara, 'that Stan Cangelosi would work on all items up to 1947. I took the succeeding years. I began with the net-worth statement of 1946. Agent John Cassidy was assigned to assist me.'

That 1946 net-worth statement was O'Hara's indispensable guide, he admitted years later. Without it, his investigation would have been extremely difficult. Eventually, as in the case of Frank Castello, trained, experienced IRS intelligence agents might have come up with a case against Longy. But even in Costello's case, luck played an important part.

Lots of legwork went into building the case against Costello. Without a lucky break along the line, creating a foolproof case could have taken years longer than it did. The case against Longy too had to have an element of luck, said O'Hara. That element was the 1946 net-worth statement signed by Longy and his wife. That was a mistake, O'Hara said, made by Longy, perhaps on the advice of his lawyers. But he never should have done it.

O'Hara's first move in Newark was to test the Zwillman defense. He asked for a meeting with Longy's attorneys. The first conference with Arthur Garfield Hays and Morris Shilensky was held in the Newark offices of the IRS on June 27, 1952. The two lawyers asked some questions, said they would confer with their client, and left.

O'Hara kept working, trying to build a case of evasion based mainly on the net-worth statement. To do this, he first had to painstakingly recreate Longy's annual expenses in order to show they exceeded his income.

'My first try,' said O'Hara, 'was to look at a real-estate transaction. I interviewed a couple, Frank and Lila King, who bought a piece of land for Longy with a mortgage from the Union National Bank.'

O'Hara's probe must have struck a nerve.

'A week after this interview,' he said, 'I was notified by I. George Goldstein, Longy's accountant, that his office would not cooperate in any way with ours.'

That was okay with O'Hara. He had hoped for co-operation, but didn't really expect it after Longy refused to reveal his income sources. The investigation went forward by the book. Two 'legmen,' agents David Spal and Pat Del Grosso, were assigned to O'Hara, and the team spread out throughout New Jersey, checking bank deposits, real-estate transfers, deeds and mortgages, stock market transactions, insurance policies, telephone records, and records at the state Division of Motor Vehicles.

Agents visited the local building inspector in West Orange to discuss alterations that had been made on the Zwillman mansion on Beverly Road. They went back to Longy's days of living in a rented apartment at 32 South Munn Avenue, East Orange, and checked the building management's records to see what renovation or extra maintenance expenses Longy had incurred there. They went into dozens of shops, asking questions about the Zwillman family's buying habits and checking their purchases.

All this took six months. In December, O'Hara took a break and met with his old sidekick in New York, agent John Robert Murphy.

'Bob was working on Frank Costello at the time,' said O'Hara 'and we exchanged notes, leads, and tips on the two, Costello and Longy.'

Bob Murphy and John O'Hara later worked in Newark together for many years. Both went to work for the State of New Jersey after their retirement from the IRS – O'Hara heading a unit investigating Medicaid fraud, Murphy in charge of a team investigating sales-tax fraud.

The federal government decided to attack Frank Costello's tax case at the same time it went into Longy's returns. In each instance, the probe was all the result of the Kefauver Committee revelations.

The Costello investigation was a textbook classic of IRS recreation. Its agents, led by Murphy and Wilfred Leach, examined thousands of vouchers, every checkbook entry, every purchase that could be traced, creating a profile of

Costello's expenses. At first, this matched perfectly with his reported income.

That didn't stop Murphy and his men. They kept digging until Murphy turned up a check made out by Mrs Costello to a flower shop. This was the piece of luck O'Hara had referred to when discussing the case. The check was for floral decorations delivered to a cemetery in Queens. At the cemetery, IRS agents found an elaborate mausoleum. Additional checking revealed that Costello had bought the burial plot and ordered the erection of the mausoleum using a fictitious name. The expense hadn't figured in his reported income.

Buoyed by this discovery, agents began checking other flower shops in Manhattan. In one owned by gambler Frank Erickson, they had another piece of luck. They found a five dollar purchase that turned out to be the lead that brought the agents face to face with Costello's mistress. She was being maintained in a manner that went far beyond Frank Costello's reported income. Costello was trapped.

Nothing so dramatic took place in Longy's case. To O'Hara, the chase was pure drudgery, a dogged digging into ledgers, checkbooks, courthouse records, and reported purchases. He visited greenhouses, tailors, and furriers. He searched records of the Federal Housing Administration (some of Longy's real-estate deals were handled with FHA-insured mortgages).

O'Hara discovered Longy's longtime friendship with Msgr John Delaney, and the fact that the clergyman had a farm in Chester, New Jersey, bought for him by Longy as a gift. He interviewed members of the Zwillman family, including John Steinbach, Longy's stepson, who by this time was out of military service and working at Public Service Tobacco in Hillside.

In June 1952, the government pulled a surprise. US Attorney Grover C. Richman filed tax liens in the amount of $940,471 against the Zwillman family. The liens were intended to cover additional taxes, penalties, and interest owed by the Zwillmans for the years 1933 to 1946.

The liens broke down into the following categories: against Longy in the names of Abner Zwillman, alias Longy Zwillman, George Long, Eli Cohen, Abe Spitzel, and George Slavin – $728,956.07. The liens against Mary Zwillman were for $100,832.47. A lien against Eugene Mendels was filed for $92,392.02, against John Steinbach, Longy's stepson, for $9,260.02, and against daughter Lynn for $9,030.82. The liens against the two children were placed because, the government charged, they had transferred property given them by their father.

This filing, Richman told a press conference in Newark, was the result of a federal grand jury probe into organized crime, fraud, and racketeering. It was a civil case, however, and had nothing to do with the IRS fraud probe into Longy's taxes.

Actually, the two cases were closely tied. The government's strategy was to tie up Longy's assets in the civil case until the IRS fraud investigation was completed. The strategy appeared to work, according to the IRS. There were loud protests from Longy's lawyers. This was prejudgment, they claimed, finding the Zwillman family guilty before any trial. They pointed to a 1939 incident in which the government had tried to attach Longy's property with liens, claiming he owed additional taxes for 1938. At that time, Zwillman had paid the amount requested, and the liens were dropped. Tell us what we owe now, said Longy's lawyers, and we'll make proper payment.

The IRS didn't respond. Its agents were too busy probing Longy's finances. In August, brokerage houses and banks throughout the East were ordered to turn over to the government any money belonging to Abner Zwillman under any of his aliases. By September, a bundle of cash and securities belonging to the Zwillmans began to accumulate in the Newark office of the IRS. The government also started proceedings to sell all the real estate in Longy's name.

At the same time, the government announced it was dropping the liens against Longy's father-in-law and his two children.

'They had been satisfied,' the announcement said tersely.

On February 11, 1953, John O'Hara prepared his first analysis of Zwillman's finances for the year 1948. Then he resumed his investigation. Obviously, he hadn't yet found the keystone of his case.

O'Hara worked well into 1953 before he again analyzed the Zwillman case for his superiors. In May, he prepared a report on the 1947-48 expenses he had turned up, with an eye to scheduling his final report for June. He hit his target.

On June 18, 1953, the IRS filed a criminal complaint against Abner Zwillman for evading $55,146 in federal taxes on his 1946 income. Longy, the IRS claimed, paid $19,686 on a reported net income of $42,896. Actually, said the government, Longy earned $114,306 that year, on which he should have paid $74,782 in taxes.

This was the first criminal complaint on taxes ever filed against Longy.

A warrant was issued for Longy's arrest. Marshals spent four hours searching for him, then reported he couldn't be found. Five days later, on June 23, Longy, puffing on a cigar, outwardly confident, walked into the marshal's office in New Brunswick and gave himself up. He was accompanied by his lawyer from the Hays office in New York, Morris Shilensky. He was arraigned before US Commissioner McCloskey, who set a hearing for the following Monday.

His surrender caught federal officials by surprise. So was his confident front. Turning to one of the marshals, Longy joked:

'Why don't we call the whole thing off, go out, and get a beer. This heat is bothering me. I shouldn't have worn this heavy suit, I guess, but I put it on because I have to go to a funeral when this is over.'

Longy didn't say whose funeral. He was released on $3,000 bail as Samuel Bressler, his Newark-based lawyer called in the press and attacked the validity of the government's case. Bressler said the complaint would be dismissed.

Bressler obviously knew what he was talking about – or made a good guess. On July 15, a federal grand jury, after listening to the evidence, refused to indict Longy. The complaint was dismissed – as far as the 1946 charge was concerned.

Longy celebrated at a family dinner in a fine West Orange restaurant. To those at the table, he appeared relaxed and confident. Inwardly, there must have been a churning doubt gnawing away at him. Longy, however, was in the habit of never letting his emotions show. He hid his doubts even from his family.

Longy knew, from reports by friends, that the IRS hadn't given up on his case just because the indictment on the 1946 charges had been dropped. John O'Hara was still out there, relentlessly interviewing, probing, checking bank accounts.

The day before the indictment against him was dismissed, Longy knew, the IRS had called in two famous Hollywood lawyers for questioning. One was Jerry Geisler, whose handling of divorce cases for Hollywood stars had always drawn sensational press coverage. But Geisler had represented other clients, including friends of Longy's. The other lawyer was Martin Gang. Both men refused to talk about their appearance. A government attorney said tersely that it was connected with the Zwillman case.

Longy knew all this. He also knew that John O'Hara had interviewed scores of others. One was Toots Shor, an old friend. Longy had loaned Shor money to help him open his famous sports-hangout restaurant. The IRS had also called in Longy's old partner, Niggy Rutkin. A man named William Dunkel, who had arranged a $23,000 loan from a bank using Barium Steel as his security was interviewed by O'Hara personally. A host of political figures in Newark and Jersey City were subpoenaed.

Longy guessed that O'Hara was preparing a schedule on all his political contributions. Actually, O'Hara had gone further; he had prepared a complete report in Longy's political financing for a grand jury sitting in September.

On September 10, Leslie Weber, Longy's old friend and

real-estate handler, was called before a public hearing in Jersey City investigating the sale of the old ballpark. At the hearing, Weber testified that he had tried to buy the park with a $20,000 loan from Longy tht was secured by promissory notes. The money, Weber testified, was repaid to Zwillman in a matter of months.

Longy mulled over this testimony, which was nothing new to him. What was new was the fact that John O'Hara had been sitting in the audience at the hearing.

Longy's worries had a real basis. Immediately after New Year's Day in 1954, O'Hara met with attorneys from the Department of Justice who wanted to know what progress he was making.

'I'll be ready for the grand jury by the end of April,' O'Hara told the conference.

He was as good as his word. On April 27, the federal grand jury sitting in Newark started hearing evidence on Longy's tax problems for the years 1947-48. On May 26, the jury returned a two-count indictment against Abner Zwillman. The charge: evasion of federal income taxes in the amount of $46,000 in 1947 and 1948. Longy, the jury charged, had underestimated his income for those two years by $89,666.

Sam Bressler was furious.

'The grand jury was deliberately confused by the government,' charged Bressler. 'They brought in 300 witnesses. Because of that crowd, the jury made a mistake, which is understandable after seeing so many witnesses. The jury overlooked proof that the IRS had in its own files that my client was innocent.'

Williams F. Tompkins, the US attorney who was to prosecute the case, was incensed. Bressler's statement, he said, was false and outrageous. Every witness called before the grand jury had vital evidence to contribute.

The two sides prepared for trial. Longy turned to Arthur Garfield Hays and Morris Shilensky to defend him. Msgr John Delaney offered a suggestion.

'It may be well,' the monsignor told Longy, 'to have a well-known local attorney in on the case. No doubt these fellows from New York are competent, but you need someone from this area respected by everyone, including prospective jurors.'

Did the monsignor have anyone in mind? Yes, he did. John E. Toolan, one of the most respected members of the New Jersey bar. Toolan, a graduate of Cornell and a former state senator, was a vain man jealous of his reputation. He hadn't handled a criminal case since his days as Middlesex County prosecutor in the Twenties. He was reluctant to appear for the notorious Longy Zwillman. Msgr Delaney, however, was insistent. Toolan signed on as counsel, with Shilensky as his assistant.

Chapter 17

The Trial

It took almost two years fom the time the original indictment was handed up for Longy Zwillman to be brought to trial for income-tax evasion. The legal maneuvering seemed endless.

Attorneys Toolan and Shilensky began by asking for a bill of particulars from the government. They wanted a list from the government of the nature and source of every item making up what the IRS claimed was Longy's gross income for 1947-48.

The government countered. In a net-worth case (which Longy's was), the prosecution doesn't know the specific sources of a defendant's income. Federal Judge Thomas F. Meaney at first upheld the government's reply, and denied the defence request for a bill of particulars. Two months later, Judge Meaney reversed himself and granted Toolan's request.

US Attorney Raymond del Tufo argued – to no avail – that witnesses listed on the bill of particulars would be subject to harassment and threats. The judge warned Toolan – if that does happen, you know the consequences, counselor, don't you? Toolan understood. His client, he let it be known, wasn't that crass or stupid.

The trial date was finally set for January 9, 1956, with Reynier J. Wortendyke chosen to sit as judge. A graduate of Princeton and Columbia Law School, Wortendyke had been named to the US District Court in Newark that same year. US Attorney for New Jersey Raymond del Tufo, Jr, had been appointed to his post just a few months earlier.

Ray del Tufo was a Newark native, son of a well-known Newark lawyer, and a brilliant young attorney himself. He was a graduate of Princeton and Rutgers Law School. He had been a football star, co-captain of the Newark Academy teams on which he played. He had been named an assistant US attorney under Bill Thompson in 1953, and made his reputation quickly, trying the case in which Albert Anastasia was charged with tax evasion. Although the Anastasia trial ended with a hung jury, del Tufo's conduct drew immediate and approving attention.

Unfortunately, by the time Longy was ready to go to trial, del Tufo was already ill with multiple sclerosis. The burden of preparing and trying the case fell on two of his young assistants, Pierre Garven and Wilfred W. Hollander. Garven did the pretrial spadework; Hollander handled the case in court.

Pete Garven was a soft-spoken Bergen County resident, a Republican who was later nominated by a Democratic governor, Richard J. Hughes, to a New Jersey judgeship. He went on to become the youngest chief justice ever to head the New Jersey Supreme Court. He served in that post only a month before succumbing to kidney disease in 1973.

Garven's father had been mayor of Bayonne and a Hudson County prosecutor who had to move to Nevada for his health. Young Pete came back to New Jersey to attend school. His education at Princeton was interrupted by World War II, in which he flew 70 missions as a bombardier for the Air Force in Europe.

After serving with the prestigious Newark law firm of McCarter and English, Garven rose quickly in GOP ranks until he was named to be first assistant US attorney to del Tufo.

Wilfred Hollander was a tall, young, hawk-nosed graduate of New York University and Harvard Law School. He and Garven, both residents of Bergen County, were very close, and after their stint as assistant US attorneys ended, joined to form the law firm of Garven and Hollander in Hackensack.

Hollander died tragically at 46. He either fell or jumped out of the fifth-story window of his law office in 1970, 11 years after Longy Zwillman committed suicide.

Before the trial began, Longy's lawyers exuded optimism. John Toolan was quiet, but Morris Shilensky kept assuring Longy that the government had a weak case. Longy was the only one who seemed to have doubts.

He had good reason. The Kefauver hearings had set him back more than he cared to show. His partners in the rackets didn't like being in the spotlight. Longy managed to shake them off, but when he was indicted for income-tax evasion, he realized that his career at the top of the heap – Big Six or not – was just about over. He had to hand his basic business duties over to a lieutenant, Gerry Catena.

Longy still maintained some control. No one as important in the rackets as he had been for 20 years is just tossed aside by his partners. Despite his legal problems, Longy continued to reap respect. This was the result of a combination of presence – Longy was still an imposing figure, brainier than most of his contemporaries, wiser, more experienced in handling the daily problems that cropped up in any illicit undertaking – and few in the rackets wanted to try and toss him aside.

Catena continued to consult with Longy on all important matters. The meetings at the Zwillman mansion at 50 Beverly Road, West Orange, went on. But Longy recognized slowly and painfully that his own glory days were over. He was too hot to be a leader any longer. Even if he beat the income-tax rap, he knew he'd be under close government scrutiny from then on. This was brought home in some pre-trial testimony.

Somehow, Longy got wind that the government had wiretap evidence against him. It may have been a tip from a member of an Essex County law-enforcement crew. Longy still had friends in local law enforcement. In any case, Morris Shilensky appeared before the court on December 14, 1955, and asked for permission to question IRS agents about wiretap evidence.

Five days later, Ed Baldwin, head of the Newark IRS Intelligence Unit, took the stand at a pretrial hearing and testified that, yes, he had obtained information on Longy from wiretap sources. But, Baldwin said, it was evidence that went back to 1936. IRS agent William Mellin at that time had planted a bug in the basement of Longy's apartment building at 32 South Munn Avenue, East Orange. It had nothing to do with Longy's income-tax problems, testified Baldwin. It had been used to investigate what he called the 'Reinfeld liquor ring.'

Shilensky moved to have this and any other wiretap evidence excluded from the upcoming trial. He also asked Judge Wortendyke to dismiss the indictment.

'On what grounds?' Judge Wortendyke asked.

Shilensky told a long and rambling story that turned out, on closer inspection, to be only a rumor that some members of the grand jury that had indicted Longy had discussed the case at a lawn party. Judge Wortendyke denied both requests. He allowed all legally obtained wiretap evidence, and he denied the request for dismissal.

The trial date, however, had to be set back. Del Tufo asked for a two-week postponement. He was looking for an important material witness, said the US attorney, who seemed impossible to find. A week later, Del Tufo reappeared in court. The witness, he told the judge, had been found, and he was ready to go to trial.

The next day, January 13, juror Harry P. Anson reported ill, unable to continue. By this time, 46 talismen had been called. Thirty had been challenged by one side or the other. The defense had used up all but two of its peremptory challenges; the prosecution had only one left.

Finally, the jury was complete. Mrs Wanda Miedziejewski, a Jersey City factory worker, was chosen to be foreman. Alexander Livingstone of Rutherford was selected to replace the stricken Anson. The other jurors were:

Louis J. Donadio of Wood-Ridge, a carpenter; Mrs Florence Nicholson of Pompton Lakes, a housewife; Mrs Roxie M. Lang, a Montclair housewife; William E. Campbell of Pompton Lakes, a shop foreman; Mrs Matilda Alzieri of Paterson, another housewife; Warren H. Andes of Harrison, a machine operator; Alexander Baker of Nutley, an assistant vice-president; Joseph J. Jordan of

Jersey City, another machine operator; Donald J. Gibson, a funeral director; and Mrs Anna Savitsky Golemme of Linden, a secretary.

Completing the jury were two alternates – Frank W. Winter of Elizabeth, an industrial engineer, and Irene Rosen of Paterson, a bookkeeper.

The number of women on the jury was a tribute to John Toolan's strategy. He knew how attractive Longy could be, and he counted on women softening any built-in prejudice on the part of male jurors inclined to stick it to Longy because of his wealth gained from the rackets, his good looks, and his good luck.

The trial began January 23. Opening remarks by the contending sides were as expected. John Toolan told the jury that Longy Zwillman was a generous but maligned family man.

'This man,' said Toolan, pointing to his client, 'lives in a glass cage. He's overpaid his taxes, if anything.'

Wilfred Hollander, in his opening address, painted a different picture. You'll get enough facts, he told the jury, to draw a fair inference that Zwillman 'deliberately cheated on his taxes. He draws $13,000 a year from the Public Service Tobacco Company. That's a fair salary. But he borrows and lends company money at will, without notes or interest.'

Hollander then turned to the IRS and how it built its case against Longy. He described how John O'Hara had made his rounds, from bank to bank, store to store, stockbroker to stockbroker.

'The government,' said Hollander, 'has proof of $40,000 spent by the defendant and his wife that is unaccounted for.'

Then came the first surprise. The next day, January 24, IRS Agent James J. Bonnano took the stand. Under questioning, he revealed that in 1947 he told Longy that he would recommend that the government settle its case against Zwillman for $105,000 – if Longy would sign a net-worth statement and submit to questions.

When Bonnano issued that statement, a spectator saw

Longy pale. This was the kernel of Longy's problem with the government. When he had talked to Bonnano, Longy had been ready to sign the statement. Paying out $105,000 to solve his tax problems was to Longy as cheap as tipping a waiter. He gladly would have paid three times that amount to be able to start with a clean IRS slate.

Longy didn't consider the net-worth statement important at first. He mentioned it to his lawyers, and they said nothing. They didn't say sign it or don't sign it. They ignored the remark. Longy, paying his legal staff a hefty retainer, depended on their advice. He didn't realize how vital the net-worth statement really was to the IRS. The government needed it to show that Longy spent more money in 1947 and 1948 than he did in 1946. And Longy, they knew, couldn't show where the extra income came from.

Too late, Toolan and Shilensky tried to keep the net-worth statement from being introduced at the trial. On January 25, Judge Wortendyke ruled the government could introduce the statement as evidence. The importance of that ruling was evident to Longy at once.

It was this ruling more than anything else that caused him to signal his faithful bodyguard, Sam Katz. Katz knew what the signal meant. Longy was hedging his bets again. He was taking no chances on the IRS having to prove its case beyond a reasonable doubt.

Katz put into motion the contingency plan. He began to probe the jury for soft spots. His object: to bribe one or two of them to make sure of a verdict favorable to Longy.

The trial went on. The big defense surprise was sprung by Toolan a week later. He revealed where Longy's money came from.

His client and Doc Stacher, Toolan brought out, had shared $1 million from the sale of Browne Vintners, not, as previously reported, a mere $358,000. That gave his client all the cash he needed for the high living the government claimed couldn't be accounted for on Longy's tax returns.

Was Toolan crazy, some spectators asked? Hardly. The big, bluff Irishman knew what he was doing – legally. The money Longy and Stacher received in the Browne Vintners deal, he believed, had been earned at a time that put it beyond the statute of limitations. The government couldn't touch Longy on it.

To try and prove his point, Toolan called John O'Hara to the stand for cross-examination. Didn't you say, he asked O'Hara, that Samuel Kessler, one of Longy's attorneys, told you in 1953 that Zwillman may have used money in 1947 and 1948 from a fund started by Stacher to take care of any future tax contingencies?

O'Hara countered. Stacher, he told the jury, denied he had ever given this contingency money to Longy. He had a signed statement to this point from Stacher.

Toolan pounced. Show us the statement, he demanded. O'Hara couldn't. Flushed with this small victory, Toolan then started to give O'Hara fits about his other testimony.

The IRS agent fought back doggedly. He told how Longy's lawyers had refused to let their client be interviewed, produce records, or cooperate in any way with agents. He said that cooperation would have been helpful for Longy. Toolan, who hadn't been in on this bit of advice, turned back to O'Hara's failure to produce Stacher's signed statement.

Why did Hays and Shilensky fail to warn Longy about the importance of the net-worth statement? This turns out to be the key question of Longy's problems with the IRS. Some say that this failure was pure hubris. Arthur Garfield Hays, they maintain, bragged about his ability to whip those young upstart lawyers at the US attorney's office – and they *were* very young.

Hays didn't pay too much attention to the fine legal points of the case, leaving the nitty-gritty to his subordinates. Shilensky was a junior in the Hays firm, to which Longy was paying big money. Shilensky was reluctant to offer any advice that would have shown up Hays, the braggart who was his boss. Toolan, who came to the case late, wasn't involved in the net-worth signing. His job, when he learned of it, was to try and minimize its impact on the jury.

On February 2, just before Mike Lascari took the stand, juror Joseph J. Jordan took ill and was replaced by alternate Frank W. Winter.

Lascari testified about the way Public Service handled loans without interest. The firm made these loans to favored customers in taverns and restaurants where its machines were installed, he said. It was a sort of good-will gesture. Lascari also testified that Mary Zwillman was paid $500 a week as a 50 percent partner in the business. Her husband was paid only $13,000 a year because his job as 'good-will ambassador' was only part-time.

The next day, Lillian Wiskind took the stand. She had been office manager at Public Service Tobacco. She testified that she had never, in all her time at the firm, had as much as a $100 discrepancy in cash or perpetual inventory. That's how well and how honestly the business was run, she maintained.

Edwin Steiner took the stand next. He had been president of the defunct E & S Trading Company once owned by Longy. He testified that Longy never took a penny out of the company.

How was it that he became president of an iron and steel scrap firm of some size. Steiner was asked? No, the former president admitted, he didn't have any experience in the field. He had been a 'liquor salesman.'

David Lieb then testified that he and a group from E & S Trading had made an investment in a brick factory. They never made any money, he said. As a matter of fact, they lost money.

The subject of Longy's West Orange mansion came up. How had he bought the place? Toolan presented documents. It had been bought by Eugene Mendels, father of Mary Zwillman, in 1946 from Cynthia and Philip Haselton. Two years later, in 1948, Mendels had deeded the property to his daughter. He was left holding a $46,000 mortgage, the money owed by Longy.

Mendels was even more generous to his daughter and son-in-law. He also had given them $30,000 as a gift in 1947-48. He gave them money for a vacation in Miami. He bought sheets for their bed at $42 a throw, handkerchiefs for his son-in-law for $5 each, and pillow cases for $6 each.

Mendels, now 82, gave this testimony by deposition from his sick bed. Where, he was asked, did he get all this money to give away?

Why, said the old man, from his earnings as a stockbroker on the old Curb Exchange, and later as a manufacturer of war goods in World War II. He felt he owed Mary and her husband that much because, after his retirement, he lived in their home and paid nothing at all for his food or shelter. He told his daughter the money was his, and he had paid all the taxes on it, so she could do with it as she wished.

Didn't you keep this money in a bank, Mendels was asked on cross-examination? Of course not, the old man replied. He remembered how he had lost a fortune during the Depression when the bank in which he kept his money went bust.

Some of Longy Zwillman's charitable contributions were exposed for the first time in testimony at the trial. His reputation as an easy mark for any sad story he came across was well known to his friends and family. Even during the trial, any tragic story in a local paper could make Longy spring into action. In such cases, local merchants were accustomed to receiving a visit from one of Longy's henchmen.

'Send a set of furniture to this address,' would be the message. The family at the address had just been burned out, it turned out, and their sad tale had caught Longy's eye.

At the trial, the charitable contributions listed in testimony were to organizations, not individuals. In 1947-48, for example, Longy had contributed $7,500 to the United Jewish Appeal, to which Mary had also given $766. The *Newark News* Christmas Fund for the needy received $1,000 that same year. The National Conference of Christians and Jews got $300; the National Probation Association, $75; the Catholic Actors Guild, $100; Congregation Beth Torah in Avenel was down for $100; the

Newark Welfare Federation, $750; the Policeman's Benevolent Association of Deal, $100. East Orange General Hospital got $100 also, as did the Sinai Congregation, a Hillside synagogue.

Testimony in the crowded courtroom dragged on, with few sensations until John O'Hara took the stand on February 14. He related the story of a $75,000 check that was sent from Longy to Los Angeles lawyer Jerry Geisler in 1945. It was a retainer for Geisler to represent Longy in the purchase of Tanforan Racetrack. The transaction was never completed. Was the money ever returned to Longy? O'Hara said he couldn't tell.

On February 22, the defense suddenly rested its case without offering a single bit of direct testimony, and without calling Longy to the stand. The decision surprised veteran courthouse reporters. Longy's lawyers, Toolan and Shilensky, really couldn't be that confident, they told each other.

It was John Toolan who rose that day to make the dramatic announcement. The clock behind Judge Wortendyke's head read 2:30 P.M.

'We have carefully considered all the testimony,' began Toolan, 'that the government has presented in this case. I am assuming responsibility for this decision. We take the position that neither in law nor in fact has the government proved that the defendant failed to report even $1 of income. On the contrary, we feel that the government's testimony proves that Mr Zwillman reported all his income. We have therefore decided to call it quits and to rest without presenting any testimony.'

Controversy swirled around the courthouse over Toolan's strategy. Later, after jury-tampering in the case was bared, some insisted that one of Longy's lawyers – Toolan or Shilensky – knew the fix was in. So, they reasoned, why prolong the trial? Most informed sources said that this was arrant nonsense. Toolan, an upright man, would never have countenanced fixing a jury. And Shilensky, if he knew about it, would have been foolish to tip his hand so early, before the case even went to the jury. He was too clever a lawyer to pull such a gaffe.

All the evidence pointed to Longy's having given the word to try and suborn the jury without telling his lawyers. As a matter of fact, the signal to fix the jury was sent even before the case began, as soon as the jurors were selected.

Toolan's reason for resting the case had solid grounding. He actually believed the government had failed to prove its case. Why, then, expose his client or any of the defense witnesses to cross-examination?

Toolan asked Judge Wortendyke to dismiss the indictments and free Longy without sending the case to the jury. The judge deliberated for three days, then decided the jury had to decide.

Toolan summed up first. He told the jury that any unusual expenditure they may have heard about came from a large hoard of undeposited money. This cash hoard – he called it exactly that, a hoard – was bootleg earnings, some of it more than 20 years old. Toolan freely admitted this, said the income was beyond the government's jurisdiction because the statute of limitations on it had expired. The prosecution, said Toolan, 'had done nothing but throw a lot of mud at the ceiling, hoping some of it would stick.'

Pierre Garven summed up for the government. He put the emphasis exactly where Longy feared it would go – on the net-worth statement signed by Zwillman and his wife. That couldn't be washed away by any statute of limitations. It was signed December 31, 1946, and it showed no large undeposited sums of cash.

In his charge to the jury, Judge Wortendyke had something to say about the use of large sums of cash in transactions. Those brought to light at the trial were a factor the jury might consider in determining the question of willful intent to evade paying taxes. But, the judge warned, the government must prove beyond a reasonable doubt that Longy had evaded paying taxes in 1947-48 in order to justify a conviction. And, said the judge, the jury had to make separate findings for each year.

The judge conceded two important defense points. The jury, in considering Longy's expenditures, had to take into account not only his reported income but any other available funds. That was a surprise concession to the possibility that Longy had stashed away his bootleg earnings, and used them in later years. The judge also told the jury it was up to the government to prove its contention that the money was spent by Mary Zwillman and Eugene Mendels, her father, came from Longy's taxable income. In other words, if the government couldn't prove that Longy had passed money to his wife and father-in-law in order to hide it, the jury had to disregard it.

The jury retired. On March 1, the jury was still without a verdict. At one A.M., they asked the judge to let them retire to the Hotel Douglas to sleep.

Shortly before one P.M. the next day, they asked the judge for a blackboard, pads, and pencils. They also asked Judge Wortendyke for renewed instructions on the duty of the government to prove that there was a likely source for the $90,000 of income that the government contended Longy had failed to report for 1947-48.

The judge denied the jury access to the 3,000-page transcript of the six-week trial. The jury members must depend on their memory, he ruled. They could ask for specific answers to points of law, but could not consult the text.

The request for blackboard and writing material suggested to onlookers that the jury was centering its discussion on the numbers in the case. The defense had put special emphasis on its contention that the government failed to show a likely source of income for 1947-48 to account for what it had called excess expenditures. The judge had dwelled on this point in his charge.

'The government had to demonstrate,' said the judge, 'either an undisclosed business activity [by Longy] capable of producing taxable income, or a disclosed business capable of producing much more than was reported, and in a quantity sufficient to account for the excess expenditures, or the increase in net worth.' The defense had contended the government had failed to show this.

One juror asked the judge: 'Your honor, could we reach conclusions from the evidence alone?'

The judge replied the jury must base its conclusions on testimony and exhibits, but that this meant they could make 'reasonable inferences' based on circumstantial evidence.

On March 4, after 30 hours of deliberations, the jury sent word to Judge Wortendyke that it was hopelessly deadlocked. The jury was dismissed. Speculation began immediately. Would Longy be retried?

That fall, the trial calendar came out. No date for a new trial for Longy Zwillman was on it.

Pierre Garven and Wilfred Hollander resigned from the US attorney's office to enter private practice. The Zwillman tax-evasion case – it appeared – was over.

Chapter 18

The Bribe

The first announcement of the arrests for bribery was made in Washington. It came from J. Edgar Hoover himself. Overshadowed during the trial, Hoover saw his chance to jump into the case when his agents notified headquarters they were ready to arrest the bribery suspect. Hoover took the opportunity at self-aggrandizement with characteristic joy.

The arrest was made after the US Attorney for New Jersey, by this time Chester A. Weidenbruner, received the sealed indictment handed up by a federal grand jury in Newark on February 15, 1959.

Arrested was Peter La Placa, at the time living in Hasbrouck Heights, New Jersey. He was picked up in the city of Englewood, New Jersey, offering the FBI agents no resistance.

At the time, La Placa was a minor figure in the rackets. He had been a bodyguard and chauffeur for Willie Moretti. La Placa's son, Dominick, was married to Moretti's daughter.

Arrested at the same time were two others, Louis J. Donadio of Wood-Ridge, an unemployed carpenter, and Anthony La Rosa, also of Wood-Ridge, who operated a gas station.

La Rosa was described by the FBI as a material witness. The agents in the arrest would say nothing more about him.

Donadio was more easily identified. He was one of the jurors in the 1956 tax-evasion trial of Abner 'Longy' Zwillman.

Two days later, the same federal grand jury handed up another bribery indictment. This one named Samuel 'Big Sue' Katz of 42 Collamore Terrace, West Orange, New

Jersey. He was charged with 'offering money to Warren H. Andes of Harrison, New Jersey, to influence the decision of the jury in the Zwillman tax-evasion case.'

Indicted along with Katz was Edward A. Goodspeed of North Arlington, New Jersey. In his announcement, J. Edgar Hoover said the bribe had been offered between January 2 and April 20, 1956. It was not the same bribe, according to the FBI chief, as the one offered by La Placa to Donadio in the same trial. The dates are significant. The trial actually began after January 2 and ended before April 20.

The FBI leaked additional information about the case. The jury, the leaked rumour went, stood seven to five for convicting Longy when it was hung up, unable to come to a decision. This was never confirmed by any of the other jurors.

The two separate indictments suggested something else. Obviously, Longy had been hedging his bets once more. Why else would he have La Placa trying to buy one juror while his close confidante, chauffeur, and bodyguard (Katz) was out bribing another? And why was Longy so unsure of his case that he felt a bribe was necessary?

Things were beginning to close in on Abner Zwillman. Gerry Catena had taken over as rackets boss in the area where Longy had once been supreme. Yes, he still consulted Longy on all important matters. Yes, Longy still had the respect of his former associates and all the newcomers in the rackets. And yes, Longy still enjoyed a substantial income from rackets activities. It wasn't as large as it had been when Longy was on top. But Zwillman still had his suits made by Fifth Avenue tailor Earl Benham. His shirts and ties still came from Sulka, on Park Avenue. His shoes were still from Bob White's in New York.

Zwillman also knew of an implacable law of the rackets jungle. No rackets boss ever lasted on top longer than 20 years. The smarter ones recognized this and withdrew gracefully, retaining the respect they had earned. The dumber ones went out on a morgue slab.

Longy's time as a top boss of the combination was over.

He knew it was time he left the stage to other people. Catena had been practically brought up by Longy. Everything the personable man from South Orange knew had been taught to him by Longy. Let him have the job, said Longy, and its headaches.

The one thing Longy dreaded was spending years in some federal prison, especially when it could happen because a bunch of stupid lawyers hadn't warned him not to sign a little piece of paper that contained his net-worth statement.

Bribing jurors was nothing new to Sam Katz. In later years, he boasted of having done it many times. He developed it into an art, he told one listener.

How do you go about finding the right juror who can be bought? After all, if you go after the wrong one, you could blow a case sky-high.

'You have to be scientific about it,' was the way Katz put it. 'You hire private dicks sometime. You go to a juror's neighborhood. You check with neighbors, friends, relatives. You claim you're a private eye, and you need information because the person you're checking may come into a large sum of money. That ain't a lie, is it?

'When you get a line on somebody – he needs money badly, he has a mistress his wife doesn't know about, he gambles or drinks, something – you have a lever.

'With this guy [Warren] Andes, for instance. I knew a guy, Goodspeed, who knew his brother, Charley Andes. I did a little checking, then gave Goodspeed the money to give to Charley, who turned it over to his brother, who was on the jury.'

Goodspeed and Andes not only lived in the same garden apartment complex; they were both members of the local police reserve squad.

The other juror, Louis Donadio, the carpenter, had been unemployed for some time. When Anthony La Rosa, a friend and neighbor, offered him money, a new house, and a steady job if he would lean toward Longy in the case, Donadio didn't refuse. The offer was made to him at a roadhouse on Route 46 in Lodi, New Jersey.

Neither Katz nor Goodspeed ever stood trial. Each plea bargained, pleading guilty before Judge Mendon Morrill on October 23, 1956. Goodspeed was sentenced to two years in a federal penitentiary; Katz received six years.

For Katz, this turned out to be six years of hard time. He was constantly being shifted from one federal detention center to another. In each case, he would be asked by FBI agents to tell what he knew about Longy. Each time, he would reply with obscenities. He finally wound up in the toughest federal prison, Leavenworth, where he served out his time in stoic silence. Had Katz cooperated with the FBI, he would have been eligible for parole in two years. His personal code, and his longtime friendship for Longy, made him keep still.

La Placa went to trial in early 1960. Donadio, the other juror, saved himself a long jail term by testifying against La Placa. He had been offered a house, a job, and $3,000, said Donadio. Anthony La Rosa turned over a first payment of $900 when Donadio was introduced to La Placa. Later, he received more money. As a result, Donadio told the jury, he voted not guilty from the start of deliberations.

La Placa assured Donadio he wouldn't be the only one sticking to a 'not guilty' verdict. La Placa's remark to Donadio suggests that he and Katz were working together. That's not too clear to this day. Longy was known for trying to make sure he would always retain the edge in any transaction. Was he hedging again in a serious trial in which he was personally involved? Katz says no, he didn't know about the La Placa bribery attempt. La Placa never talked about it.

La Placa's trial ended abruptly when he announced he would plead guilty, although he insisted he was innocent. Judge Richard Hartshorne sentenced La Placa to eight years in a federal prison. The sentence, said the judge, was more severe than the one handed out to Sam Katz because Katz had no previous record, while La Placa had serious convictions going back to 1921.

As for Longy Zwillman, another fate awaited him.

FBI files reveal how easily federal law-enforcement

authorities got wind of the bribe offer to two of the jurors in Longy Zwillman's tax-evasion trial. On September 3, 1958, W.B. Welte, a top-echelon official in J. Edgar Hoover's office in Washington, sent an urgent request to his boss.

'Newark Division . . . requests authority to install misur [microphone surveillance] in an office of the Supreme Beverage Company, 470 S. 10th Street, Newark. This is the office of Herman 'Red' Cohen, a close associate of [Abner] Zwillman, whom Zwillman visits regularly during business hours. The possibility exists that Cohen is a 'front' for Zwillman in the Supreme Beverage Company. Cohen is closely associated with Zwillman in other matters.'

Several lines that follow this memo in the files are obliterated under a section of the Freedom of Information Act that permits the agency to withhold information about its informers. A second paragraph follows:

'Zwillman is the subject of an active top hoodlum investigation in the Newark Office. He has been extremely notorious as a top level hoodlum for many years and numbers among his close associates many of the top hoodlums in the US. Newark states he is generally regarded as the most powerful underworld figure in the State of New Jersey and among those of first rank in national underworld prestige.'

This description was overstated hindsight. The FBI's Newark office knew, even before Zwillman's tax-evasion trial, that Longy had 'retired' from active participation in the 'combination,' as the Big Six was known when it no longer had the six original members who had ruled organized crime for 20 years. Longy was still considered an elder statesman whose advice was sought by the younger men when special problems arose. His acumen commanded tremendous respect, as did his connections in the legitimate business world and among people in high places. But Longy had relinquished active control of his end of the rackets soon after the Kefauver hearings exposed him as a top gang leader. All his rackets undertakings were in the hands of his trusted former aide, Gerry Catena, when the FBI memo was delivered to Hoover.

The hyperbole in the memo asking for misur installation was merely an effort to convince J. Edgar Hoover that Longy was still important enough to warrant illegal electronic surveillance. The memo – with more deletions – continues:

'The proposed misur installation will be made with the assistance of [here two sentences are deleted] and will be monitored [more deletions]. Trespass will be necessary in the installation if made. As to possible risks of detection involved, the Newark Office advises that there are no foreseeable risks.'

Welte recommended that authority for the illegal tap be granted for 30 days. Its continued use would have to be justified by the Newark office every 30 days.

A week later, Hoover responded with a message to the agent in charge of the Newark FBI office:

'Provided full security assured, authority granted to install misur for 30-day period in Herman 'Red' Cohen's office at the Supreme Beverage Company, 470 S. 10th Street, Newark, NJ. Advise immediately of time and date of installation made and symbol number assigned. Submit justification prior to end of 30-day period with your recommendation in event misur desired for longer period.'

Planting the bug evidently took some time. It wasn't until December 12, 1958, that Director Hoover received a confidential memo from the Newark special agent in charge.

'Misur completed 12/18/58 and will carry symbol number [deleted], and will be monitored . . .' The rest of the memo is deleted.

On January 21, 1959, the misur struck paydirt. The exultant teletype went directly to J. Edgar Hoover in Washington, with the name of the agent in charge of monitoring the bug deleted.

'. . . this date advised he had overheard conversation between Herman 'Red' Cohen, a lt. of Zwillman and unidentified male. In conversation re 1956 income-tax evasion trial of subject, Red stated that "we had two jurors that is how we won." This trial resulted in hung jury. Red discussed how unidentified members of original jury panel were approached and that two of them were chosen to serve on the jury. "Sue" paid off one of the panel who was not even chosen for the jury. She believed identical with Sam "Big Sue" Katz constant companion of Zwillman. Informant further advised that Red implied that should subject's motion to dismiss above indictment be unsuccessful, similar steps to bribe jurors must be taken. Subject's motion to dismiss indictment has been under advisement by Judge Reynier J. Wortendyke, USDC, Newark, for approximately three months. Bureau requested to advise action taken on above.'

The bug was kept active. In the next few days, it revealed a few additional tidbits concerning Red Cohen's operation. On Christmas Eve 1958, the listener heard Cohen threatening an unidentified man who owed him $2,200. The threat contained a warning – by implication – that Longy's muscle would be used to collect the debt. On New Year's Eve, the bug revealed information that Longy's GMC truck franchise in Newark seemed to be in some financial trouble.

On January 6, 1959, the listener on the tap heard the names mentioned of several shylocks operating in the Newark area. A cryptic note follows; Red Cohen, it said, feels that two top hoodlums (names deleted) would move into the area if Longy died. No indication why Cohen spoke about the possible death of Zwillman.

There's little doubt that the misur shows an FBI informant buried deeply in Longy's organization. The use of the word 'informant' as distinct from agent makes this clear. The informant must have been the person who drew Red Cohen into casual conversation about the tax-evasion jury, eliciting the information about the bribe.

Did the informant know a bribe had been offered? Evidently. Why else would the conversation turn to bribery, especially on the telephone? And why was Red Cohen's office selected as the site for the bug? Did the informant know Red Cohen's blabbermouth tendencies? He – or she – must have known that most of Longy's other associates were close-mouthed to a paranoic point. Only Red would be indiscreet enough to talk openly about such delicate matters.

How did the FBI find out that Longy used Red Cohen's office as a quiet hangout? Zwillman's moves for years were closely monitored by a shrewd, experienced agent in the Newark office, John Connors.

The relationship between Connors and Zwillman was a strange one. They never met formally, never spoke to one another. Yet a grudging respect grew between the two men, watcher and watched. Longy's attitude toward his 'tail' was one of wry amusement. He admired Connors' tenacity.

'It was as if Longy recognized that Connors had a tough job, and was doing it in a thoroughly professional manner,' recalls a former FBI agent who worked with Connors. 'And John respected his subject because Longy was quiet, reserved, never showed anger or annoyance, never tried to use muscle (as some less powerful racketeers often did). John considered Longy a good businessman, and very personable. He felt sorry for Longy's family, especially the children.

'Connors is quite a guy. After he retired from the FBI, John was chosen by Brendan Byrne, then governor, to be security chief at the huge sports complex in the Hackensack Meadowlands, where they have Giant Stadium, the race-track, and the arena. The two men met when Byrne was Essex County prosecutor, at the time Longy died. Later, John became security chief for Caesar's Hotel on the boardwalk at Atlantic City. I think he's still there.'

Longy Zwillman may have guessed, when Sam Katz and Pete La Placa were arrested and charged with bribing the two jurors, that the FBI had planted a bug. But where? Did he guess Red Cohen's office? Red was a boyhood friend. The two grew up together in the Newark Jewish ghetto. Longy trusted Cohen implicitly. That's why he used the offices of the Supreme Beverage Company for some sensitive meetings.

If Longy *did* guess where the tap had been planted, he took the information to his grave.

Chapter 19

Over the Edge

The call came to West Orange Police Chief Thomas F. Mulvihill about 11 A.M. on February 26, 1959. It was from Eugene Mendels, who lived with his daughter and son-in-law, Abner Zwillman, at 50 Beverly Road. There had been, said Mendels, 'an accident,' at the house.

Lt George Bamford was dispatched at once. 'Accidents' at Longy Zwillman's house could be serious. The lieutenant was let into the house by Mendels. Bamford took one look at the 'accident' and called the prosecutor's office and the medical edaminer.

The Essex County prosecutor at the time was Brendan Byrne. Later, he achieved a reputation among gangsters – they called him 'Boy Scout' and 'the guy who can't be bought' – that led him right into the New Jersey State House for two eventful terms as governor.

That cold February morning in 1959, Brendan Byrne's attention was fixed firmly on the death of Longy Zwillman.

'I'd been prosecutor for only a month,' Byrne recalled years later. 'The first thing I knew about Longy's death was when Dr Edwin Albano, the medical examiner, called me. He and his assistant, a man named Kaehler, were at Zwillman's house with the West Orange police. He said Zwillman was hanging in the basement, and that it looked like suicide.

'Dr Albano asked me if I had any special instructions. I said yes, I wanted a post-mortem done immediately. I also told him I was sending down a long-time member of my investigative squad, George Meagher, to stand by while the autopsy was being done. I wanted an immediate report of the findings.'

Byrne did more. He asked Meagher to reconstruct Longy's movements for the days immediately preceding his death. The family, especially, was to be questioned closely.

'The rumors were circulating at once,' said Byrne. 'Longy's position in the rackets was the cause, I guess. The stories going around were to the effect that Longy had been murdered on gangland orders, and the death made to look like a suicide. Or that he had hanged himself, but was forced to do it on orders from the Mob because they feared he would give damaging evidence because of his IRS troubles.

'From all our findings, that was nonsense. The autopsy, the man's actions on the night before his death, the fact that at 55 he was still strong enough to raise quite a racket if someone tried anything funny, everything pointed to suicide due to temporary insanity.'

The night Longy died, he had gone to a late dinner with his wife and his sister, Ethel, at the Westwood, a restaurant not too far from his home. He seemed upset. He had two whiskeys before dinner, didn't eat much. At about 10 P.M., he excused himself, saying he had an important engagement, and left with his driver.

Longy Zwillman was agitated. He had been to see his personal physician, Dr Arthur Bernstein, in Newark that afternoon. Longy was told he was suffering from a serious heart ailment and high blood pressure. Dr Bernstein later told the prosecutor's investigators that Longy was also deeply depressed.

That night after dinner, his depression led Longy – alone – to the home of Gene Catena, brother of Longy's longtime aide and pal. Gerry Catena, who had replaced Longy at the head of the Zwillman organization, was in Florida. Longy needed to talk to someone, and since he couldn't reach Gerry, he turned to Gene Catena. Longy Zwillman had come to the edge of the precipice.

Zwillman arrived home from Catena's house, and he and Mary went to bed. At about two A.M., Mary awoke to find her husband pacing the floor. She started to get up. He told her to stay in bed. He was having chest pains, said Longy, the usual pains he'd had for a year or more. He'd be all right.

He told Mary the doctor had given him some pills, and he would take them. She said she was worried about him and wouldn't be able to sleep, so he gave her a sleeping pill, and she fell asleep.

Mary Zwillman awoke at about seven A.M. Longy was gone. She saw his money lying on the dressing table, and thought he went to work without it. She called his office at the Public Service Tobacco Company in Hillside and found out he hadn't yet arrived. It was then about eight A.M. She left word to have Longy call her when he came in.

At 10 A.M., Mary Zwillman needed some facial tissues. She went to get them in the basement storeroom where the family kept toilet supplies. As she walked down the steps, Mary could see into the storeroom. The door was open, and through the doorway she saw her husband, a rope around his neck, slumped so it seemed his knees were touching the floor. Her screams brought her father running.

Longy Zwillman was hanging, a plastic electric cord around his neck, one part held in his left hand. The cord had been looped around the small supports under the ceiling that construction people call 'cats.' He was wearing a checked bathrobe made by A. Martin of New York and striped pajamas from Battaglia of Milan, brown leather slippers, and socks. In the pocket of his dressing gown were 21 tablets of reserpine, a tranquilizer. On a small table near the body was a half-empty bottle of Kentucky bourbon whiskey.

The police weren't called at first. Instead, Longy's physician was called, and Dr Sidney Franklin arrived at the house at about 10:15. Dr Franklin was Dr Bernstein's associate. He pronounced Longy dead.

When the police appeared about 10:45 A.M., Mary was still sitting on the steps leading to the cellar, sobbing. Dr Bernstein arrived later and was questioned. He gave the police the information about Longy's visit to his office the day before, and about his depression.

In those early months of 1959, Longy Zwillman was a man at war with himself. The years – and the money – he had spent building a façade of respectability had been all but wiped out by events apparently beyond his control.

That was a novel experience for Longy. From the time he was 14, he had always held his destiny firmly in his own hands. He had determined where he was going, and how he was to get there. Nothing would be allowed to stand in his way.

Longy wanted wealth, and he got it through bootlegging and gambling.

He wanted power, and he got it through his creation of the combination, the Big Six, the first real organization of crime into big business in the country.

He wanted respect, and he got it through his investments in legitimate business, and his philanthropy, his concern for the poor.

When Prohibition ended, Longy could have continued on his course to wealth, power, and respect by remaining Joe Reinfeld's partner, importing liquor legally, building a business empire as big as Joseph Kennedy's – all legally. He could have been honored openly for his philanthropy, could have lived a life free of entanglements with the IRS, the FBI, the watchdogs of Congress.

He chose, instead, to stay in the rackets. Was it fear that legitimate enterprise could never provide the immense riches that illicit activities had given him? Was it a nagging doubt that he wouldn't be able to provide for the dozens of families that depended on his largesse?

Or was it a tragic flaw in his character, the failure to realize that a shining path was open to him, if he only had the courage to take it?

Longy Zwillman learned early in life to remain inconspicuous, although he was a power in the rackets. Let the others hog the spotlight;he'd rather work in the shadows. He had learned from Msgr John Delaney that he could educate himself to a point where he was truly a cultivated individual. Longy also learned to hedge his bets by investing in legitimate businesses.

By these means, Zwillman built an elaborate personal façade that swept him almost effortlessly into the best social circles, as well as intimate contact with powerful political figures.

He learned to enjoy the role of cultivated, affable lord of the manor, respected equally in the world of legitimate business and in the rackets. He would stroll with unconcealed satisfaction through the rooms of his mansion on Beverly Road, sit with friends at the opera and at dinner, enjoy the company of people who never guessed what it had taken for their host to claw his way into their circles from the streets of Newark's Jewish ghetto.

Longy's passion was his family above all else. He adored his socialite wife, Mary, a woman who had helped bring warmth, care, and hospitality into his private life.

'When Longy died,' said James J. Sheeran years later, 'there was a feeling of genuine loss around town.'

Sheeran, a war hero and mayor of West Orange in 1959, recalled the atmosphere when word of Zwillman's suicide leaked out.

'People knew about Longy, although they may never have met him personally. They felt the town had been deprived of a man who had done much for the community. There was a real sense of pity and sorrow, feelings seldom if ever expressed at the death of a racketeer.'

Why, then, did Abner 'Longy' Zwillman, a man who had everything to live for – it seemed – go over the edge and take his own life?

Begin with the Kefauver Committee. Longy's appearance at the televised hearings ripped away the veil from his gangland activities, stripped him of the mask he had so carefully worn for so many years since Prohibition days.

Strangely enough, Longy hadn't been deserted by his friends in the legitimate world. They remained remarkably loyal, despite the bad publicity. But Longy, somehow, didn't trust this loyalty. His public image had been dealt a blow, and Longy assumed this would strip him of his friends' approval, the admiration that meant so much to him.

Longy had 'retired' from the rackets. Oh, the boys still considered him a valuable asset, a counselor to be consulted on major decisions. But the decisions were no longer his to make. The money kept rolling in, but the concept of command was gone.

The old insecurities of his childhood surfaced. The drop from the mountaintop of racketeering after the Kefauver exposure must have taken a great psychological toll on Longy's self-esteem. It was hard to give up the trappings of power, even though Longy more than once had voiced a desire to get out of the rackets.

When the IRS hit Zwillman with a tax-evasion charge, his depression deepened. He had made it a point to stay out of legal trouble ever since his conviction for assaulting a pimp in 1927. Now, he was being besieged, amid great publicity, by the tax people. Worse, because of poor legal advice, Longy had almost sealed his own conviction by signing a net-worth statement that the government would use against him at the trial.

His mistrust of his lawyers led Longy to arrange for the bribing of two jurors. The FBI planted its bug, the bribe offer was uncovered, and Longy's world began to cave in. The worst part of this descent was the effect it was having on his family.

Longy's daughter, Lynn, was one of the victims of her father's troubles. He was proud of Lynn, of her artistic talent. It hurt Longy deeply when Lynn was refused admission to certain art schools because she was a Zwillman. Longy was extremely protective of his moody daughter.

When she began to be harassed at her high school after the Kefauver hearings, Longy was disturbed. When the tauntings increased after the bribe was revealed, Zwillman was almost beside himself. Longy could be tough – except when his child's happiness was involved.

The final blow came after that visit to Dr Bernstein. In

those days before open-heart surgery, a cardiac problem such as Longy's must have sounded like a death sentence.

All these elements – exposure to the public, the fall from power, his health troubles, and especially the effect of his troubles on his family – took their toll. Longy Zwillman went over the edge.

One prominent law-enforcement official felt that Longy, by killing himself, thought he could ease the pressures on his family. Zwillman, of course, was mistaken. The stress – and the sorrow – remained with them long after Longy died.

Gerry Catena got the phone call from his brother with the news of what Longy had done. He was vacationing at the Doral Country Club in Miami. Local police officers appeared almost at once, anxious to learn if Catena had any information about Longy's death. They said that Catena looked shaken, pale, almost bewildered. They reported later that he sat for several days in front of his luxurious bungalow, not speaking, not reading, barely moving himself to go inside for meals. It was as if, said one policeman, Gerry Catena had lost a close member of his family.

In Rome, Lucky Luciano was taking coffee with a guest, a visitor from America. Jean Lascari was the widow of his old friend, Mike. They were sitting on the sunny balcony of Luciano's apartment. He was leafing through a day-old copy of *The New York Times* that Jean Lascari had brought with her.

Jean heard her host gasp, then cry out:

'My God, look at this!'

Luciano's finger was pointing to the account of Longy Zwillman's suicide.

Epilogue

Longy Zwillman's funeral took place, as Jewish tradition dictates, within 24 hours of the time he was pronounced dead. It was a simple rite held at a funeral parlor just a few doors down from Longy's boyhood home in Newark's Third Ward.

A prayer, a short eulogy by Rabbi Joachim Prinz, and the mourners moved out, some to go on to the cemetery, others to go about their business. Following the family's wish, the rabbi did not speak of Longy's life. He asked, instead, for compassion for the dead man's family.

'They deserve the right to mourn,' said Rabbi Prinz, 'the right to the love, understanding, and comfort of the people who sit here. We bring our years to an end as a tale is told. There is a human being lying dead in this coffin. I plead with you for respect of the majesty of death. I plead that what the people here need, what they need very badly, is the privilege of every human being – to have the right to mourn.'

About 350 people were inside the funeral parlor. Another 1,500 crowded the street outside, trying to get a glimpse of the family – and the celebrities they thought might attend.

Few did. Toots Shor left his Manhattan restaurant and was there.

'I don't forget friendship,' was all Shor would say to the dozens of reporters who gathered outside Philip Apter's funeral home on Stratford Place in Newark.

A few others from the world of politics, entertainment, and the rackets were also there. Some, like movie producer Dore Schary, a boyhood friend of Longy's, came and later denied they were present, although newsmen saw them.

The FBI and the county prosecutor's men were there, taking note of those who showed up. The rackets characters who came to pay their respects to the family behaved themselves, for the most part. A few of the tougher souls forgot their manners and tried to rough up photographers as the family walked into the funeral parlor. Although arrangements by the family were made for a ten A.M. funeral, it was announced to the public that services were to be at four P.M. This was a ruse to keep the curious away. Still, when the family arrived at Apter's Funeral Home, a large crowd was on hand.

Rabbi Prinz, president of the American Jewish Congress, and a leader in American Jewish spiritual life, kept the service short.

Longy's mother, a tiny, frail 80-year-old worn by grief, sat huddled in a front pew. As Rabbi Prinze spoke, she cried quietly.

Before the services began, the family – one by one – was led to the bronze coffin, which was covered with a blanket of 100 red roses. All floral tributes from sources outside the family had been sent by Longy's widow to hospitals in the area.

Longy's mother, on the arms of her son Irving and his wife, almost collapsed as she came to the coffin, crying: 'Abele, Abele, my son, my son.'

Mary Zwillman stared down at her husband's casket, her face drawn, and said nothing. Her son, John, stayed at her side, his face immobile. Daughter Lynn, copper-haired, tall, and beautiful at 15, wept uncontrollably.

Seven chauffeur-driven limousines and 27 private cars led the cortege to B'nai Abraham Memorial Park on Route 22 in Union, New Jersey. After the *kaddish*, the traditional Hebrew prayer in praise of God, said at graveside by the deceased's nearest male relative, the casket was lowered into a concrete vault sunk deep in the ground. It had room for three more bodies.

As the coffin was lowered into the grave, Rabbi Prinz reached down and plucked two of the roses from the top. He turned and handed one to Mary and the second to her daughter, Lynn. The mourners went their own way out of the memorial park.

Three days later, a long, rambling editorial about Longy's death, 'Beyond the Law,' appeared in the *Newark News*. The writer couldn't seem to make up his mind whether Longy was to be mourned or his death celebrated. The editorial ended by remarking how strange it was that Longy had an apparent immunity to the law.

'No federal, state, or local agency has brought him to justice after a brief youthful visit to jail. And when retribution finally came, it was at his own hand.'

No mention of the Kefauver Committee, of the IRS trial, of the bribe.

Mary Zwillman sold the house on Beverly Road and moved away. Before the sale, but after she'd left the mansion, Mary had an auctioneer come in and dispose of everything in the house. The proceeds were donated to charities.

The announcement of the two-day auction brought a near-riot to the secluded, winding, ravine-ringed street in West Orange where Longy and other powerful local figures lived. Police had to block off surrounding streets for fear that fire apparatus would be unable to get through the crush of parked cars.

Inside the house, the scene was even wilder. Women were stripping sheets and pillowcases from Longy's bed, and snatching half-filled perfume bottles from Mary's dresser, then rushing over to a cashier to pay for the memorabilia. Long before the two-day sale was ended, almost every stick of furniture, every curtain and drape in the place had been sold.

About a year after Mary sold the house at 50 Beverly Road, the new owners returned from a visit to the theater in New York. They discovered to their horror that the house had been broken into. The burglar entered through a rear window and left the same way.

Curiously, a careful check of the contents of the house revealed that nothing – absolutely nothing – was missing. Money had been left in a night table. Some jewelry was in a dresser drawer. Silver was in a bureau in the dining room. Nothing was taken.

One theory at the time had it that the thief – or thieves – had been looking for a bigger haul, 'Longy's stash,' as one put it. Of course, it should have been known that Longy Zwillman never kept a cache of cash at home. He had enough bank accounts.

Another theory had the FBI breaking-in in order to remove a bug planted earlier. FBI files refute this. Telephone taps *had* been placed to check on Longy, but not in his home.

In 1964, a thief did steal $700 worth of jewelry from Saul M. Shapiro, who had bought 50 Beverly Road. The Shapiro family wasn't at home when the thief, posing as a plainclothes detective, showed a fake badge to Hyda Hernandez, the Shapiro housekeeper.

The fake cop wandered around the house carrying a writing pad, pretending to take notes. After a time, he pulled a gun and asked the housekeeper where the valuables were kept. All he could find were some jewels in the bedroom.

The thief made a fuss. He didn't believe that a man as powerful and rich as Longy Zwillman wouldn't have more valuables around the house. The maid had trouble convincing him that Mr Shapiro was not Longy Zwillman, that Longy was indeed dead.

STAR BOOKS BESTSELLERS

CHILLERS

COME THE NIGHT	Nick Blake	£1.95
SHADOWS	Shaun Hutson	£2.25
SLUGS	Shaun Hutson	£1.95
SPAWN	Shaun Hutson	£1.80
EREBUS	Shaun Hutson	£2.25
SLIMER	Harry Adam Knight	£1.80
THE PARIAH	Graham Masterton	£2.25*
THE PLAGUE	Graham Masterton	£1.80*
THE SPHINX	Graham Masterton	£1.50*
THE DJINN	Graham Masterton	£1.50*
THE MANITOU	Graham Masterton	£1.50*
THE DONORS	Horvitz & Gerhard	£1.95*
THE SENTINEL	Jeffrey Konvitz	£1.65*
HALLOWEEN III	Jack Martin	£1.80*

STAR Books are obtainable from many booksellers and newsagents. If you have any difficulty tick the titles you want and fill in the form below.

Name ______________________________

Address ______________________________

____

Send to: Star Books Cash Sales, P.O. Box 11, Falmouth, Cornwall, TR10 9EN.

Please send a cheque or postal order to the value of the cover price plus: UK: 55p for the first book, 22p for the second book and 14p for each additional book ordered to the maximum charge of £1.75.

BFPO and EIRE: 55p for the first book, 22p for the second book, 14p per copy for the next 7 books, thereafter 8p per book.

OVERSEAS: £1.00 for the first book and 25p per copy for each additional book.

While every effort is made to keep prices low, it is sometimes necessary to increase prices at short notice. Star Books reserve the right to show new retail prices on covers which may differ from those advertised in the text or elsewhere.

**NOT FOR SALE IN CANADA*